BHUTAN
AND THE BRITISH

Simtokha Dzong

BHUTAN
AND THE BRITISH
Peter Collister

SERINDIA PUBLICATIONS
with
Belitha Press

British Library Cataloguing in Publication Data

Collister, Peter
    Bhutan and the British.
    1. Great Britain — Foreign relations — Bhutan 2. Bhutan —
    Foreign relations — Great Britain
    I. Title
    327.410549´8 DA47.9.B47

ISBN 0-906026-18-0

Distributed in India by
U.B.S. Publishers' Distributors Ltd, 5 Ansari Road, Delhi 110002

Published in association with Belitha Press by
SERINDIA PUBLICATIONS, 10 Parkfields, Putney,
London SW15 6NH

Printed and bound in Great Britain by
Biddles Ltd, Guildford and King's Lynn

CONTENTS

LIST OF ILLUSTRATIONS

Line drawings on pages ii, vii, xi, 6, 24, 41, 53, 74, 118 and 199 are by Julian Burton.

The photographs, taken between 1905 and 1907, are reproduced from the personal albums of John Claude White and Captain Harold Hyslop (private collection, London).

Ugyen Wangchuk with Royal Bodyguard, Tongsa, 1905.

Ugyen Wangchuk with senior ministers and officials, Tongsa, 1905.

Ugyen Wangchuk with his family and personal servants, Wangdi Chöling, Bumthang, 1905.

Ugyen Wangchuk with his sister, daughters and niece at Wangdi Chöling, Bumthang, 1905.

"The Lhasa Doctor", Ugyen Wangchuk's personal physician.

ACKNOWLEDGEMENTS

I am grateful to Mrs A. Commander at the India Office Library for her assistance over the selection of documents; to Mr Yoshiro Imaeda, National Library Adviser in Thimphu, who lent me his extensive bibliography; and in particular to Dr Michael Aris of Wolfson College, Oxford, not only for help with the bibliography but also for much constructive comment; also to Anthony Aris of Serindia Publications whose knowledge of the country, illustrative material and careful editing were invaluable.

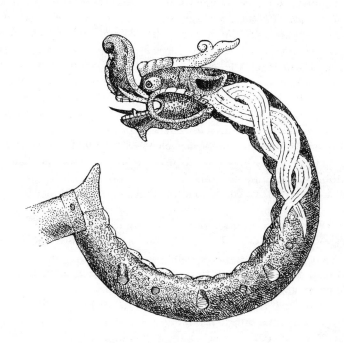

PREFACE

This book is not a history of Bhutan. Very few foreigners, certainly not Westerners, are qualified to write about a country whose history, religious and secular, has been so complex. A few Indian scholars have written books on Bhutan's history and government, but there is no work devoted solely to the two hundred years' association between Bhutan and Great Britain although one or two, published in India, cover parts of the period. There is fortunately, however, a good vein of source material, in the form of travellers' diaries, official reports and governmental correspondence. Unfortunately, though, this is almost entirely confined to the British side, mainly because a series of disastrous fires destroyed some of the Bhutanese archives and others remain inaccessible. Inevitably therefore this is a book about Bhutan as seen through British eyes although I have tried to set the record straight wherever possible.

My interest in Bhutan was first aroused in 1975 when I led a small British mission to discuss possibilites of aid to education and fell in love with the country and its people. On my return I read John Claude White's *Sikhim and Bhutan* and was surprised to discover that the first British mission had been undertaken by George Bogle just over two hundred years before ours and that his was the first of a series including White's own journeys in the early years of this century and continuing until the end of the second world war. I was not surprised to learn that with some notable exceptions the magnificence of the country and the charm of its people had had the same effect on most of my predecessors as on my companions and myself. The exceptions had been those whose 19th century missions had not been welcomed by the Bhutanese during a period of internal dissension and strained relations with the British over frontier problems. Ultimately this led to a war in which the ill-armed Bhutanese soldiers displayed a courage that was the admiration of their enemies.

When I returned to Bhutan on another official visit in 1982 I was a little less ignorant and was able to look at places through the eyes of my 18th and 19th century forerunners and to compare my impressions with theirs. I found the impact of the country even greater than before. In 1984, two years after starting the research for this book, I was fortunate enough to be invited to return, this time for a longer period, to do some work for the government of Bhutan, and to see some of the remoter areas through which one or two of the missions had passed.

Although my main intention has been to introduce the Kingdom of Bhutan to the general as well as the academic reader, mainly through the writings of British travellers and official correspondence and not attempt anything more than a sketchy outline of Bhutanese history, I have had to deal at rather greater length than originally intended with political relationships as these were generally either the cause or the outcome of successive missions. Towards the end of the book I have attempted to summarise the benefits accruing to both sides from this long relationship as this does not seem to have been done before at all objectively and has inevitably been overlaid by the much greater and more obvious benefits to Bhutan from the association with the Government of India since 1947

In the main however this is not a political book. It has the more modest objective of introducing readers to a kingdom whose people have considerable respect for Britain, where increasing numbers of Bhutanese officials and educators are now being trained, and to extending knowledge of a country which has so much in common with our own, including a universally revered hereditary monarchy, respect for the law, tolerance of others and a robust sense of humour. Admiration for these attributes, as well as for the breath-taking beauty of the scenery and the splendour of the architecture, become apparent in the recollections of many of the British officials, soldiers and others whose memoirs form a substantial element of this book.

The sturdy personalities of these travellers in a virtually unknown land are matched by the eccentricities of their spelling. Bhutan becomes at times Bootan and Bhotan and its inhabitants Bootaniers, Bootias and Booteahs. For the most part I have only retained their versions of the names of places and people when quoting from source. Otherwise I have adhered to contemporary spelling in the interest of continuity. Even modern maps vary and the few scholars who have written histories of Bhutan differ considerably over the spelling of most proper and place names. I have just had to pursue my own course going for contemporary concensus as far as one exists. In many case I have accepted Dr Michael Aris' corrections of my original versions.

Another problem has been to identify on the few modern maps available, the locations of smaller places, rivers and mountains, referred to in the memoirs, partly because of the authors' sometimes bizarre phonetic spelling, partly also because names seemed to have changed quite often. On several occasions missions camped in or passed through places mentioned by their immediate predecessors and found different names in use. Quite frequently also villages were abandoned as the forests were cut down or the soil worked out or as a result of the semi-perpetual state of civil war; and it has been impossible to identify them at all. Wherever possible I have tried to avoid mentioning these but have sometimes had to retain them in the text for the sake of the context. I apologise to readers who look for them in vain on the map.

I have also, wherever possible, used the English spelling customary in Bhutan today for the names of institutions and buildings and, for the most part, of official titles where these are still in use. For titles no longer in use but frequently referred to I have often retained the Anglicised versions of the memoirs. Readers are referred to the Glossary for definitions of titles and other words. These were mostly based on the Indian experience common to all the 18th and 19th century travellers, the most important being the names they accorded to the spiritual and secular rulers, the Dharma and Deb Rajas, although Raja was not a Bhutanese term. Dharma is a sanskrit word and Deb was the Bhutanese pronunciation of the Tibetan 'depa' (sde-pa) or civil ruler.

I must reiterate that this is neither a history of Bhutan nor an account of the country's complex and distinctive culture which is woven into the history and religion of the region. Nevertheless in the impressions recorded by visiting Britons, their reactions and their descriptions, varying in emphasis over the centuries, a picture emerges of a unique kingdom. It is interesting to note not only the changes in attitude of the Bhutanese towards these strange intruders but also the differences of approach amongst the British themselves whose descriptions of geographical features, bridges, buildings and artefacts are more trustworthy than their assessments of people and institutions, influenced by their own cultural background, and without much understanding, in most cases, of Buddhist values.

Their attitudes reflected not only their own societies but also the current relationship, at the time of their visits, between British and Bhutanese authorities and the state of the frontier. The eighteenth century visitors wrote as agents of an expanding trading company, scholarly accounts of privileged visits, which aroused enormous interest in the west, where the age of enlightenment comprehended a thirst for knowledge about far away places. Early twentieth century officials represented a great imperial power with benevolent but, on the whole, empty-handed intentions towards a country from which there was nothing to fear. The nineteenth century missions were very different. The British Indian governments which they served were usually at war somewhere or other on the Indian sub-continent or in Asia, either within India itself, in the complex and shifting alliances of Princely states or on the periphery, in places as far apart as Afghanistan, Persia, Burma and Nepal. There was an ever present fear of Russia and preoccupation with the north western frontiers, and anxieties about China. The perpetual feuding between Bhutanese and British Indian subjects in the border areas, the interminable civil wars within Bhutan and the resultant power vacuum were seen therefore within a wider framework of imperial diplomacy. This affected, in their official capacity, the outlook of

nineteenth century visitors, who were also influenced in their personal
reactions to Bhutan by the evangelistic and moralising spirit of the times.
They represented a nation whose interests clashed with those of the
Bhutanese; and official criticisms of Bhutanese actions were reinforced
by personal moral judgements on a society so different from their own.
Their uninvited missions occurred during periods of internal crisis and
they were not made particularly welcome. Consequently, they were, not
unnaturally, prejudiced against their reluctant hosts.

In normal, times however, the Bhutanese are the most hospitable people.
The century of Anglo-Bhutanese tension, culminating in war in 1864, has
long since been forgotten and the modern traveller is assured of an
almost embarrassingly friendly reception. Although they are indebted to
the Government of India for assistance in almost all fields of economic
aid, without which they could not play a proper role in the modern
world, nevertheless they also welcome help from other sources and it is
good to know that the British hostility of the past has been replaced by
co-operation in the field of education and that the English language now
provides a major tool for development and international contact.

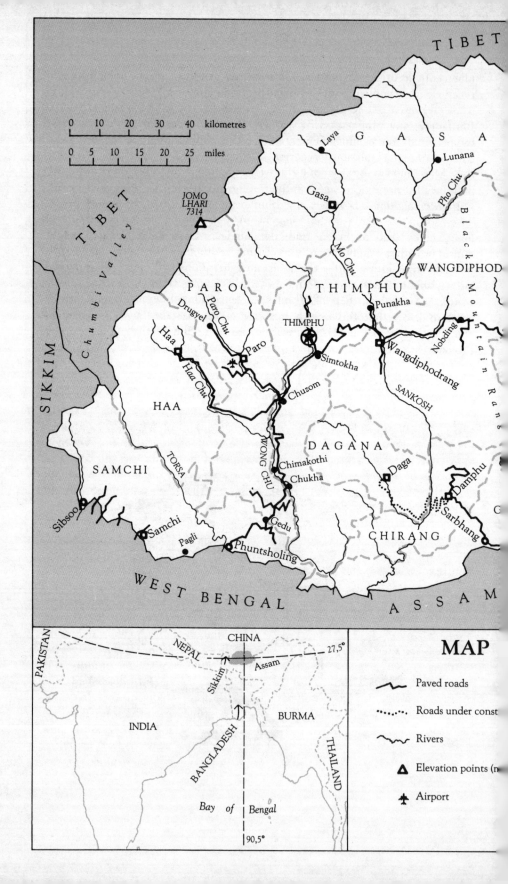

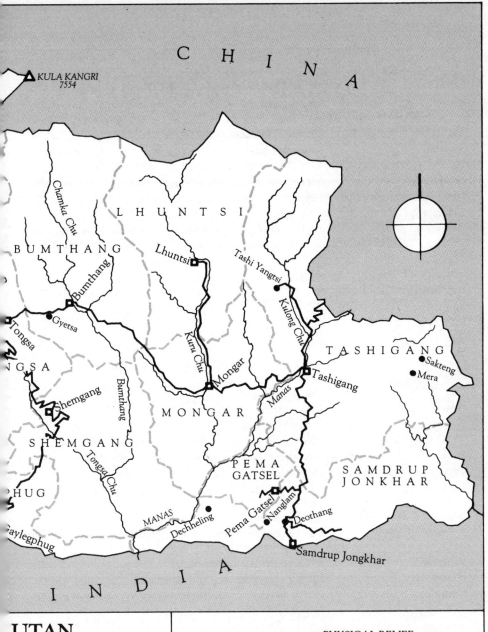

CHINA

△ KULA KANGRI
7554

L H U N T S I

B U M T H A N G

Chamka Chu

Bumthang

Lhuntsi

Tashi Yangtsi

● Gyetsa

Tongsa

N G S A

Kuru Chu

Mongar

Kulong Chu

T A S H I G A N G

● Sakteng

● Mera

● Tashigang

Shemgang

Bumthang

M O N G A R

Manas

S H E M G A N G

Tongsal Chu

P E M A
G A T S E L

S A M D R U P
J O N K H A R

P H U G

MANAS

● Dechheling

Pema Gatsel
● Nanglam

Deothang

aylegphug

□ Samdrup Jongkhar

I N D I A

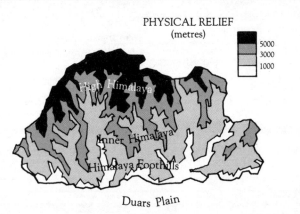

PHYSICAL RELIEF
(metres)

	5000
	3000
	1000

High Himalaya

Inner Himalaya

Himalaya Foothills

Duars Plain

GLOSSARY OF TERMS

Amban	Chinese representative in Lhasa.
Amlah	Council of State, a term found only in 19th-century records.
Dasho	Title of all senior government officials (= Red scarf officer).
Deb Drönyer	Senior government official (orig. Deb Raja's Guestmaster).
Deb Raja	Head of secular government, Regent.
Deb Zimpön	Chamberlain to the Deb Raja.
Dharma Raja	Former spiritual ruler of Bhutan, successive incarnations of Shabdrung Ngawang Namgyal; the Bhutanese equivalent of the Dalai Lama.
Druk Gyalpo	King of Bhutan.
Drungpa (Doompah)	Government official with authority over a group of villages, junior to Dzongpön.
Duar	Mountain pass, leading from Indian plains to the Bhutanese interior, and adjoining territory.
Dzong	Fortress-monastery, administrative centre of a valley-district.
Dzongpön	Fort commander with authority over a civil district, junior to Pönlop.
Gap	Village headman.
Gelong	Fully-ordained Buddhist monk.
Gosain	Hindu pilgrim-trader.
Jemadar	Viceroy's junior commissioned officer, Indian Army.
Jingal	Primitive form of shotgun.
Lama Khembo (Je Khembo)	Head Abbot of Bhutan.
Lama	Spiritual 'superior', equivalent to 'guru', sometimes with high position in hierarchy.
Lopon	Senior monastic teacher.
Nyerpa	Government bailiff with responsibility for taxation in the 18th and 19th centuries.
Paharias	Hill dwellers (Indian term).
Pönlop	District governor, largely autonomous.
Sanyasis	Hindu ascetics, a term here referring to a group of mendicant traders, moneylenders and mercenaries who were in conflict with the British in the area of Bengal adjoining Bhutan in the second half of the 18th century.
Shung Drönyer	State treasurer.
Subadar	Viceroy's senior commissioned officer, Indian Army.
Tshogdu	National Assembly.
Zemindar	Landlord with extensive property (Indian term).
Zimpön	Chamberlain or Master of Ceremonies in the service of Dharma Raja, Deb Raja, Pönlop, or Dzongpön.
Zingap	Court attendant or messenger.

INTRODUCTION

Drukyul—Land of the Thunder Dragon

Embedded beneath the snow white folds of the high Himalayas the ancient kingdom of Bhutan has preserved its independence from time immemorial, untainted by the baser aspects of the outside world. Although today it is classified as one of the poorest and least developed countries in the world, it has, unlike most others, retained its integrity and distinctive way of life virtually intact.

Only 250 miles long and 90 miles wide, landlocked and bordered by its powerful neighbours, India and Chinese Tibet, as well as Nepal, Bhutan's main line of communication is southwards to the Indian border although the development of a road suitable for wheeled traffic is comparatively new. Until a hard surfaced road was completed in 1962 the only means of transport between the capital, Thimphu and the town of Phuntsholing near the border was by pony or mule and the journey took up to ten days.

Geography has exercised a stronger influence over national history than in most countries. The great natural barriers of this rugged land led to such a physical isolation that the Bhutanese have developed national characteristics which have remained unchanged throughout the centuries. These include self sufficiency, determination, an unaggresive pride, good humour and courtesy. Even their one great national import, the Buddhist faith, has been moulded to a distinctively Bhutanese form.

Although the mountain ranges of the north and the forests of the south contributed to inaccessibility, the river valleys provided links with the outer world and so there developed a few regular trade routes to neighbouring countries which were utilised by everyone, be they merchant, lama or private traveller.

Three great lateral divisions divide the country geographically and so determine the centres and nature of population: the lowlands north of the Indian border, the central highlands and the snowy heights. In addition to these, a mountainous spine down the centre has also, until recently, effectively separated west from east reinforcing existing linguistic and ethnic differences for which, and for whose continuance, it was in large measure responsible.

The first of the three lateral zones lies to the north of the plains, adjoining the Brahmaputra basin, fed by rivers rising high in the Bhutanese Himalayas. It is a land of dense tropical vegetation in places and an average rainfall of 100 inches a year. Although mostly in the plains the area also includes some high peaks arising out of the foothills, in between which lie lush tropical valleys with evergreens and bamboo clothing the hillsides which, in places, are bright with huge pink and blue rhododendrons, snow white magnolias and wild orchids of many sizes, often growing from trees. In the hot steamy jungle, laid back from the roads, there is an abundance of wild life including elephant, buffalo, tiger, bison, rhino, musk and barking deer. It is the only known home of the golden langur monkey and is a paradise for butterflies of every shape and hue, some of them as large as small birds.

The main centres of population, such as they are in this under-populated kingdom, lie in the central area, like the filling in a sandwich. No less than nine rivers flow through it coming down as mountain streams from the north, through narrow valleys forming enormous rocky gorges in places and in others broadening out into fertile valleys where a large range of crops and vegetables is grown. There are terraces of rice and fields of maize and wheat as well as orchards and pasture land. Home of the Himalayan bear, of wild boar, of pheasant and partridge, it is scenically magnificent with tempting and well stocked trout streams tumbling their way through blueish purple mountains before widening out into emerald green valleys, flowing sedately past solidly built villages, little townships and ancient monasteries, before narrowing and tumbling again through rocky defiles. Some of the hillsides are covered in vegetation, including oaks and giant rhodo-dendrons, but there are occasional patches where the forests have been cleared for cultivation. In the fertile valleys lie most of the major towns: Thimphu, the capital; Punakha, the old capital, marvellously sited at the confluence of two rivers; and the townships of Bumthang, Paro, Ha and Tashigang. Most of them are situated on the routes taken by traders who, although not numerous, from earliest recorded times passed between India and Tibet. The same routes into Bhutan were taken by the Buddhist monks who so changed the course of national history, as well as invaders from Tibet.

The third and most impressive of the three lateral regions is one of vast mountain formations, rising to 24,000 feet, where in the great Himalayas the ancient Gods are enthroned in icy splendour. Many of peaks remain unexplored and most of them never lose their snow white mantles, including the sacred peak of Chomolhari. All but two of Bhutan's rivers rise amongst these peaks before cascading down to the valleys below. In these high places there are enormous and forbidding rock faces and glistening glaciers, at the foot of which lie the blue glacier lakes, an area of dwarf rhododendrons and azaleas, the home of the snow leopard, musk dear and the Tibetan white eared pheasant.

The awe-inspiring hand of nature is almost matched by the works of man, for in every part of Bhutan can be seen perched on the highest of peaks, tiny shrines, isolated temples and towering dzongs – monasteries which are usually also the seats of local government. They were nearly always sited in commanding positions on high ground at strategic points and were heavily fortified. The oldest, at Simtokha, was built in 1629, (some say 1627 but the most authoritative sources prefer 1629) by Shabdrung Ngawang Namgyal, the founder of modern Bhutan. It was the first seat of government and became the model for all the others. Constructed of wood and hard earth, no nails were used, a pattern that was followed everywhere.

The people of Bhutan, who number no more than 1.3 million in an area of 18,000 square miles, have been so cut off from the world by natural barriers apart from their comparatively slender religious and commercial contacts with Tibet and India, that they have developed a unique lifestyle extending not only to religion and government but also to architecture, dress and even sport, in which archery is the national pastime and is as much in evidence in township and hamlet as in medieval England.

Until the beginning of the last century very few travellers had penetrated the country, apart from Tibetan monks, a few holy men up from the Indian plains, a trickle of hardy Indian traders and the Portugese Jesuits, Cacella and Cabral, in the early seventeenth century; and from the late eighteenth century onwards official missions from British India. All travelled on foot or with mules or ponies.

Most Bhutanese still live in ways that would be recognised by those early travellers; in small hamlets beside the rivers and in isolated and surprisingly large farmsteads similar in appearance to those in Austria and Switzerland. They are usually made of wood, stone and clay, without any nails, and have shingled roofs held down by large stones. Animals occupy the ground floor.

The people are meat eaters, enjoying pork and beef with rice, fresh vegetables and herbs, accompanied usually by incredibly hot spices, especially chillies and red peppers. They are also great chewers of betel and enjoy local liquors called chang and arak (and more recently a quite congenial whisky).

Physically, they are, with some notable exceptions, not particularly tall but almost all of the hill dwellers are very sturdy. The plains men are thinner and look more like Indians of Bengal. Like the descendants of the 9th century Tibetan immigrants and the Indo-Mongolian inhabitants of the Eastern border, they are of a different ethnic origin to the Bhutanese of the central zone. The typical Bhutanese of this area which includes the major centres of population and government, is of medium height, well built, with mongoloid features, a well developed sense of humour and an absence of 'hang-ups' over alcohol, sex or other aspects of social life, unusual in the sub-continent. There is no caste or class system and women do not have to live in seclusion. Their costume, of blouse and long finely woven dress formed by a multi-coloured square of cloth secured at the waist by a belt and at the shoulders with silver buckles, is the most attractive of any national dress and is universally worn except on the plains (and nearly always adopted by the few European women in Bhutan). The men's dress is a sort of highland plaid with a huge fold above the belt forming a pouch which becomes a resting place for cigarettes, tobacco, car keys, even the office file. Under it is worn a silk or cotton vest with broad white cuffs. On special occasions men wear knee length boots of embroidered cloth. Ministers and government officials also wear scarves of different colours denoting their rank and no official will ever call on a senior without wearing his scarf. Most respected of all, after the orange of the Royal Family is the red silk scarf of the Dasho, a title conferred by the King on the most senior officials.

The national language is Dzongkha, a polished version of the speech of Western Bhutan, originally a dialect of central Tibet. The classical written language taught in the dzongs is literary Tibetan. Nepali is generally spoken in the south and there are about eleven or more different dialect languages in the east. Consequently the development of Dzongkha as a unifying force is a national objective and about 80 percent of people speak it although it is native only to about 25 percent of them.

Another unifying force is the use of English as the medium of instruction in the schools from the infants school upwards and those who emerge from the top of the system are highly articulate in English and freely use it as a means of communication within the country and for international contacts.

The great unifying forces are cultural, for art and drama, music and dance, all have a religious foundation in Bhutanese Buddhism. To the music of traditional instruments, including drums, trumpets and shawms, there are many occasions for religious dances whose performers wear colourful costumes. These are not, as in some countries, merely quaint revivals but living manifestations of a long tradition and a national faith. Almost all representation in art or music is designed to show the perennial struggle between good and evil. Ever present is the contemplation of enlightenment through the medium of painted scrolls in temples and wall paintings in monasteries.

Although nothing is known of the religion of Bhutan before the 8th century it is said by some writers to have been animistic and for elements to have been retained even after the introduction of Buddhism by Guru Padmasambhava, a monk from Swat (now in Pakistan) who is credited locally with introducing the Mahayana school of Buddhism. Over the centuries a distinctive faith developed and this process was accelerated when some members of the older monastic schools took refuge in Bhutan from political strife in Tibet. The greatest of these and the founding father of modern Bhutan, both ecclesiastical and civil, was Ngawang Namgyal who entered the country at the age of 23 in 1616. After many struggles and much opposition he became undisputed spiritual and temporal head of the land. He laid down its code of law based on Buddhist principles and established an independent theocracy which continued after his death, with ten incarnations of his spiritual successors, lasting nearly three hundred years until the foundation of the modern hereditary kingdom in the early years of this century.

Although Bhutan is no longer a theocracy, Buddhism is still woven into the fabric of society in a way for which there is no modern western comparison. Buddhist perceptions of non-violence are integral to the way of life (although this has not prevented the Bhutanese from being determined and successful soldiers when their country has been threatened and from giving Tibetan invaders and troops from British India a good drubbing on occasion). Monks still play a leading role in Bhutanese life and have an honoured place in the state with statutory representation in the national assembly and the royal advisory council. In every part of Bhutan the physical aspects of Buddhism can be seen: great dzongs, temples, small shrines, prayer wheels, and prayer flags straining and fluttering in the almost permanent winds of the highlands.

The history of Bhutan is inseparable from religion. After the time of Guru Padmasambhava there followed a difficult period of constant Tibetan incursions before the arrival of the refugee lamas which was followed by the spread of their faith and the establishment of powerful monastic overlords in various parts of the country. There was no central authority until Ngawang Namgyal imposed it after decisively defeating the Tibetans in 1639. It was after this time that he took the title of Shabdrung. He was the supreme authority in both spiritual and temporal matters and only after his death were the two powers separated between the 'Deb' (temporal) and 'Dharma' (spiritual) rulers. Shabdrung Ngawang Namgyal's rule lasted 35 years until his death, said to have been kept secret for 50 years in an attempt to prevent disruptions when the civil war he had suppressed broke out again and the attacks from Tibet were resumed, until in 1647 the Bhutanese defeated a combined Tibetan and Mongolian army. Ngawang Namgyal's work was to stand the test of time and the many dzongs that were built at his behest are a physical reminder today of his rule. These include the Tashichodzong in Thimphu, which remained intact until rebuilt in traditional style between 1962 and 1970 in order to house the government. Of no less importance was his introduction of a system of local government through the 'Pönlops', the rulers of regions, and the Dzongpöns, the district administrators. He established the rule of law and the collection of revenue. By the time of his death all the western part of Bhutan was united and not long afterwards the eastern area was incorporated to form a state whose boundaries did not

differ greatly from those of the modern kingdom, apart from the
frontier territory later annexed to India by the British.

The history of Bhutan throughout the 17th and 18th centuries was of
the struggle for supremacy between the spiritual rulers, The Dharma
'Rajas', successive incarnations of the Shabdrung, chosen after a long
search to find the right child, and the Deb 'Rajas' who, in Shabdrung
Ngawang Namgyal's time had only been his appointed subordinates; and
the increasing power of the Pönlops, some of whom used the Deb Rajas
as their pawns in a power struggle. Although the secular suzerainty of
China and the spiritual overlordship of Tibet were always claimed and at
times acknowledged, the conflicts remained internal and there were
fewer invasions from Tibet and an increase in traders from India. After
the disclosure of the death of the founding Shabdrung in 1705, who had
in fact died in c.1651, power in the 18th century passed increasingly to
the Pönlops who indulged in endless civil wars.

The main external cause of conflict in this period was not in the north
from Tibet but on the southern border with the Indian state of Cooch
Behar which had been periodically invaded by Bhutanese whose actions
were often neither known by nor approved of by the central authority.
The government of Bhutan paid an annual tribute to the Raja of the
state, but by the end of the 18th century they had become powerful
enough to neglect this obligation and even, in 1772, to abduct the Raja. It
is at this point that Britain enters the story for the first time.

CHAPTER ONE

1771–1775: Conflict and Reconciliation: George Bogle and the First Mission

In 1757 Clive's victory at Plassey opened a new chapter in Britain's relationship with the Indian sub-continent, an association that had begun in the 16th century with delegations from the courts of the Tudors to those of the Moghul Emperors who had agreed to the founding of the East India Company in 1601 as a staging post on the west coast for the spice trade from the East Indies. India only became the Company's main area of operation after the Dutch had driven the English away from the East Indies and they in their turn had defeated the Portuguese in sea battles off the west coast of India. In 1674 the Company's Headquarters moved from Surat to Bombay which Charles II's Portugese bride had brought in her dowry. The Company had by then already set up a 'factory', as the trading depots were known, at Madras in 1640; and in 1690 they moved from Hughli to Calcutta which later became their main centre. By the turn of the century, therefore, although still subject to the Moghul Emperors in Delhi from whom they received their permission to trade, the British were not only well established on both coasts but had also been granted rights of administration within the area of their factories from which they exported cotton goods, indigo, pepper and spices from the west coast and cotton, sugar, silks and saltpetre from the east.

The decline of the Moghuls in the 18th century led to the establishment of many emergent states ruled by former vassals of the Empire. Chief amongst these were the Rajput Princes in the north, the Mahrattas in the south west, the state of Hyderabad in the south and later on the Sikhs in the Punjab. It contributed also to the rivalry between the French and English companies not confined to the periods of war in Europe, to their political support of rival states and ultimately the extension of the areas under their direct administrative control. Despite French successes under Dupleix the British East India company had by 1757, after Clive's victory at Plassey, established a supremacy that was only really endangered again by the French during the war of American Independence (1776–1783). By then also the British company had become so involved with the succession problems of the Indian rulers of Bengal in the east that it had already begun to administer areas outside the factories. Although nominally ruled by the Nawab, Bengal was

virtually controlled by the Company because of the military and fiscal
powers delegated to it by the decaying Empire. Warren Hastings, who
succeeded Clive, continued the process of reforming the administration,
of revenue collection and of curtailing the money grubbing activities of
the Company's servants. He was arguably the greatest of all British
administrators in India although his position, as ostensible representative
of a merchant company, still mainly concerned with profitability, was far
less secure than that of his 19th century successors. He was well aware of
the distaste of his Court of Directors in London for anything that did not
lead to profits. Consequently his correspondence with them on the
subject of Bhutan was understandably cautious.

The court was no respecter of persons and the abrasive tone of some
of their letters to a man whom posterity was to remember long after its
own collective oblivion, is in striking contrast to the euphemisms of
modern bureaucracy. For example, in response to Hastings' promotion
of a military officer in the Company's service, they wrote: "We cannot
supress our indignation at your conduct . . ." and a number of their
letters contain phrases such "We cannot but be displeased with . . ." and
display a remarkable tetchiness towards their chief representative in
India. No wonder therefore that Hastings had to probe very carefully
their likely reactions to possible involvement with Bhutan and to
emphasise the profit element so dear to his masters, who took the bait
and replied, on April 4th 1771: 'It having been presented to us that the
Company may be greatly benefited in the sale of broadcloth, iron and
lead and other European commodities by sending proper persons to
reside at Rungapore to explore the interest of parts of Bhutan and
Assam and other countries adjacent to Gaulporah and as you well know
our earnest desire to extend the vend of the staples of this kingdom to as
great a degree as possible we are surprised you have not already made an
attempt to carry so desirable an object into execution. You are therefore
required to procure the best accounts possible and give us your opinion
thereon.'

Even before the abduction of the Raja of Cooch Behar by the
Bhutanese there had been frequent border incidents; and in writing to
the Court about possible trade with Bhutan Hastings had anticipated a
future need to turn his attention northwards. Local Bhutanese officials
were becoming powerful and increasingly independent of their divided
spiritual and temporal rulers many days march away in the central
highlands. Consequently when the rulers of small Indian border states
were weak they invited attention from marauders, sometimes with the
connivance of minor Bhutanese officials. This situation was accentuated
by the geographical location of the 'duars', a series of mountain passes,
whose name like the English 'door' and the Hindi 'dwar', (a gate or
entrance) has a common Indo-European origin. This is precisely what

they were: gateways to the more fertile plains; and as such were to prove a source of contention over the next hundred years when the term came to be applied to the whole area of level plain into which the duars opened.

Whilst the Bhutanese held captive the ruler of Cooch Behar, the Nazir, or Regent, of that state, installed the Raja's son on his father's throne, to the annoyance of the Deb Raja of Bhutan, Deb Yadhur, who again invaded the state. After an initial reverse he was successful, with assistance from the ruler of another small Indian state, the Raikat Darp Deo of Baikunthpore, and installed his own nominee as king. The Nazir fled and appealed to the Company for assistance, offering to pay half the state revenues in return. Hastings accepted the offer and in December 1772 a force of four companies of Indian troops and two field guns was sent to Cooch Behar under Captain John Jones. After a battle in which Jones was wounded and only after considerable losses amongst his sepoys were the Bhutanese forced to withdraw, deserting their ally. The boy king returned with the Nazir to his capital and ratified a treaty with the Company acknowledging its supremacy, accepting annexation to Bengal, agreeing to pay the expense of military operations and making over half the annual revenue; the other half was to be retained only so long as the state's loyalty was assured. This was a fierce price to pay, especially as there was no end to the frontier incidents.

Now, nearly two years after the Court had first written about trade with Bhutan, Hastings was able to report the expulsion of the Bhutanese from the Company's territory, but even so took care to justify his actions on the grounds of security, writing on January 15th 1773 about 'Boutanners (sic) a nation who inhabit the mountains of the north of that province (Cooch Behar) . . . who have of late years, partly by force and partly by treachery, obtained a dangerous influence in those parts . . . In deliberating on these affairs we had more in consideration the peace and security of our present possessions than any advantage to be derived from the new acquisition we were flattered with; for as your district of Rungapore [Rangpur] has been frequently exposed to the incursions of the Boutanners and the collection of revenue drawn from part of Cooch Behar which depends on Rungapore thereby rendered very precarious, it became a matter of direct interest to embrace any opportunity which offered of expelling these people from these countries and confining them within the limits of their mountains . . .'

He went on to describe the success of the military operations in Cooch Behar and reported his intention "for the better protection of the districts of Rajanal and Boglepoor from the depradations of the banditti who inhabit the neighbouring mountains, to raise a new corps of light infantry under Captain W. Roberts".

The following month a new war broke out as the Darp Deo had now allied himself with the Sanyasis, a lowland people who had long been in

league with the Bhutanese and had, at the Company's insistence, been
dismissed from the service of the Raja of Cooch Behar. In a letter of
1773, Hastings had described them to the Court as people who 'under
pretence of religious pilgrimage have been accustomed to traverse the
chief part of Bengal, begging, stealing and plundering wherever they go'.
Captain Jones was again successful, reaching Baikunthpore in the middle
of February and capturing Dalingcote. Meanwhile Mr George Purling, the
Collector of Rangpur, an administrative and revenue official, decided to
go on the attack, having had intelligence reports of a renewed Sanyasi –
Bhutanese alliance, on the grounds that the Darp Deo could not be
crushed until his allies were defeated. He therefore accompanied
Lieutenant James Dickson and a detachment of Indian troops to
Chichacotta where the Sanyasis retreated from the fort and fought their
way into Buxa Duar. They were closely pursued by Purling and Dickson
who then found themselves in danger of being cut off. They had to
withdraw, losing fourteen sepoys and an English sergeant.

Shortly after this, marauders from Bhutan once again entered the
Rangpur district. This time the Collector sent Captain George Thomas
with a small party of 'Pergunnah' sepoys, a locally recruited paramilitary
force, normally only used for revenue collection, who unsuccessfully
attacked the Bhutanese 'imprudently expending their ammunition',
Thomas being killed.

Other military operations showed up the inadequacy of the Company's
border troops as well as the robustness of the Bhutanese. From a camp
near the border Captain Robert Stewart wrote, in an order to his
command on February 2nd, a few weeks after Thomas' death: 'From the
behaviour of the troops this morning in front of the united army of the
Raja and the Sunassie, Captain Stewart is sorry to say that his utmost
efforts to their honour and safety must fall far short of their interest', a
garbled way of telling them they had not done well. He went on to
impress on them the importance of obeying orders . . . '400 disciplined
men would have defeated the battalion as it behaved that day . . . As
regularity and obedience are our grand and only superiority they cannot
be too rigorously enforced'. However, in a covering letter to Warren
Hastings he said that the enemy had been completely routed although
they had got to within 50 yards of the Company's forces, of whom he
wrote, rather surprisingly in view of his strictures, 'never did men behave
with nobler or steadier resolution'. He had, nevertheless, chosen to
upbraid them for 'being ambitious in pursuit as the smallest tendency to
irregularity in soldiers cannot be too palpably stigmatised'.

This little victory was described to the Court of Directors on March 1st
1773: 'We have the pleasure of informing you that everything has
succeeded to our wish. The Bhutanese retired before Captain Jones and
Captain Stewart took the capital of the Zeminder of Bycunpore (sic) in

league with the Bhutanese'.

The Court's response, received many months later, was to order Hastings to report 'in what manner and to what extent the Company may be benefited by opening trade to these countries'.

In the meantime however, Hastings had realised that he had been rather too sanguine and wrote on March 31st to report that the Sanyasis were still active and that 'despite severe orders to Zemindars [landowners] and farmers', they were assisted by local people. 'We meet obstacles every day', he wrote, 'in the superstition of the inhabitants'. Captain Timothy Edwards had met the same fate as Thomas and had been deserted by his sepoys . . . 'We fear that the revenue may suffer . . . ' Describing the events in Cooch Behar however, he wrote that the operations had 'gone on with the same success with which we began . . . express orders had been given to Mr Purling not to listen to any overtures of negotiation from the Boutanners till he has obtained entire possession of the low countries . . . ' He was directed to 'regard the hills as the boundaries of Bengal'.

Ten days after the despatch of Hastings' letter the Bengal government ordered Mr Purling to take over the low lying cultivated land right up to the foot hills which were to be regarded in future as the frontier of Bengal and would thus be secure from attack. The Bhutanese were informed that no treaty would be signed until this land was in the Company's hands. Although the Dharma Raja professed a desire for peace the Deb Raja, Deb Zhidar, sent a force to attack Chichacotta which was defended by Dickson and over two hundred sepoys. The Bhutanese charged with great ferocity and the defenders fought for their lives, losing five killed and thirty three wounded before the Bhutanese withdrew into the hills after losing more than two hundred men.

The Deb Raja was forced out of office after this set-back, and his successor sued for peace, the emissaries asking only for the return of some of the lowlands. Purling recommended agreement as much of this country was said to be very unhealthy.

A few days before this, on 29th March 1774, the Panchen Lama of Tibet (called 'Teshoo Lama' by the British) wrote to Hastings. He was probably aware of Hastings' reputation for fair dealing and was prepared to be surprisingly frank over the shortcomings of subordinate rulers such as those in Bhutan over whom he was supposed to exercise a degree of spiritual overlordship, despite Bhutanese military success in repelling invaders from Tibet. Consequently the Bhutanese had asked him to mediate in their conflict with the British. 'I have been repeatedly informed', he wrote, 'that you have been engaged in hostilities against the Dah Terrea (The 'Deb Raja', as the British called him) to which it is said the Dah's own criminal conduct in committing ravages and other outrages on your frontiers, has given rise. As he is of a rude and ignorant race, past

times are not destitute of instances of the like misconduct which his own
avarice tempted him to commit. It is not unlikely that he has now resumed
those instances, and the ravages and plunder which he may have
committed on the outskirts of Bengal and Behar provinces have given
you provocation to send your vindictive army against him; however his
party has been defeated; many of his people have been killed, three forts
have been wrested from him, and he has met with the punishment he
deserved; and it is evident as the sun your army has been victorious; and
that if you had been desirous of it you might have entirely extirpated
him, for he had not power to resist your efforts. But I now take upon me
to be his mediator, and to represent to you that as the said Dah Terrea is
dependent upon the Dalai Lama who rules this country with unlimited
sway, (but on account of his being in his minority, the charge of the
government and administration for the present is committed to me)
should you persist in offering further molestation to the Dah's country, it
will irritate both the Lama and all his subjects against you. Therefore
from a regard to our religion and customs, I request you will cease all
hostilities against him and in doing this you confer the greatest favour
and friendship upon me. I have reprimanded the Dah for his past
conduct, and I have admonished him to desist from his evil practices in
future and to be submissive to you in all matters. I am persuaded that he
will conform to the advice which I have given him, and it will be necessary
that you treat him with compassion . . . ''

Warren Hastings wasted no time and on the 25th April a treaty consisting of ten articles was agreed to by which Chichocotta province was
restored to the Deb Raja who was to pay the Company a tribute of five
Tangun horses (described on page 14). Bhutanese merchants were
allowed to send an annual caravan to Rangpur and in return they promised
not to shelter Sanyasis or harbour criminals from the Company's territory and to allow Company troops to pursue over the border if necessary.
Hastings' hand was strengthened by the knowledge that the Court of
Directors was prepared to support limited military action and to leave
ultimate responsibility to him as they had already written to that effect,
saying 'Although we shall by no means depart from the rule laid for
confirming our view to our present possessions, yet as the peace and
security of them appears to have been the chief object of our President
(i.e. Hastings) and Council in agreeing to the proposals of Nazir Dev,
minister to the young Raja of Cooch Behar, we approve of the measures
they have taken to drive the Boutanners from the Raja's country and
consider the advantages proposed to the Company as an equivalent only
to the charges we may incur in assisting him. At the same time we are
pleased with the attention our President and Council have paid to our
declared sentiments respecting new acquisitions, in referring to us the
ratification of the treaty they thought it advisable to make with the Raja

upon their affording the assistance he desired; but as you have the local means of enquiring how far such an alliance may be necessary we leave this matter to your final determination and permit you to rectify the said treaty as you shall find most for the interest of the Company'.

By the time this letter was received the treaty had been signed, military action taken, and agreement reached with the Bhutanese. Only two months later the first and possibly the most significant British mission set off into the unknown country of Bhutan. Its leader was George Bogle of the Bengal civil service who was accompanied by Alexander Hamilton, as assistant surgeon. Warren Hastings wrote to Bogle on the 13th May 1774 to say "The design of your mission is to open a mutual and equal communication of trade between the inhabitants of Bhutan and Bengal and you will be guided by your own judgement using such means of negotiation as may be most likely to effect this purpose".

A more fundamental purpose of the mission was to take advantage of improved Anglo-Bhutanese relations by establishing contact and consequently trade with Tibet, as Hastings told the Court of Directors, ever mindful of their commercial interests. Bhutan was then regarded as little more than a means to an end.

Bogle was also commanded to take sample articles for commerce, to ask about the acceptability of other commodities and to inform himself about Bhutanese goods 'especially such as are of great value and easy transportation.' Hastings' letter ends on a familiar civil service note: 'you will draw on me for your charges and your drafts will be regularly answered . . . I need not recommend to you to observe a strict frugality and economy when the good of the service on which you are commissioned shall not require a deviation from these rules'. On his return he was commended for the meticulous accuracy of his accounts, not only for the maintenance of daily expenses, but also on his accounts for the bestowal of presents which included a string of pearls said to be worth 4500 rupees, a snuff box, a pair of pistols, a spy glass, as well as mathematical instruments made in Bengal and 'samples of Birmingham ware'.

He was also asked to undertake a number of private commissions for Warren Hastings; for one or more animals called 'turs' which produce 'shawl wool', one or two yaks and 'any curiosities, whether native production, manufactures, painting or what else may be acceptable to persons of taste in England.' The mission was also bidden to find out all they could about Bhutanese modes of government, 'areas of excellence, climate; roads, manners, customs, building and cookery, to bring back samples of coins and to report on the main characteristics of the people'.

In May 1774 at the hottest time of the year, Bogle and Hamilton set forth, crossing the border river between Cooch Behar and Bhutan in canoes. Once on the far bank they had little idea of what to expect and Bogle wrote 'As none of the Company's servants, and I might say almost no European, had ever visited the country which I was due to enter, I was equally in the dark as to the road, the climate or the people'.

They passed the recently destroyed Chichacotta fort and spent their first night in a thatched house built on stilts four foot off the ground. The walls were made of reeds tied with slips of bamboo without any iron or rope used in the building; 'the space below being turned into a hogstye contributed little to its pleasantness'. Nevertheless the evening was not uncongenial for they drank a bottle of rum with the headman and his neighbours and a female pedlar who lived with the headman and shared his taste for rum.

They set out early the next morning towards a chain of mountains about eighteen miles away which seemed to be looming over them. The people in this low lying area looked more like Bengalis but as they approached the hills there were marked signs of climatic changes. Here were forests, beautifully clear rivulets flowing over sandy river beds, and little springs to drink at; and they halted at 'a grand natural amphitheatre with the noise of waterfalls'. Continuing on their way they reached Buxa Duar where the local official, the Subha, visited them with presents of white scarves, butter, rice, milk and tea.

On 9th June they entered the hills where they were now well away from the Company's jurisdiction and were in Bhutan proper where the people looked very different from the plainsmen and where they were furnished with a pass from the Deb Raja, by whose orders they were provided with carriers who were pressed into service at each village, and with a couple of Tangun ponies. Bogle thought they had rather a mean appearance but changed his opinion of them when they turned out to be patient and sure footed and could 'climb a monument'. Most of this hardy breed were piebalds of about thirteen hands. Their tails were usually docked when sold at Rangpur, unless the English purchasers specially requested otherwise.

They wound their way up Mount Peachokum climbing steadily up a steep, narrow and winding path and felt chilly even at midday. Before crossing the pass at the top they turned to look back at Bengal and Bogle commented: 'It is impossible to conceive any change of country more abrupt or any contrast more striking'. To the south was a vast tract of lush flat land but to their north were mountains, glens, valleys and hills covered with 'lofty and luxuriant trees'. Before descending there was a religious ceremony and 'standards or banners were set up of white cloth with sentences written upon them'.

At every halt Bogle carried out Warren Hastings' instructions to plant potatoes, the first batch of ten being at a place called Jaigugu which consisted only of three houses. At Maridzong which they reached after a journey including many descents and steep climbs, passing three water-falls, he planted fifteen.

From thence they went by six difficult stages to Chuka and on towards Tashichodzong with the air growing colder at each stage. They were now climbing steadily through country whose vegetation was surprisingly familiar including huge walnut trees, elderberries, holly, willow, ash, aspen, sweetbriar, roses, brambles, juniper, wormwood, turnips, leeks, shallots, water and marsh melons, cucumbers and brinjals. The houses were made of stone and rammed earth, several storeys high, and there were numerous wooden cantilever bridges carrying tracks across the streams, as well as an iron suspension bridge built by the great Tibetan saint Thantong Gyalpo (1385–1464).

At one point they had to cross the Chuka river by a bridge 150 foot long, which consisted of five iron chains stretching from one side to the other, covered with bamboo matting placed on top of laths for the floor which swayed when stepped on. More often they encountered rivers which could only be crossed by a couple of ropes, of which one was for the feet or knees and the other for hand hauling.

At last after a march of over 150 miles, most of it following river courses, they reached Tashichodzong where the party was accomodated in a substantial house near the dzong (which Bogle referred to as 'the palace') where they felt so cold that they had to hang up Bhutanese blankets round the walls for insulation. Looking out from their residence they could see that they were in a valley about five miles long and a mile broad surrounded by mountains. On the low ground near the river there were rice fields and the area looked fairly prosperous and well populated with villages also scattered on the hill tops.

Not long after Bogle's arrival the Deb Raja returned from a journey and all of the balconies of the dzong were crowded with priests wearing red robes of Bhutanese woven cloth. 'The character of a Fakir is held in great esteem in this country' wrote Bogle, using the terminology of Muslim India. The loud playing of castanets, tabors, fifes and trumpets signalled the arrival of a procession saluted by the firing of thirty matchlocks. First came twelve led horses, then about a hundred and twenty men dressed in red and blue, thirty matchlock men, thirty archers, thirty horses laden with cloth, forty men on horseback, some wearing bushy hats, and six musicians, all preceeding the Deb Raja, also on horseback in scarlet cloak and large yellow hat, men waving fly whisks on either side of him and others carrying a white silk umbrella with coloured fringes which protected him. As the procession reached them the onlookers lit roadside fires of aromatic pine needles before prostrating themselves.

Two days later Bogle was sent for and his entry to the dzong was watched by about three thousand people as he was led through the three courts of the great building. After climbing a couple of iron plated ladders he came to an antechamber hung with weapons and from there was led into the audience chamber where the Deb Raja, in scarlet satin and wearing a mitre on his head, sat on a throne like a gilded pulpit surrounded with silver ewers and vases, whilst a servant twirled an umbrella over him. Twelve high officials were seated on cushions near the wall. Bogle bowed, although aware that according to the custom of the country he should have prostrated himself, before laying his presents in front of the Deb Raja and seating himself on a cushion in the centre of the room. No one spoke whilst copper platters of rice, butter and treacle were brought in, as well as tea, walnuts, Kashmiri dates, apricots, cucumbers and other fruit, all of which were set out before him in silence. Then a man with a silver kettle of buttered tea poured some into his own palm before filling the dishes of the Deb and the officials who provided their own wooden cups which were glazed black on the inside and wrapped in cloth as they were carried in the owners' tunics next to the skin. Bogle was given a china cup.

After the Deb Raja had said grace he spoke a few words to Bogle whilst the tea was being drunk and then Bogle was dressed in a flowered satin gown which he subsequently likened to the 'water tabby gown' worn by his aunt and a red 'handkerchief' was tied round his waist. He was then conducted to the Deb who bound his head with another hankerchief, squeezing his temples and placed on his head an image of Buddha, intoning prayers as he did so. Then, tying two silk handkerchiefs together he threw them over Bogle's shoulders before leading him back to his cushion.

Two or three more dishes of tea, two glasses of a spirit that Bogle referred to as whisky but was probably arak and betel nut, were passed round before the presentation came to an end and he was ushered out of the chamber.

A similar reception took place with the acting Regent, in his room at the top of a tower in the middle of the dzong; but after the first visit subsequent meetings with him were conducted without any of the formalities and he showed much more intellitent curiosity in the visitors than his secular counterpart or anyone else in the country. Bogle and Hamilton, with whose microscope he was fascinated, dined with him on several occasions, usually on stew made of pieces of kid with cucumber, seasoned with red pepper and served with boiled rice, sugar and butter.

One of the very few available accounts in Tibetan of Anglo-Bhutanese meetings has been translated by Michael Aris and his wife and quoted in his *Views of Medieval Bhutan*. It is a letter of rebuke sent to the Regent by the retired head abbot, on his return from pilgrimage in Tibet. He attributed recent disasters to the Regent's forgetfulness of a fundamental Tantric rule. The initiate must never have relations of any sort with those who oppose his teachings. 'The barbarian demons have disturbed your mind, Holy Being, to the extent that you are enamoured of the goods of the English . . .'

Bogle was very interested in the dzong and its inhabitants and described both in some detail. The building was divided into several courts, flanked with galleries supported on wooden pillars all the way round, which he likened to the architecture of an old English inn. The monks lived in a monastery within the dzong and from a gallery their ceremonies could be watched by visitors. He saw some of the dances which were performed daily. About twenty 'gelongs' (priests) dressed in many-coloured satin cloaks, sat on a bench, each holding a large tabor or a drum, beating time which they took from a priest who stood in the middle clashing two silver cups against each other, whilst other monks, wearing masquerade dresses, with visors like the beaks of birds, horses' heads, and other grotesque figures 'danced and capered with whimsical gestures'.

The walls of the dzong were two or three storeys high, inclining inwards and were entirely made of wood. Consequently the hills around were stripped of timber. At dusk the gates were shut and no one could enter until the following morning. Once every eight or ten days a string of five or six hundred monks left the dzong to bathe in the Chinchu river, 'They seem to lead a joyless, and I think, an idle life' wrote Bogle. A Bhutanese visitor to 18th century Britain might have said the same of the Dean and Chapter of most English cathedrals.

According to Bogle, Bhutanese social life was very democratic as masters lived on a friendly footing with their servants and dependants; and life was organised on common-sense lines. Marriage was easy and entailed no ceremony and if there were no children divorce was equally simple. Polygamy was not allowed.

The obsequies of death were rather more ceremonious, especially when the corpse was burnt. Bogle attended the burning of the body of a priest at which forty of his fellows recited offices whilst tea was served, bells tinkled and tabors and trumpets played. Keeping a respectful distance, old women counted beads and repeated the prayer 'Om mani padmi hum' which Bogle translated as 'Oh the jewel of the lotus, Amen', the lotus being the symbol of highest perfection. When night fell the body was wrapped in a linen sheet and laid on a funeral pile for which workmen had all the time been cutting wood. The dead monk's relations set fire to the pile which two priests fed with more wood whilst another threw spices, salt, butter, oil, betel and leaf. On the third day the ashes were collected and thrown into the Chinchu. There was no suttee, as in Hindu India and wives could not only outlive their husbands with impunity but were also free to marry again.

Other aspects of Bhutanese social life Bogle thought worthy of mention were that all the inhabitants of the country were dirty in their persons with the exception of the Deb Raja. On the other hand he found them remarkably free from the many taboos which distinguished Muslim as well as Hindu India and they had no caste system. Families were mostly self-contained, bartering their produce in exchange for wool from Tibet which was spun, woven and dyed by the women of the family. They ate bread made of unsifted flour, and coarse lean beef which was hung up to dry. The main food, however, was pork, and dried fish which came from Bengal and was eaten with rice and butter. As well as salt, fish and hogs the returning caravans from Rangpur brought coarse linen, broadcloth, dyes and spices.

Bogle reckoned that there were three classes in Bhutan: priests, government officers and people who worked on the land, land holders and husbandmen. The priests were trained from an early age, took a vow of chastity and swore also never to kill any living creature. Hence the Regent's horror when he thought that Hamilton was going to kill a fly that he wished to show him under the microscope.

Unlike the priests, government officers took no vows of chastity, but as marriage seemed to be a bar to promotion many remained single. They too were trained from a very early age and, according to Bogle, 'seldom arrived at places of trust or consequence till far advanced in life; and having passed through all the difficult gradations of service, it is no uncommon thing to see a minister as expert in mending a shoe or mending a tunic as in settling the business of the nation'. How admirable.

However the priests were the most important members of society and even the Deb Raja was accountable to them for the exercise of power and held office at their pleasure for they were responsible for electing him in the first place. They often became the governors of provinces; and the path to high office lay more in the priesthood than in the secular bureaucracy, as in the England of Cardinal Wolsey two centuries earlier.

Provincial Governors (Dzonpöns) had considerable powers, including those of policing their areas, levying taxes and the administration of justice. Taxes were very moderate, each family being rated according to their means and paying in kind; of which Bogle wrote: 'This mode of collection, however repugnant to the refined ideas of European policy, leaves them unencumbered with a heavy expense for tax gatherers and precludes the necessity of employing a numerous body of subjects in a vocation so useless to the state and so vexatious to the people'. In accordance with its limited revenue the expenses of government were small. Officers received no salaries and lived on the proceeds of presents and patronage. There was no standing army; but, as in medieval Europe, troops were called out to follow their landlords, and were all trained in the skills of archery. The main drain on the economy was the annual payment to the Panchen Lama in Tibet.

Of the people, Bogle wrote; 'The simplicity of their manners, their slight intercourse with strangers, and a strong sense of religion, preserve the Bhutanese from many vices to which more polished nations are addicted. They are strangers to falsehood and ingratitude. Theft, and every other species of dishonesty to which the lust for money gives birth, are little known. Murder is uncommon and, in general, is the effect of anger, not covetousness. The celibacy of a large part of the people however, is naturally productive of many irregularities; and the coldness of the climate inclines them to an excessive use of spiritous liquors'.

During his stay in the country the political situation was in a state of turmoil. The previous Deb Raja had been ambitious for more power, at the expense of the Dharma Raja, and had strengthened his connections with the Panchen Lama in Tibet and the Raja of Nepal as well as with the Emperor of China; but he over-reached himself when he attacked Cooch Behar and was repulsed by the Company's troops. This and his attempt to rebuild the dzong in a single year after it had been burnt, imposed great burdens on the people; and during his absence with the army the Dharma Raja's party took control and the current Deb Raja elected. However, some of the former ruler's supporters were still in the dzong and although some were prisoners many others were allowed their freedom and were in touch with their former leader, now living in Lhasa. They had attempted to regain power and rebel forces had reached Simtokha where they were reinforced by others before advancing towards Tashichodzong where Bogle and his party were still awaiting permission to go on to Tibet.

Just before the rebels were routed on the edge of the town he received the long awaited letter brought by a messenger from the Panchen Lama. This was to the effect that he would not be permitted to go to Lhasa as the Emperor of China would not like it and desiring him to return to India. Meanwhile a Gosain (a trading Hindu pilgrim), who acted as an intermediary between the Company and the Tibetan authorities, had received quite different information, that the prohibition was due to an outbreak of smallpox. Bogle refused to accept the presents brought by the Lama's emissary or the letter addressed to Warren Hastings on the grounds that it would constitute acceptance of the refusal. He was also disappointed in the attitude of the Deb Raja who put further difficulties in his way. He now placed all his hopes on the Gosain who was permitted to go on to Tibet. Bogle thought that the Tibetan attitude was due to a deep rooted suspicion of Europeans and detected a similar approach in Bhutan where he suspected that some of his journeys had been made unnecessarily difficult by the Deb Raja's people in order to discourage him. Consequently, although he had many questions to ask, he tried not to appear publicly curious in order not to arouse suspicions, especially in the vicinity of the Deb. However, when the ruler went off with his troops because of the civil war Bogle felt much freer to carry out his mission of enquiry into the details of Bhutanese life. Amongst other things he learnt that most of the trade between Lhasa and the low lands in the south of Bhutan was by way of Patna and Nepal and was carried out by Moghuls and Kashmiris.

At length his persistence paid off and the Deb Raja read out a letter from the Panchen Lama to say that the Dalai Lama, the spiritual ruler of Tibet, had agreed to his continuing his journey provided he took only a few attendants with him. Even then the Deb Raja, who Bogle now regarded as the main opponent of his going, still tried to dissuade him, possibly because his predecessor, the rebels' chief, had fled to Lhasa where the Lama was acting as intermediary for peace. Bogle was convinced that he would find the Panchen Lama more receptive to Hastings' proposal for trade and that the Deb Raja would then also accept them. He decided therefore not to press anything until his return to Bhutan, especially as he had learnt that the Deb was the main beneficiary from the existing trade and therefore had a vested interest in the status quo. The annual caravan sent by the Bhutanese to Rangpur in the Company's territory was mainly subscribed by him together with some of the ministers and provincial governors. Each sent an agent with Tangun ponies and a selection of musk, cow tails, coarse red blankets and striped woollen cloth in half yard widths. The imported goods, consisting of broadcloth, spices and dyes, were mostly sent on to Tibet, either as part of the annual tribute or for trading in return for Tibetan handkerchiefs (Bogle probably meant the scarves required for all official occasions) flowered satins, tea and wool.

Despite his disappointments Bogle wrote, 'The more I see of the Bhutanese, the more I am pleased with them. The common people are good humoured, downright and I think, thoroughly trusty. The statesmen have something of the art which belongs to their profession. They are the best built race of meen I ever saw; many of them very handsome with complexions as fair as the French.'

Whilst waiting at Tashichödzong for further news, he began to suffer from the increasing cold and the Regent gave him a yellow satin gown lined with lambskin and the Deb Raja a dozen blankets. Meanwhile in India Hastings was acting in response to Bogle's comments about the encouragement of trade and issued a notice to the effect that officers in Rangpur and district should offer every assistance to the caravans.

At last, the long awaited permission arrived and as the insurrection seemed to have ended with the rebels abandoning their siege of Simtokha, Bogle was free to leave, taking with him only Hamilton, Mirza Setta, a Kashmiri who had come up from Rangpur and spoke the language, the messenger from the Panchen Lama and an attendant of the Deb Raja. En route they met an officer and some soldiers in pursuit of rebels and Bogle was able to observe the Bhutanese military system. The hall of every public office in the land was hung around with matchlocks and shields with which the retainers were armed in time of war. Other weapons included: broadswords with shagreen handles, 'targets', or shields made of coiled cane, bamboo bows and quivers and arrows made of reeds, often with poisoned tips, and a few pikes. Soldiers wore quilted caps, iron netted hoods or helmets; some had coats of mail and most wore woollen hose soled with leather and gartered under the knee. Over their tunics they carried several striped blankets. They slept in the open keeping themselves warm with their plaids and their whisky.

Before leaving Tashichodzong Bogle set down his thoughts on future trade possibilities remembering that the main objective of his mission was to establish free trade between Tibet and Bengal. 'The foreign trade of Tibet is considerable', he wrote, but there was a need for more imports to pay for the many commodities the country was able to export. Trading conditions were good and many merchants settled in Lhasa, especially Kashmiris who fulfilled the same functions in the Tibetan, Nepali, Bhutanese and Bengali trade as the Jews in Europe. They had agents everywhere, especially on the Coromandel coast, in Bengal, Benares and Nepal, who sent supplies up to them. There were also the Gosains, who adopted a humble manner, procuring them easy entry into Tibet, of whom Bogle wrote; 'Though clad in the garb of poverty there are many of them possessed of considerable wealth'. The Chinese were also large scale traders. However, little of this trade benefited Bhutan. The Tibetan merchants who managed to get to Paro, were only allowed to exchange their salt and wool for Bhutanese rice; any trade in more valuable goods was entirely for the benefit of the Deb Raja and principal officers. Consequently if permission were to be obtained for Bengal merchants to travel only as far as Paro, a place well suited geographically to be a centre of communication, their goods would only be purchased by the same people and, with the exception of tobacco, betel and bacon, on a fairly modest scale. The only real difference would be that Paro would become the market for Bengal goods instead of Rangpur, which would not lead to increased trade with Tibet.

Unfortunately the fear of another insurrection by the former Deb, possibly with Tibetan support, was such that Bogle could not ask for the Deb Raja's consent for Tibetans to trade freely at Paro without incurring the suspicion that he was implicated. He decided therefore to refer everything to do with the Tibetan merchants to the Panchen Lama and to try and obtain permission for Bengali merchants to have freedom of passage, selling their goods in Paro as well as in Tibet. He therefore proposed that in addition to the existing caravan arrangement in Rangpur, for which all duty should be abolished, the Bhutanese should be free to sell their horses anywhere in Bengal free from duty or any other hindrance, as already suggested in Hastings' letter to the Deb Raja; and that in return the Deb should allow 'all Hindu and Mussulman merchants freely to pass and repass through his country between Bengal and Tibet'; but that no English or European merchants should be given permission, as Bogle knew that this would never be granted. He was convinced that if the Bhutanese could be encouraged to trade freely, seeing all the goods available in Calcutta, and finding the price of broadcloth, coral and spices, to be lower than in Rangpur, they would start trading there. This would increase the sale of English broadcloth and reduce the large amount of French cloth purchased by the Bhutanese for the Tibetan market.

Meanwhile, two weeks before Bogle was writing down his thoughts on trade, Hastings had written to him on much the same lines stressing his willingness to abolish all duties. He was also astute enough to suggest that Bogle should find out where the Deb's personal interests lay and how far they might be affected by the new proposals: 'an encouragement of any hopes of advantages he may entertain, provided his particular profits from it will not interfere with or obstruct the general plan may greatly facilitate your negotiations; and for this purpose you will be equally solicitous to remove his objections and calm his apprehensions of detriment to his interests or danger to his country, should any such arise in his mind'. Hastings went on to say that the Deb should be shown the great advantage of his capital becoming the centre of a lucrative commercial link between Bengal and Tibet.

Bogle replied that until the fear of insurrection was over little could be done but that when this had been lifted he was sure that permission for Tibetan merchants to go to Paro could be obtained from the Panchen Lama.

Bogle's mission to Tibet is another story but suffice it to say that the Panchen Lama did respond as anticipated and issued instructions to the merchants of Lhasa and Tashilhunpo. A number of Kashmiri and Gosain merchants then told Bogle that they intended to send agents to Calcutta to purchase goods as soon as the rains were over; and a wealthy Gosain merchant took the opportunity to accompany him back to Calcutta on his homeward journey.

Hastings' compliance with the Panchen Lama's wish to found a monastery on the banks of the Ganges helped Bogle in his mission. It was hoped that it would remove Tibetan and Bhutanese fears about the heat and unhealthiness of Bengal; and that pilgrimages could lead to the development of a substantial trade. The Lama also offered to use his good offices with the Emperor of China to procure leave for the Company to send a deputation to Peking.

Although he spent all his time at the Panchen Lama's palace and was never able to go to Lhasa partly because of the jealousy of officials there and also because he would have had to incur great expense in procuring presents for them, Bogle compared the Panchen Lama of Tibet favourably with the Deb Raja of Bhutan. He was more accustomed to dealing with strangers, enjoyed negotiating, spoke Hindi and was therefore easier to converse with; and he knew of the reputation of the Company, with which apparently he had long wanted to be associated. He supported Hastings' and Bogle's plans for trade which he realised would increase his own influence. He was very candid and told Bogle all about the opposition to his journey by the people in Lhasa and even gave him the correspondence to read. Although a spiritual leader, he seemed to Bogle to be a more understanding and enlightened administrator than the Deb Raja of Bhutan, who, despite being a secular ruler, was difficult of access, 'stiff and ceremonious in his manners and indecisive in business. He is guided entirely by his officers who are reserved, suspicious and evasive'. All important matters had to be discussed, not only with the Lama Rimpoche but also with several hundred priests. Consequently the Bhutanese authorities made many objections to merchants passing through their territory, insisting, not unreasonably, that their people were not used to strangers and that if a merchant was robbed it would cause problems with the British. Bogle thought that this was just a pretext in order to keep the Tibetan trade in their own hands. No doubt motives were mixed but throughout their recorded history the Bhutanese have always welcomed those whom they wished to see and been wary of others who invited themselves. The result has been the preservation of national independence.

However, when Bogle was able to reassure the Bhutanese that no Europeans would be allowed in – a step most assuredly leading to ultimate take-over, as was to happen to their neighbours in Assam and further afield in Burma and had already occurred in parts of India – and that the concession would be for Indian merchants only, the Deb Raja was at length persuaded to agree. Bogle admitted that he was much indebted for this outcome to the Panchen Lama's people who had accompanied him back to Bhutan and he sent a copy of his proposed treaty to the Lama who replied, approving of it.

Before returning to India Bogle wrote again to Hastings to say that there was now a great opening for the sale of English broadcloth to the wealthier Tibetans and that Tibetan merchants might also act as carriers for selling it to their neighbours, the Tartars, to the detriment of the French, with whose East India Company the English had been at war for much of the century, and were to continue so for another forty years. He also thought that a new trade could be developed in cutlery and glassware and that the best way to increase both the existing trade in cloth and coral beads as well as starting new kinds was to encourage Kashmiris, Gosains, Bhutanese and Tibetans to go to Calcutta in the winter months where they could buy English broadcloth at the lowest prices in addition to other goods, and for them to have passports and escorts to and from the Bengal frontier.

Bogle's return journey to India by the same route as his outward journey was uneventful. After his return he continued his Bhutan connection, becoming Collector of Rangpur where the Bhutanese caravans traded in sight of what he called 'my Bhutan hills', but died in 1781 at the age of thirty five. He was to have joined his friend the Panchen Lama in China in order to pursue trading possibilities at the court of the Emperor but the Lama also died whilst in Peking. Bogle was a gentle, good humoured and tolerant Scot who believed in adapting himself, as far as possible, to the custom of any country he was in. His mission could be said to have been successful in its main objective for in 1786 the Company's agent in Tibet, Purangir, a Gosain, reported that many Bengal merchants had made their way through Bhutan to Tibet. Given the slowness of communication between the Bhutanese central authorities and lesser officials and the length of time it took to mount trading caravans this was more likely to have been the result of Bogle's mission than that of the next British expedition to Bhutan in 1783.

CHAPTER TWO

1775–1783: Consolidation: The Journeys of Alexander Hamilton and Samuel Turner

Before the end of the year Dr Hamilton returned to Bhutan as Warren Hastings wished to maintain and strengthen the contacts already made. This time Hamilton's brief was simply to adjudicate on the claims made by the Bhutanese to the districts of Ambarree Fallacottah and Julpesh.

He followed the previous year's route to Punakha where he arrived on April 6th 1776 and went on to Tashichodzong the following month. As a result of his discussions he recommended the return of the two areas to Bhutan which was accepted by Hastings. The next year he returned for the third time in order to offer Hastings' congratulations to the new Deb Raja, Jigme Senge.

Even so there was not yet much evidence of greatly increased trade between Bengal and Tibet via Bhutan and the arrangements were therefore made for the Peking meeting which never took place because of the deaths of the two Principals.

Some further contact was also necessary as boundary disputes had not ceased despite the treaty which had been ambiguous in some respects. According to its provisions the districts of Paugola Hat in the east and Kyountee, Murragaut and Luckipore in the west were returned to the Bhutanese in return for their annual tribute of five Tangun horses. However, the Raja of Cooch Behar objected to this loss of territory and was supported by the Collector, who considered that parts of these districts had never properly belonged to Bhutan and should be returned to Cooch Behar. The situation was further complicated by the Bhutanese sending an envoy to Calcutta to complain that the Nazir of Cooch Behar and his old ally the Darp Deo of Baikunthpore had, in fact, never permitted the land to revert to Bhutan after the signing of the treaty. Hastings ruled in favour of the Bhutanese, mindful of the need to keep the peace with them in order to secure a route to Tibet and the Chinese markets beyond.

Once again in 1783 Hastings upheld Bhutanese complaints about Ambarree Fallocottah and Julpesh although Cooch Behar's case had some validity and it was by no means a clear-cut issue. The time had obviously come to mount another mission to settle all these vexed problems and Captain Samuel Turner of the Bengal army was appointed to take charge.

Accompanied by Lieutenant Samuel Davis who was to act as draughtsman and surveyor and Mr Robert Saunders, a surgeon, they set off from Calcutta in January 1783. They rode through the low lands of Cooch Behar carried in palanquins, camping in the evenings beside the rice fields, and once across the border they followed the same route as Bogle, for whom Turner had a great respect referring to him as a man 'eminently qualified for his mission by a discerning capacity and uncommon gentleness of manners'.

Their first halt over the frontier was at Chichacotta where they saw the high bank and thick stockade which the Bhutanese had defended in 1772. They continued in palanquins through the flat country and only alighted when they were half way up Buxa Duar hill. The road now became very steep and narrow, intersected by masses of coarse marble. Of the view as they ascended Turner wrote 'the prospects . . . were inconceivably grand . . . the tops of the highest mountains lost in the clouds, constituted altogether a scene of extraordinary magnificence and sublimity'. At the foot of the final ascent the mission was met by a herald who preceded them sounding a trumpet and near the summit they were joined 'by five mountain nymphs with jetty flowing tresses', Zingaps and other officials who presented white scarves and offered them tea and chang, a spirit made from wheat or rice which Turner, like Bogle, called a 'kind of whisky', and described in meticulous detail the method of preparation which Davis sketched. Hastings was going to get his money's worth from this mission. That afternoon a tent arrived for their use as well as an elephant for the onward journey. Under the fascinated gaze of a crowd of 'Booteas' they paid an evening call on the 'Subha', the provincial governor of Buxa Duar with whom, according to the custom of the country, they exchanged scarves. The Subha sat in ceremonial state on a tiger skin laid on a scarlet cloth holding a silver vessel containing the fire made from the burning of aromatic woods. When they returned the call the Subha and Zingap, who had been sent by the Deb Raja, raised objections to their onward journey despite the Deb's obvious interest in the mission. They all dined together and the Subha ate 'to the manner born' and drank claret as well as beer.

The next day the party accompanied the Subha to the top of a nearby hill to set up prayer flags. They were joined by a cavalcade carrying five white flags on bamboo poles; standards, twirled by their bearers, fluttering with silks; and seven young girls with loose hair, chanting as they walked. The procession was led by the head lama wearing a deep crowned cap and scarlet vest riding a Tangun horse, followed by the Subha in blue satin with gold embroidery, and two Zingaps. The crowns on their hats were shaped 'after the European fashion with brims three or four inches broad' decorated at the top with crests of yellow metal. Other priests and officials made up the rest of the party. At the top of the hill three lamps were burning on an altar which had been erected in front of a large tree. The priests chanted, prayers were intoned, tabors and trumpets were played and cymbals were clashed; and whilst rice was scattered, the Deity's protection was invoked for the mission's journey through Bhutan.

At last, on 22nd May the Deb Raja's permission having been received, they were on their way, following the steep pathway towards the summit of a mountain where they were told by their hosts to be silent lest they should disturb the elements and bring down rain.

Their route took them to Okoo mountain with threatening boulders hanging above them, and on the other side a steep precipice down which they lost a fine Arab horse intended as a present from the Governor General to the Deb.

The passed a night at a place called Gugoogoo where they heard 'the loud and hoarse murmers of the Chinchu (now called the Wang Chu or Thimphu Chu), rolling in a deep channel at the foot of the mountain 'and at least twenty miles to the north they could see snow capped peaks'.

On the rough and rocky roads the Tangun horses scrambled 'with wonderful felicity'. As they marched, the British officers noted the ingenious way that water was conducted to the roadside through hollow bamboos. They were well served for refreshment as some of the Bhutanese carried hollow buffalo horns filled with a fiery spirit called arak, although more to Turner's taste was chang which, although slightly acid was 'a grateful liquor', and they were regaled with tea and fruit by villagers.

The very steep ascent up Mt Murichom had to be done on foot for even the Tangun horses had their limitations. On the way they saw women and girls engaged in the laborious task of bringing water from the springs below up to Murichom village which consisted of about twenty houses in whose construction clay had been used as a form of cement. Inside each house the roof was clear of the walls and very low pitched, made of 'fir boards placed lengthways and cross beams and joists of fir and confined by large stones laid on top'. The lower part of the house sheltered hogs, cows and other animals; the family occupied the first storey and the space between the ceiling and the roof was used as a granary. From the windows could be seen a vista of cultivated land with cinnamon trees, strawberries, raspberries and well laden peach trees.

The next day they reached a waterfall which Davis sketched. Then after a steep climb they reached the summit of yet another high mountain after passing through a chasm in solid rock only just wide enough to admit a man on horseback. They crossed the chain bridge referred to by Bogle, which was meticulously sketched by Davis who also drew sectional and elevation plans. Turner compared the system of chains supported on a bamboo platform covered by bamboo matting to an ancient description of a similar bridge over the river Tees. They halted at Chuka Dzong, a large square building made of stone with walls of 'prodigious thickness', and were lodged in a 'lofty apartment' with two or three loopholes.

On the next day's march the roadside was covered with strawberries which apparently ripened and decayed unnoticed by the Bhutanese. Turner wrote 'I could not view them with the same apathy but dismounted from my horse and loitered away much time in culling the ripest from the banks'. He was delighted to recognise familiar English plants including even docks and nettles as well as primroses and dog roses in full bloom and 'the cuckoo's call brought strongly to my imagination the seasons in which I had formerly listened to the harbinger of spring'.

The air was now distinctly chilly and the tops of the mountains were hidden in cloud. In the evening they sat around a fire made from turpentine fir. The next day they ascended through a forest of pine trees and half way up a mountain saw a castle 'in a bleak but beautifully romantic situation'.

They crossed the summit on the 29th after studying another chain bridge en route and on the next part of their journey saw more dog roses and sweet briars as well as willows and maples and in the distance mountains clothed with pines. They passed well cultivated fields with oxen yoked to the plough and reapers with sickles.

Their next lodging was at a place where they stayed in a spacious house whose interior walls were black with smoke from fires made on flat stones without any chimneys. They visited an orchard well stocked with walnuts, apples, peaches, pears, apricots and 'barberry trees'.

The following day the route led through more open country where the Chinchu ran less rapidly watering a beautiful valley 'in which no spot of land was unemployed'. 'Their labour', wrote Turner of the Bhutanese 'merited a more grateful soil but I never saw lands cleaner or better dressed. Heaps of manure in every field at proper distances lay ready to be scattered amongst the corn; yet with all their care the crops were thin, running much to straw. In addition to this the bareness of the hills and the diminutive size of the pines were evident indications of an unkindly soil'.

On the next day's march they saw Simtokha monastery perched on a mountain side and reached Tashichodzong down in a valley with the river running through the middle of it. From their apartment they had an extensive view up and down this valley which was 'in a higher state of cultivation'. The banks of the river were lined with willows and many of the houses and monasteries had orchards and fields of corn.

The next day Turner sent the Purangir Gosain, his interpreter, to the dzong (which he always referred to as 'the palace') to arrange for the ceremony of introduction to the Deb Raja and the delivery of the Governor General's despatches. This Gosain must have been a man of considerable influence as he was used and trusted by the Tibetans as well as the British and was well established with the Bhutanese. The Deb proved to be unavailable as he was engaged in religious rites and Turner declined the offer to see offficials. At the time he thought the Deb Raja's response to have been a diplomatic ploy to magnify his importance; but on later acquaintance he realised how genuine was the piety of Bhutanese religious leaders whose 'religious zeal . . . in the performance of any prescribed duty will never admit of interruption'.

On June 3rd, accompanied by Davis, Saunders and their attendants, Turner went to the dzong where balconies, doors and avenues were crowded with people gazing at these strange visitors. Nine years had passed since they had seen Bogle and the recollection had no doubt dimmed. Eventually they were conducted from a waiting room by a large number of Zingaps through long passages and up ladders to a small room near the summit, a third of which was taken up by a silk screen decorated with portraits. The walls were blue and the arches, doors and pillars were painted vermilion and gilt. The Deb Raja (successor to the one known by Bogle) sat cross-legged on a pile of cushions in a corner with an escritoire on one side, a cabinet containing religious figures on the other and a low painted bench in front of him. Each member of the mission presented a white silk scarf fringed at the ends and Turner delivered the Governor General's despatches.

The three British officers were then seated on cushions with their attendants ranged behind them. The three high officials who had entered the Deb Raja's quarters with them remained standing as did the interpreters. First there was an exchange of courtesies opened by the Deb who asked after the health of the Governor General, the supreme Council and the Chief Justice. Turner responded by thanking him for the civil reception they had received en route. The Deb Raja then took him aback by asking bluntly if there was any object in their visit other than the delivery of the letters. He replied that their contents would show the mission's objectives. They could not be read until later as they were in Persian, the language of courtly exchange, and the only other language known to most Bhutanese was Bengali.

Three small benches were then placed in front of the visitors and a huge yellow teapot brought in. A servant poured a little in to the palm of his hand and sipped. which Turner later noted was customary and presumed it was to test for poison. Small lacquered cups were filled for the three visitors and the Deb, who gave a long invocation in a 'low and hollow tone of voice', dipped the tip of his finger into the cup three times and threw a few drops on the floor as a sort of libation before sipping. The tea was made of water, flour, butter, salt and 'Botea' tea 'with astringent ingredients and was not to the Europeans' taste. 'We had hitherto shunned as much as possible', wrote Turner, 'these unpalatable libations, yet we now deemed it necessary to submit to some constraint'.

Whilst the Deb spoke of Bhutan's lack of resources trays were brought in filled with oranges, dried apples, walnuts, vegetables and Chinese and Kashmiri preserved fruit which were placed before them. When they had eaten, the Deb gave the Master of Ceremonies, a silk scarf for each of visitors. These were thrown across the shoulders before they took their leave. Turner learned later that equals exchange scarves on meeting, with a slight inclination of the body.

He was very favourably impressed by the meeting and by the Deb in particular. Tall and muscular in appearance, grave and dignified in manner, he was nevertheless good humoured and animated, articulate and urbane. Turner found this surprising 'in one separated from inter- course with the world by a mass of imperious mountains and who was almost totally secluded from the sight of any other than his own subjects'.

The following day there was another meeting at which the British took presents for the Deb Raja. He was fascinated by Turner's clothes but disapproved of the way they showed the outline of the body, although he liked the pockets. He also commented on the similarities between Bhutanese and British; in their use of wool, spirits, meat and tea. Turner agreed that "the Bootea, like ourselves, is an utter stranger to the subtle niceties and refinements of the Hindu which constitute the infinitely absurd perplexity that results from caste'. The Deb then told his servants to leave so that they could have an informal talk. He had understood the content of the letter and claimed that he and Hastings had a spiritual alliance. He asked about the picture he had sent the Governor General, a view of the Punakha dzong, and Turner was able to say that he had seen it in Calcutta where it had been much admired. When his host asked if Turner could let him have a picture of Hastings' palace the interpreter began a flowery evasive answer. Turner was able to understand enough to stop him in full flow and to tell the Deb Raja that he was unable to draw but that Davis, who was a fine artist, had a view of Calcutta from Fort William which would be given to him when some slight damage from the journey had been repaired.

At the next day's meeting the three chief officers of state were called in: the Thimphu Dzongpön who was provincial governor and fortress commander; the Shung Drönyer, treasurer and Captain General; and the Zimpön, the Chamberlain or Master of ceremonies . The first was cor- pulent and good humoured although not very polished; the Shung Drönyer, tall and athletic, and the Zimpön young and helpful.

Despite all these civilities Turner encountered 'an inexhaustible succession of obstacles' relative to the business of his commission, to surmount which took up all his time.

One evening he dined with the Deb Raja, an honour never bestowed on any Bhutanese. The Deb had requested that the table should be laid with his guests' camp cutlery and that their dinners should be prepared by their own servants. He himself ate a frugal meal of roots and boiled rice, using chop sticks. He declined the offer of sweatmeats and wine and gave Turner to understand that monks were forbidden to touch alcohol. Nevertheless Turner left some on the grounds that his host might be tempted to try a little as he had the power of absolution as well as a lively curiosity: and a few days later there was a request for more. During the dinner the Deb Raja expressed astonishment at the amount and variety of European food, the ingredients for which he was told had come from all over the world. His own food came from grain, the roots of the earth and fruit. He never ate anything that had breath, unlike his secular countrymen for although he was the secular ruler he was also a priest.

There were 500 gelongs, celibate monks, within the dzong, whose frequent services included much chanting and a clamorous noise of instruments which the British did not particularly appreciate. Turner noted that although the monks were celibate, the water carriers for the dzong were the prettiest of the local girls; also that the monks were, surprisingly, fairer and more athletic looking than any other Bhutanese he had seen, despite their sedentary lives. All Bhutanese, he wrote, had close cut black hair, broad, largely hairless faces, and many were remarkably fair. Many also went unwashed although for the monks their ablutions appeared to be part of their religious practice. Like Bogle before him he watched their processions to the river, led by their senior carrying an iron pot suspended by a chain to the end of a long wand, smoking with aromatic woods. Each was dressed in a loose robe to below the knee, a short sleeveless woollen vest and a large oblong mantle of deep crimson cloth folded around the body in an artful but apparently negligent and easy manner, holding rosaries in their right hands.

Turner and his companions had plenty of time to explore the valley. The river flowed through the middle, bordered by rich soil sown with rice and in the centre stood the dzong. It was in the shape of a quadrangle, built of stone with slightly sloping thirty foot walls, very small windows and a single row of projecting balconies. From the main entrance a flight of stone steps led to a huge gateway with massive doors studded with iron knobs which were closed by a bar of timber. Inside the central square was· a citadel seven stories high on the top floor of which stood a statue of Buddha under a guilded canopy. The lama's apartments were on the fourth floor and the other monks were housed on the lower floors. Below ground level were store rooms and kitchens.

The British mission's quarters were comfortable but cold compared with the heat of Bengal to which they were accustomed; and like Bogle, they had to make their own arrangements for warmth, lining the wainscots with woollen cloth and making curtains to keep out the piercing winds which howled through every aperture. Otherwise they

were very satisfied with their abode which was in the form of a square
courtyard with a house on one side for the officers, buildings on the
other three sides to house their staff and stores; and their cattle in the
central yard. From their rooms on the top floor they had a balcony with
a fine view over the river.

They made daily excursions and went walking every evening when they
picked wild strawberries, to the amazement of the monks who spurned
them. They visited the Deb Raja's stud of Tangun ponies, mules and
Tartar geldings; and saw aqueducts from which conduits made of hollowed
tree trunks carried water for two miles from the springs to parts of the
valley. 'The most perfect comprehension of the science of hydraulics'
wrote Turner, 'could hardly, in the present instance, have suggested to
them any improvement'. Occasionally they walked to a small shrine in
front of which there were flagstaffs flying narrow banners of white cloth
bearing the words 'Om mani padme hum', a phrase that was also carved
on rocks and in some places displayed on hillsides by the positioning of
large boulders. On their return to the dzong of an evening they sometimes encountered a large and pampered bull to which they gave a wide
berth and passed furnaces where men were forging the brass items used
in religious practices. In another place they watched paper being
manufactured from the bark of trees. They often also wandered through
orchards filled with apricots, peaches and wild raspberries.

They enjoyed the healthy and bracing climate and whilst Davis was
sketching Turner and Saunders went climbing up in the mountains that
they could see from their quarters. Looking back from the upper slopes,
dotted with stunted trees, they could see the beautiful valley they had left,
watered by the winding Chinchu. At the summit of one of the mountains
they came to a stone building where a small boy sat in the courtyard. He
took them up a flight of wooden steps at the top of which a monk was
waiting for them. They were ushered into his room where they sat on
cushions and drank buttered tea. The monk spoke in glowing terms of
the Governor General and of the English. They stayed so long that they
had to do the last part of their homeward journey in the dark. The Deb Raja
was very worried when he heard this and spoke of wild beasts and evil
genii in the woods. He thought that his fears had been realised when
Saunders fell ill with fever and said that a very powerful demon lived on
the mountains and sent a priest to the house to repeat solemn incantations
around a cauldron of fire. Saunders recovered soon after.

During their stay the members of the mission watched a civil war from
close quarters, led by the Dzongpön of Wangdiphodrung, who a few
days earlier had sent them a basket of fruit and a respectful letter. He
had been joined by a disgruntled officer and some displaced nominees of
the former Deb Raja and as his forces were reported to have captured Punakha
dzong the British watched the preparations made at Tashichodzong for

the approach of the rebels. Several squads of ten or twelve men were sent off into the mountains, presumably to reconnoitre the enemy positions, and a large party took up a defensive position on the bridge opposite the mission's house. The next day news was received of the defeat of some of the Deb Raja's forces only six miles to the south and later that day the rebels advanced to within two to three miles of the dzong. That night the British began to make their own defensive arrangements and the following day the enemy could clearly be seen on the brow of a hill. An attacking party of the Deb Raja's forces was sent out, creeping forward in small groups until they came within bowshot and matchlock range when they opened fire, the enemy replying with the same weapons. The rebels counter-attacked and the Deb Raja's men withdrew bringing three of their wounded to be treated by Saunders. All three men had been hit by arrows and in one case when Saunders pulled the shaft out the man cut a deep incision with his own knife and removed the arrow head. They all took it for granted that the arrows would be poisoned and that they would have no chance of recovery but Turner does not mention their subsequent fate.

By the next morning the rebels had built a stone breastwork in front of their defences stretching between three villages and that day, after Turner had inspected the defenders' two small cannons, at the Deb's request, he advised against their use as they were so old they would endanger their own side if fired. Shortly afterwards the bells of the dzong rang as a call to arms and a mass of the Deb's armed men rushed out brandishing their weapons and shouting. The rebels came out to meet them and in the ensuing battle a number of shots whistled past the building from which the British were getting a grandstand view of Bhutanese methods of warfare. These reflected the civilised and sedate nature of the people. There was no foolhardy and unnecessary exposure once within range of the enemy and both sides availed themselves of every inch of cover, firing occasional shots and then withdrawing. If the rebels, who originally showed much greater vigour and courage than the loyalist forces, had pressed home their advantage and continued the momentum of their attack they would have taken the dzong, especially as they had received reinforcements of men and ammunition.

The following morning the Deb Raja's forces advanced in three divisions, pausing to make an irregular and slow discharge of musketry before continuing their forward movement. Throughout the day there was intermittent firing and Turner wrote: 'It is curious to observe the mixture of defiance and of fear displayed in the conduct of these combatants . . . both parties are so careful to conceal themselves that seldom anything is visible but the top of a tufted helmet or the end of a bow'. However, despite their cautious tactics the Deb Raja's forces had defeated their enemy by the end of the day and Turner wrote: 'No magic exhibition could display a more sudden and striking change of scene. In an instant the whole place and the rice fields were covered with an innumerable host; every bank and bush gave up their proportion'. The weary soldiers climbed out of their hiding places and vantage points and some withdrew to the dzong, whilst others occupied the villages formerly held by the rebels, in which the villagers were calmly going about their normal business. There was little damage and few lives had been lost, although a few prisoners had been taken and others had been badly wounded. Turner wrote: 'Thus ended this long conflict which impressed on us a very mean idea of their military accomplishments whatever other qualities they may possess'. Despite this disparagement he thought that the Bhutanese were 'a strong and hardy race by no means deficient in manly courge' and ascribed their feeble modes of attack and defence to want of discipline, lack of tactical organisation, not fighting in compact sections or platoons, their distrust of each other and their general lack of military experience as most of them were peasants called in from their fields to join the forces. A more important reason perhaps was that the Bhutanese were, and still are, an essentially civilised race with Buddhist respect for human life, their own as well as their enemies', and had no wish to shed more blood than was strictly necessary by the circumstances forced on them. Eighty years later Turner's countrymen were to experience the courage of the Bhutanese in defence of their country and to encounter their innately chivalrous approach to warfare.

Their weapons and equipment had not changed much either in the intervening years and Turner's description differs little from those of British officers in 1864. Most of the soldiers wore a quilted jacket over a tunic with a blanket over the top. Their helmets were made of stained cane coiled conically over cotton rope, quilted between two pieces of cloth with flaps that sometimes turned down over the ears and a piece to cover the nose. Over one arm a convex shield of painted cane was carried and a long straight sword was worn across the body, thrust into the belt. A bow and quiver was slung on a belt behind the back, the arrows being drawn from over the left shoulder. The bow, which was six foot long and held in the right hand, was made of bamboo and was perfectly straight. Only a particular type of bamboo from the hills was used as it was remarkable for its elasticity and strength and was made of a split piece or two pieces fixed together by bands. The bow string, a small hempen cord, was drawn by the thumb armed with a ring of bone or thick leather bent round it. The arrows were made of dwarf bamboo, also only from the mountains. They had flattened barbs of pointed iron and the sides were sometimes grooved to contain poison made from a vegetable juice. Some of the soldiers had matchlock muskets and carried forked sticks to rest them on when aiming. They were only usable in fine weather when the matches would burn and the priming in an open pan could take fire. The greatest attribute of Bhutanese troops was undoubtedly their accurate archery and skilful use of shield and sword.

After the battle the rebels withdrew to Wangdiphodrung over twenty six miles to the east where they were blockaded by the loyalist forces and ultimately defeated although the Dzongpön and his retinue managed to escape, taking with them most of the gold ornaments from the shrines of the dzong.

During all this time Turner had continued to have audiences with the Deb Raja who went to Wangdiphodrung when it fell and sent for him to join him there,

He set off the next day with Davis and Saunders, travelling light with only a single servant each. They passed Simtokha in misty rain and ascended narrow paths winding through tree-covered mountains: beech, birch, maple, pine and yew, and bushes loaded with blackberries. At midday, thoroughly drenched by then, they met up with some of the Deb Raja's retinue who were keeping dry in shelters made of branches of trees. They sat with them round a fire drinking hot buttered tea which under these circumstances they actually enjoyed. They set off again refreshed and had to ford a stream where the horses had great difficulty and only just managed it but once on the other side they were on firm gravel and had an easy ascent under skies that were now blue and so clear that the 'mountains displayed a regularity and softness of feature that is seldom seen in the wild but sublime scenery of Bhutan'. They met one of the Deb Raja's brothers preceded by many attendants and a man playing a reed instrument like an hautboy. This was the usual custom when senior officials were on the move and the player was expected to blow the whole time. On several occasions Turner saw people blowing continuously for five minutes at a stretch without pausing. Eleven hours after setting out they reached Wangdiphodrung where the dzong stood on a rock between the Pochu Mochu and Chinchu rivers and found their billets in a house nearby where they ate with some difficulty, despite the abundant provisions, as their culinary equipment had not caught up with them. After all their exertions they had a poor night's rest as their billet had been occupied by both armies and was a home for rats as well as fleas and mosquitoes.

The next day they looked over the loyalist forces' entrenchments, constructed when they invested the castle, before inducing the enemy to surrender by obstructing their water supply. The dzong was built at the southern end of a rocky hill with huge solid walls and only one entrance. A hundred yards in front stood a round tower with loopholes affording a good field of fire. The Deb Raja's troops were fortunate not to have had to make a frontal attack. The bridge leading to the dzong was particularly fine, made of turpentine fir about a hundred and fifty years old, and formed the subject of one of Davis's sketches.

The following morning they visited the Deb Raja and then spent the next few days walking around the area. He suggested that they should visit Punakha, an offer that they accepted readily. Turner thought that this was 'the most pleasing testimony of the Raja's having totally thrown aside that jealousy and distrust which we had been taught invariably to expect'. He even offered them money for their expenses as they were still without the bulk of their equipment, gave them roasted grain for which they had acquired a taste and sent them fresh butter daily.

'The weather was serene, the atmosphere clear, and the sun shone full upon the distant mountains' when they set off. Their road wound through a verdant valley, as smooth and fresh as a bowling green, dotted with fine old trees. Corn was growing on the lower slopes and the breeze brought them wafts of jasmine as they walked through this sylvan scene. On arrival at Punakha they saw that the dzong was very similar to the one at Tashichodzong, only even more spacious. It was sited on the point of a peninsula between the Mochu and Pochu rivers and a wooden bridge had to be crossed in order to enter the courtyard.

They were unable to see inside the dzong because an over-zealous gate-keeper had not had his orders rescinded since the end of the rebellion and refused to let them in; but they were able to admire the gardens which were well stocked with oranges, lemons, pomegranates, peaches, apples, pears and walnuts. There was also a large mango tree bowed down with fruit. The vegetables, on the other hand, were poor things, some bitter lettuces, a few cabbage leaves, and potatoes like marbles. According to Turner the Bhutanese had no skill as gardeners and were not interested in caring for anything that bountiful nature did not offer them on a plate. He was more impressed with them as farmers and admired the 'neatly dressed' corn fields where most of the work was done by the women, planting, weeding and using sickles and flails. The British found the strong sun very congenial after the cold and it was even too warm to walk except in the evenings when they explored the area. One evening they explored the Deb Raja's villa and, returning late, their guide insisted on appeasing the local 'genii loci' as Turner called them, at sacred places where he deposited a few Narainees, the base silver coins struck in Cooch Behar one of which was worth about a third of a Company's rupee.

On their return to Tashichodzong they learnt that the last remnants of the rebels had been defeated and a few days later the Deb Raja himself returned. His approach was heralded by numerous heaps of fire smoking by the roadside, the usual token of respect customary when great personages passed through an area. He was very interested to hear of their experiences and Turner, as always, told him all the details as a way of gaining his confidence, knowing that he would in any case hear them from others.

During this period the three officers were delighted to meet their old acquaintance, the Buxa Subha, who, in audience with the Deb Raja, had to prostrate himself nine times, as all Bhutanese subjects had to do, from the lowest to the highest. After the presenttion of scarves Turner told the Deb Raja how helpful the Buxa Subha had been to the mission.

Amongst the many articles they had brought for entertainment and to give as a present was an electrical hand grip which became a great source of fun. Unwilling volunteers were regularly called for by the Deb Raja to offer themselves to be electrocuted and when the time came to leave they left it with him as well as a few mathematical and optical instruments. Saunders also displayed his surgical instruments to the Deb 'who had versatility of genius and a spirit of enquiry' and left a supply of drugs with him. Saunders was impressed by his host's knowledge of medicine and was interested to learn about the natural remedies known to the Bhutanese.

On their way to the Deb Raja's country house a few miles out they received the depressing news that the Bhutanese servant carrying all their dinner service had had too much to drink and that their equipment had been destroyed when he stumbled allowing it to fall into a ravine. Despite this tiresome news they continued on their way and found the Deb Raja seated in a pavilion on the edge of a deep precipice commanding a beautiful view of the valley, the dzong and the river. They sat on a level space dotted with all kinds of trees, aware of some noisy and savage Tibetan dogs in kennels nearby. Below the pavilion were beds of hollyhocks, sunflowers, African marigolds, nasturtiums, poppies, a few 'weakly' larkspur and some rather poor roses. Whilst drinking tea and eating strawberries they talked about foreign countries in which the Deb Raja was intensely interested. He told them that in his kingdom there were said to be some enormously tall people over in the east and that north of Assam there were others with short straight tails. He also told them of his pilgrimage to Lhasa dressed as a mendicant monk on foot all the way living a simple and austere life far removed from the cushioned formalities of his court. Inside the building there was a superb temple where monks were reading sacred writings and where the wall hanging depicted scenes of Lhasa and·Kathmandu. They dined off cold chicken with the Deb Raja, washed down with chang, and afterwards watched a fight between two bulls, one of which was the strongest and fiercest Turner had ever seen. In accordance with Bhutanese custom the weaker of the two was led away before the fight was ended.

At last a message was received from the Panchen Lama of Tibet to the effect that he would see them but only two people would be received as that was the number seen on the previous occasion when Bogle and Hamilton had gone there. Turner wrote 'It is extraordinary what absurdities and prejudices I had to combat'.

After paying their last respects to the Deb Raja, Turner and Saunders set off for Tibet, parting from Davis with considerable regret knowing that they had to accept the conditions brought by the messenger. On their way they ascended the highest mountain they had yet encountered, from the top of which they were able to take bearings on most of the places they had seen. They also saw in the distance the monastery where the Shabdrung had spent his early years. They descended on their way to Paro where the dzong was an oblong entered by a wooden bridge built beside a mountain. Three stone outposts in the form of a triangle defended the routes from Tashichodzong and Buxa Duar. The Paro valley was even larger than that at Tashichodzong.

At Paro they were visited by the Bhutanese Agent who conducted the annual caravan to Rangpur and spoke highly of the assistance given by the British Collector and the commercial resident there. They also watched a Bhutanese archery contest of which Turner wrote that it was 'impossible to behold their sport without admiration'.

At last they set forth on their way to Tibet, halting to be entertained at the birthplace of the Zingap whom the Deb Raja had sent to accompany them. They passed the night at Drugyel dzong where the fort crowned a low rocky hill with two round towers on the north side commanding the road to Tibet. They awoke to see a light covering of snow in the valley and on the tops of the mountains. That day they reached the last village in Bhutan and spent the night in a room hung with martial equipment, caps, shields, quivers and bows. Passing a guardroom on the way to the frontier they saw a 'yak of Tartary' making a low grunting noise and Turner later sent two of these beasts to Hastings who kept the one survivor on his country estate in England and had it painted by the famous painter of animals George Stubbs.

Later that day they crossed the border into Tibet where they saw the new Panchen Lama, an engagingly intelligent infant of eighteen months, and ultimately, like Bogle, had an uneventful return to India.

The mission had followed a surprisingly similar course to Bogle's, even encountering an insurrection led by the same person and suffering equally long and frustrating delays in getting to Tibet. Nevertheless they succeeded not only in consolidating Bogle's work but also in bringing Bhutan to the notice of the western world.

Davis's main contributions were his magnificent drawings and water colours of Eastern scenes, including a large number from Bhutan, but he also kept a diary, complementing Turner's report, in which he described many aspects of Bhutanese life with the same tolerant respect that Bogle had shown. For instance, although amazed by the monks' adherence to celibacy he was impressed by their tolerant view that many roads led to heaven, including those of other faiths. In the arts he thought that the Bhutanese had the potential to surpass even the skills of craftsmen and artists in India. He admired the democratic nature of society and the absence of caste as well as the lack of ostenttion by the rulers and their subjects' ease of access. His only major criticism was of Bhutanese attitudes towards women who he thought were treated worse than anywhere except in Tibet. They were, in his view, constantly at work and their sole purpose in life seemed to be to relieve the men of their need to do anything. As a result they took little interest in their appearance, rarely bathed and hardly ever changed their clothes.

Davis also considered that the comparative absence of money contributed to the virtues of Bhutanese society, writing: 'The absence of money in a society excludes, in a proportionate degree, depravity of morals and vices'. The rulers were unable to amass wealth 'which excites envy and greed'. (In contrast to this, two later visitors, Captain Pemberton and Kishen Kant Bose both referred to the swingeing tithes paid by the poor in order to enrich their rulers) 'The mass of the inhabitants' wrote Davis, 'are most nearly upon an equality than they are in most other civilised parts of the world'.

He was interested to note that all government officers wore a prescribed uniform (national dress is still obligatory; and, indeed foreigners working in government departments also adopt it) and therefore had no chance 'to wear fine feathers'. The Bhutanese were 'strangers to cruelty, extortion and bloodshed . . . not unlike that described in the golden age'. This is in such stark contrast to the very harsh criticisms of Pemberton, Griffith and Eden in the next century that there must be a number of contributory reasons including the accident of personality as well as the differing moral attitudes of the 18th and 19th centuries. Although this can be overstressed it is a striking fact that Bogle and Davis, and to a lesser extent, Turner, all spoke of the Bhutanese with respect, and indeed affection, working, as they did, in a sub-continent in which the English were, as yet, still mainly concerned with trade, and were merely one power amongst others, and in which it was quite common for Europeans to take employment with local rulers. Also at that time, there were few European women, whose numbers substantially increased in the next century, bringing with them the moral and social attitudes of their homeland. In the eighteenth century European men cohabited quite openly with local women. Bogle, for instance, is supposed to have had two daughters by a Tibetan lady, who were sent home to Scotland to be brought up after their mother's death. Fifty years later British society in India would have been less tolerant. It is hardly likely that the Bhutanese themselves had changed so much in the course of half a century or so and the other most likely explanation for such contrasting descriptions is that, not unnaturally, they showed a very different face towards those whose visits they welcomed, or at least, did not actively oppose, to those whom they did not wish to see, as in the case of the 19th century missions, for reasons which will become apparent in the next chapter.

Davis contrasted the Bhutanese favourably with the inhabitants of India and was impressed by the fact that even in warfare 'they showed a

tenderness of each others' lives, which, without scruple, I should have
attributed to their want of courage, had they not given proof of the
contrary in their war with us'. (i.e. in 1774). They were poor, but on the
whole, a happy people, 'living without any outrageous oppression at
home nor of invasion and slavery from abroad'. On the other hand he
thought that they were 'for ever excluded by the nature of the country
from making any considerable progress in arts, manufactures and commerce'. Given the nature of communication in his day this observation is
understandable, certainly in respect of manufacturing industry and
exports. Even today, despite greatly improved roads and a very recent air
link, geographical factors and low population still inhibit the development of
industry.

He was interested in the Buddhism of Bhutan which he thought owed
something to the proximity of Hindu India and thus differed in some
ways from the religion practised in Tibet, although contemporary scholars
now consider these difference to be due to geographical factors. He was
much impressed by the religious ceremonies he witnessed, in particular
an annual one held each September, lasting about twenty days, including
a number devoted to sacred dancing, performed entirely by gelongs in
the quadrangle of the dzong, to an orchestra of their fellows, all dressed
in satin robes with large embroidered caps. He described in some detail
the seven days of dancing integral to this festival, including the famous
'black hat' dance, based on the story of a murder of a king of Tibet who
had persecuted Buddhists; and another well known dance of malignant
spirits who control the phenomenal world and who were tamed to act as
protectors of Buddhism. In this a dancer whose face was surrounded
with skulls was followed by others in pairs wearing various masks including
one with a head like a frog. Another dance included figures wearing
masks of tigers as well as frogs and fantastically beaked birds each 'gar-
nished with little ivory skulls': and another, the very last one on the
seventh day, in which sixteen monks, all dressed as females, performed
the dance of 'the sixteen Rigma goddesses'.

Davis, who was only twenty three when he went to Bhutan, transferred
soon after his return from military to civil service and became the Collector of Burdwan in Bengal. He had a successful career in the Company's
service, not without excitement, for he was lamed by a bear who attacked
him as he was sketching some ruins; and on another famous occasion
had to defend his family, armed only with a pike, during civil disturbances
in Benares. He became an acknowledged expert on Hindu astronomy and
was elected a Fellow of the Royal Society. Before leaving India he served
for a time as Accountant General and after returning to Britain was
appointed a Director of the Company, dying in 1819. He outlived by 17
years Samuel Turner who died in London in 1802 of a paralytic stroke
at the age of 42. After his mission to Bhutan he served in the Third

Mysore war at Seringapatam and, still, only a Captain in the Company's service, retired to England in 1797; and the year before he died he also was elected F.R.S. on the strength of his journals. Robert Saunders continued in the Company's service until 1800 when he retired.

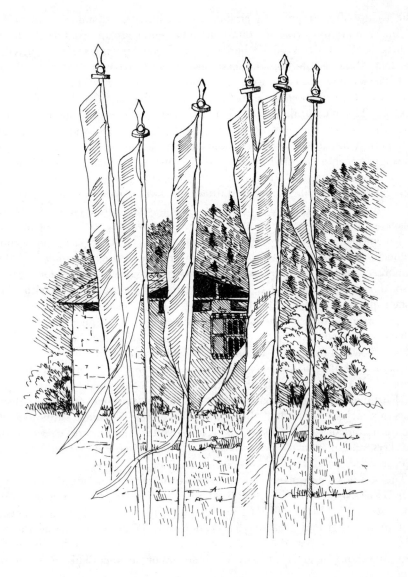

CHAPTER THREE

1783–1838: Frontier Troubles and the Report of Kishen Kant Bose

The treaty of 1774 and the ending of hostilities owed much to the efforts of the remarkable Gosain Purangir who enjoyed the confidence of the Lamas of Tibet. In 1773 he had gone to Bengal to intercede on behalf of the Deb Raja of Bhutan and had subsequently accompanied both Bogle's and Turner's missions as well as leading one himself to Tibet in 1775 on behalf of the British, remaining in Lhasa for five months. Later he visited Peking. The favourable reception he had been given on his journey through Bhutan had impressed the Court of Directors who wrote to give him permission for a Buddhist monastery to be built in Calcutta of which Purangir became the first Abbot. Alas, some years later he was killed by robbers searching for treasures. In the same letter to the Governor General in which the Court permitted the building of the monastery they also wrote; 'You must studiously avoid affording the least cause of suspicion to any of the country powers that we have any schemes of ambition to accomplish, which in truth we have not . . . Our views in forming connections with any new states or powers are merely commercial.' This reinforced a previous letter in which they had written 'It has long been a wish of the Company that a trade route might be opened with those distant parts of India.' The Court of Directors considered that the reports of the various British missions 'afforded much useful information on the subject from whence we entertain the most sanguine hopes' and they asked to see samples of Tibetan wool. These sanguine hopes suffered a set back in 1792 when the Nepalese invaded Tibet to whose assistance the Chinese sent a force which drove the invaders back almost to their capital at Kathmandu. Unfortunately the Chinese suspected that the British Government in India had been supporting the Nepalese, although this was unfounded. As a result the passes into Tibet were closed to all travellers and merchants from India; and, to a large extent, have remained so ever since.

The Chinese had exercised a loose form of acknowledged sovereignty over Tibet, as Tibet did over Bhutan, whose rulers showed considerable deference to Chinese officials in Lhasa. These sent messengers once a year to the Deb and Dharma Rajas and chief Pönlops instructing them to rule carefully, to put down any revolt and to report any imminent foreign invasions, neglect of which would incur a fine. This was on one occasion actually imposed. Twenty gold coins accompanied the Imperial Mandate annually and the Bhutanese sent each year twenty-three coolie loads of fine rice, silk and cotton goods valued at 3000 rupees. Flowered scarves, silk, cord, gold and silver were then received from the Chinese. Although not normally exercising any direct authority China was obviously regarded as a distantly suzerain power even though Bhutan was not tributary in the accepted sense. The Chinese did occasionally intervene physically as on one occasion when they despatched troops to decide between the claims of rival parties.

It was easier for the Court in London to insist on the solely commercial nature of the Company's relations with neighbouring states than for its servants on its frontiers to obey such a ruling when confronted with a tangled web of problems arising from ill defined frontiers and a long history of cross-border relationships and movements. In particular the successive Collectors of Rangpur found themselves increasingly involved with apparently intractable problems. In 1779 the then Collector gave a border decision in favour of the Raja of Cooch Behar, of which the Deb Raja complained to the Governor General, who set up a commission to investigate. It was decided that seven disputed villages should go to Bhutan and eleven to Cooch Behar but the Bhutanese refused to accept this. A few years later the Raja of Cooch Behar complained that the Bhutanese were refusing to return offenders who had taken refuge in Bhutan on the grounds that they were Bhutanese citizens. In such an indeterminate area where many people were of mixed blood nationality could be claimed as and when it was convenient.

Most of the disputes were comparatively minor but every now and then a major incident arose which necessitated the use of troops. Such a one occured in 1808 at Maragahat, a fairly large area consisting of several taluqs (districts) of which, according to the Raja of Cooch Behar, only one had ever formed part of Bhutan although they had been awarded to the Bhutanese in the treaty of 1774.

In 1808 a party of armed Bhutanese had crossed the border and had killed five people and a detachment of the 7th Native Infantry had been sent, under Captain William Slessor, to keep the peace. A Bhutanese deputation was despatched to Rangpur but the Collector gave his judgement in favour of Cooch Behar which was not accepted by them and Maraghat remained in Bhutanese possession.

For about a hundred years until the war of 1864 both sides had frequent recourse to arbitration which neither accepted unless the decisions were backed by force of arms. A further complicating factor was the invoking of the treaty by the rulers of Cooch Behar under which the British were legally bound to give assistance although in a number of cases the Bhutanese were the injured party.

In 1811 there was another affray in the same area, troops were sent

again and the land was deemed to revert to Cooch Behar but this was not
acceptable to the Bhutanese who again formally laid claim to Maraghat.
They refused to accept a British suggestion the following year that
boundary disputes should be settled by the erection of frontier posts;
understandably enough if, as seemed probable, they were put up to mark
irrevocably a border which they did not accept.

In 1815 Kishen Kant Bose, an Indian official in the Company's service,
was sent on a fact finding mission to Bhutan. Unlike his predecessors, he
gave only a brief description of his journey. He entered the country
further to the east than Bogle and Turner and followed a track to Sidlee
through long grass and high jungle which was 'attended with innumerable
inconveniences'. There were elephant and rhinoceros all around, the
whole area was infested with leeches, it was intensely hot and the mosquitoes proved to be an absolute torment every morning and evening.
He crossed the 'Champamatee' river and continued through thickly
forested country until crossing the 'Sarabangha' (neither of which are
marked on any map, possibly one was the Tongsa Chu) and on to the
Pochu Mochu rivers which he followed to Punakha and Wangdiphodrung.
He described this part of the journey as 'the worst he had hitherto
travelled, running in many places along the sides of preciptious banks'.
Nevertheless he returned by the same route.

The main part of the report is devoted to factual, detailed and useful
descriptions of the country and its inhabitants. Of the land itself he wrote
that the low lying areas could produce a good revenue if well cultivated.
Of the institutions of Bhutanese society he wrote: 'All the people of
Bhutan considered the Dharma Raja as their spiritual guide – an incar-
nate deity – and implicitly obeyed his orders'. The present incumbent
had, as a tiny child in Lhasa, insisted that he was the Dharma Raja of
Bhutan, much to the consternation of his parents. Eventually, after many
tests, the Lhasa authorities were convinced of his authenticity.

He was then taken to Bhutan where he had no trouble in recognising
articles belonging to the previous Dharma Raja although they had been
mixed up with others. He was then held to be the reincarnation of his
predecessor and ceremonially installed. He was freed of all secular duties
and cares of government and was able to live a life of pious contemplation and holiness. His domestic circumstances were, however, strictly
controlled, being allowed a ration of only four pounds of rice daily and a
precisely stipulated number of servants to minister to him.

The Deb Raja was described by Bose as a 'Prime Miinister' whose chief
officers included a counsellor who spoke on behalf of the Dharma Raja,
as well as the governors of Punakha and Tashichodzong, Paro, Tongsa
and Dagana. He could only act with their concurrence and had no
authority to deviate from established customs including those regarding
perquisites from presents, revenue collection, trade, fines or the disposal

of government servants' property after death.

He went into even greater detail about the subordinate officers naming their titles, even listing their allowances of rice, issued by a storekeeper who had to ensure that amongst other things, the chief of the buttermen received one pound of rice whereas the chief physician had no less than four and the three secretaries who dealt with correspondence in the languages of Bhutan, Persia and Bengal, each had two pounds.

Kishen Kant Bose made it clear why, although Punakha was the capital, the Dharma and Deb Rajas moved from there to Tashichodzong outside Thimphu for half the year. This was because Punakha was at a much lower altitude and the summer months became uncomfortably hot. Thimphu only became the captial in 1960; and the monk body still spends one half of the year there and the rest in Punakha.

He also described some of the functions of the governors of provinces starting with the governor of Punakha whose writ ran for two days north and south of Punakha and rather less from east to west. In a mountainous country like Bhutan distances were measured, not in miles but in walking time. Another official collected tithes in the form of rice, wood, wheat and grass according to custom which he forwarded to the Deb and Dharma Rajas. Once a year there was a meeting of the Pönlops and Zimpöns, together with many peasantry, at which officers were appointed to and removed from their posts. The Punakha Zimpön had many horses and much cattle and traded with a capital of about 5000 rupees, neither receiving nor paying any revenue in cash. His colleague, the Thimphu Zimpön was the governor of Tashichodzong and was responsible for feeding the court during its six months sojourn there during the summer months. Under him was the governor of Gacha to the north and the Subha of Buxa Duar in the south, who had to pay him 800 rupees annually. He also received grain and other taxes in kind from various subordinate officials, to enable him to defray the expenses of the great annual council when the Deb Raja appointed and dismissed officers.

The Paro Pönlop was described by Bose as 'an officer of great conse-quence' who had under him the Zimpön of Dalingcote and the Subhas of several of the duars as well as the Phari Pönlop who ruled this side of Tibetan border. They all paid him revenue in kind except the Zimpön of Dalingcote who was responsible for the maintenance of the garrison where a fighting force was kept in readiness for emergencies. For this reason the Paro Pönlop was the most powerful of them all. Six out of the eighteen duars came under him and he ruled a quarter of the country.

Other officials included: the Wangdiphodrung Zimpön and the Cherrung Subha in the south who controlled Sidlee and Bijnee; the Dagana Pönlop who controlled the area between Buxa and Cherrung; and the Tongsa Pönlop who lived at Tongsa, six days journey to the east of Punakha, whose jurisdiction included eight of the duars.

Kishen Kant Bose gave a list of the major dzongs and described the life of their inhabitants. The Tashichodzong remained empty during the winter; and even in the summer, if the weather became particularly hot, officials and monks moved even higher up into the hills, to Desiphuta. The Tashichodzong area was snow-covered during the winter and, according to Bose, the snow lay up to three feet thick on the roofs of the houses. The few remaining people who did not migrate with the court kept themselves warm by wearing many layers of clothing, huddling round fires and drinking plenty of tea and wine. Even many of the ordinary people spent the winter months at lower latitudes where they had second houses and farms.

Turning to military matters, Bose reckoned that there were about 10,000 men capable of bearing arms but didn't think much of their abilities with matchlocks as they could barely hit the targets. They were afraid to fire with more than two fingers of powder; and if they had to use more they tied the weapons to trees and discharged them from a distance.

Their method of fighting with bows and arrows was for each side to fire and then rush forward and struggle for any dead bodies from which, according to Bose (whose informant must surely have enjoyed pulling his leg), they would extract the livers to eat with butter and sugar. They also mixed the fat and blood with turpentine in order to make candles for shrines. The bones were used for musical pipes and the skulls for beads. They were also mounted in silver to make receptacles for sipping water at religious ceremonies.

The accuracy of Bose's description of Bhutanese customs cannot easily be verified as so many of the national archives were destroyed in the series of great fires. In some ways he was more likely to have been accurate than the British officers as many Bhutanese spoke Nepali or Bengali but he may also have been rather more gullible. Nowhere else is there any mention of cannibalism and it seems hardly likely in a Buddhist country.

He explained the reason for the incessant internal conflicts, with which the country was wracked in the 18th and 19th centuries, as being due to the Deb Rajas either staying too long in office or of arousing in some other way the jealousy of the chief officers of state. If the Deb refused to resign and was defeated in battle the assembly of notables chose a Pönlop or Zimpön to succeed him, with the Dharma Raja's consent. He always had to come from either the Sha district round Wangdiphodrung or the Wang region that included Thimphu and Punakha. If there was no one suitable they selected a priest, a gelong, and if they couldn't settle matters amicably they sent to Lhasa for a successor.

A boy could become a novice monk between the ages of five and ten. If found acceptable, the child was invested with a red cloak and a piece of cloth placed round his neck; and thereafter he no longer belonged to his parents. The gelongs fed him, taught him to pray and read the holy books. He had to renounce all connection with women and with any form of cultivation but could engage in trade or serve the Government. If found with a woman he was expelled but if he wished to renounce his vows he could do so by crying out aloud 'Dumshobdai' or 'my covering has fallen off' and had to fly from the monastery although allowed to take his property. The gelongs were obliged to perform religious worship in public, to read holy books for private individuals and to burn the dead. The chief abbot was second only to the Dharma Raja and officiated during an interregnum between the death of a Dharma Raja and the identification of a new one, for whose instruction he became responsible. His deputy usually succeeded him on his death with the concurrence of the gelongs' council of elders, to which the Deb Raja, the four chief councillors and the three Pönlops always belonged. Bose reckoned that there were about two thousand gelongs altogether in the main dzongs and over three thousand elsewhere. Those who lived with the court, at Tashichodzong and Punakha, or with the chief officers in the other dzongs, were fed by the government but those who lived in solely ecclesiastical monasteries had to support themselves. When a rich gelong died, part of his property went to one of the Debs and the rest was divided amongst his brethren. Gelongs did not bear arms unless they were in government service. According to Bose they were not even permitted to sleep or lie down and members of the order kept watch with whips to ensure compliance.

The Bhutanese have a well developed sense of humour and perhaps Bose's informant about this and the eating of human livers was enjoying himself at the expense of a credulous foreigner. On the other hand there are references elsewhere to a rubric forbidding monks to indulge in much sleep.

The gelongs abstained from fish or flesh on the 8th, 14th, 24th and 30th of each month and were forbidden to take wine, although some drank it in secret. They were forbidden to kill any living creature, whether fish in the river or lice in the head. Bose thought that the Dharma Raja was worshipped as a God and that Bhutanese Buddhist deities had their counterparts in the Hindu Pantheon. He saw many similarities between the two religions. Both worshipped the images of deities, counted beads at prayers and offered clarified butter to the gods by throwing it into fire. He noticed the manifestations of religion everywhere he looked: the stone walls with 'om mani padme hum' inscribed on them and the innumerable, ever flapping prayer flags, even flown outside the dwellings of the poorest people where they were little more than rags.

Turning from monastic to domestic life, Bose wrote that when a child was born he was first washed with warm water and then the next day plunged into a cold river, whatever the weather, and the mother also bathed there wrapping the boy up and carrying him home. Marriage was by mutual contract without any celebration and husbands usually lived in their wives' houses. A rich man could keep as many wives as he could afford and conversely a poor man could buy a part share in a wife with his brothers, of whom the eldest was considered to be the father of any children, the younger brothers being called uncles. Apparently it was no crime for a man to sleep with any of his female relatives except his mother although copulation with sisters or daughters was frowned on. According to Bose pre-marital chastity was not considered much of a virtue and most women were married at about twenty five. Old women were quite often married to boys who ultimately married their deceased wives' daughters.

The death of a notable was usually an occasion for feasting and drinking; and during the three days that the body was kept in the house the usual allowances of food and drink were placed beside it. They were later taken by the officiating gelong. There were two stone-built areas near Tashichodzong and Punakha where bodies were burnt. Afterwards the ashes were placed in brass pots, covered with silk and taken in a procession to the river where they were thrown into the water and the pot and silk given to the gelongs who were then regaled with rice and tea. Finally flags inscribed with 'Om mani padme hum' were erected at the house of the deceased.

The Bhutanese were self-sufficient and would do most forms of manual work except killing animals which was done by people described by Bose as being 'of mean caste' although, as there was no caste system in the Hindu sense, he was probably being more accurate when he later referred to them as slaves. Occupations followed by the Bhutanese included, in addition to farming, shop keeping and carpentry and there were also potters and blacksmiths although the potters had no wheels and the carpenters no saws. Presumably they used axes and sharp knives.

Exports included Tangun horses, blankets, walnuts, musk, cowtails, oranges and madder, all of which were sold at Rangpur from whence the traders returned on their annual caravan with woollen cloth, indigo, sandalwood, 'assafoetidan' (resinous gum used in medicine and cooking), nutmegs, cloves, and coarse cotton cloths, some of which they exported to Lhasa in exchange for tea, silver, gold and embroidered silk goods. Similar Bhutanese exports were sent to Nepal and Assam. From the duars bordering Rangpur itself and from Cooch Behar they also obtained pigs, cattle, betel (or pan), tobacco and dried fish. All this external trade was in the hands of senior officials.

The staple forms of agriculture included rice, wheat, barley, mustard, and maize. Walnuts, apples, peaches, pomegranates, limes and melons were also grown.

The population of the country comprised fifteen different ethnic groups as well as Muslims and Hindus in the low lying areas adjoining India. They were ruled by various grades of official of whom the lowest were Zingaps. Then came Drungpas, Dzongpöns, Subhas, Zimpöns, Pön-lops and finally the Deb Raja. The ruling Deb at the time of Bose's visit had begun his official career as a lowly Zingap. Officers were changed at the annual gathering when the Deb, whose office was as insecure as anyone else's tried to pack the posts with his own nominees.

Bose thought that the Bhutanese were fraudulent intriguers who would not scruple to murder their own families if it served their own interests but that their slaves were amazingly loyal despite ill-treatment. Their laws took no account of assault, minor wounding or adultery; and in the latter case a husband was free to kill the culprit. Other forms of murder demanded a fine of 126 rupees to the Deb Raja and payments to various officials as well as to the victim's heirs. If a man could not pay he was tied to the corpse and thrown into the river with it. 'No distinction was made', wrote Bose 'between what is called murder and manslaughter in English law' – an interesting observation on the state of law in British India with which he would have been familiar.

Robbery, which only occurred on the roads as the houses contained little of any value, was punished by confiscation of property, incarceration for six to twelve months and sale into slavery, not only of the criminal but sometimes also of his relations. Complaints to the courts were not productive of justice for, if substantiated and debts collected, the money went to the judge. If the claim proved to be unfounded the judge took it from the plaintiff who lost out either way. As officials always found an excuse for extracting money from anyone who appeared to have become affluent, people were afraid to wear fine clothes or to eat and drink too well. The gelongs, on the other hand, waxed fat on the collections for charity and the perquisites of office as well as their trading ventures and the return of debts which had to be repaid with interest. Bose considered that the peasants were oppressed on all sides, their rice crops, grass and straw all being handed over to the government, although they were allowed to retain some of their wheat and all their 'dhemsi'. The government also took, at a low price, the blankets they wove and any colts produced by their mares. They were obliged to furnish firewood, spirits, grain, husks and straw for government officers and to act, without payment, as porters for senior officers' trading ventures unless they could obtain exemption from the Deb Raja for which, inevitably, they had to pay. The usual currency was the Narainee rupee which was stamped with the dies captured from Cooch Behar when the Raja had been taken prisoner. Each new Deb and Dharma Raja coined his own rupes with differing weights.

Kishen Kant Bose returned to India the same way he had come, despite its hardships and hazards. Later this remarkable man become a Collector in the Company's service.

In Bikrama Jit Hasrat's *History of Bhutan* (Thimphu, 1980), Bose's account is rightly called 'one of the finest, chronicling Bhutanese religious and historical legends, the country and its people'. In the same book Captain Pemberton's report is dismissed as 'full of fantasies and fallacious observances about Bhutan, its system of administration, its people and their social and religious customs'. However, no extracts are given to allow the reader to form his own opinions. In the absence of Bhutanese records and the necessary reliance on English documentary sources it is essential to strive for historical objectivity by not being too selective, by putting aside national prejudice and present day values and by quoting fairly extensively from contemporary reports, to allow the reader to form his own conclusions on their validity: but they cannot just be ignored because they offend current susceptibilities.

Although both Bose's and Pemberton's reports included some very tall stories Bose's has the wildest exaggerations and in some ways equally unpleasant reflections on Bhutanese character as Pemberton's. On the other hand it does have the most detailed and useful account of life and customs in Bhutan and is unblemished by the sort of supercilious value judgements made by Pemberton, whose report will be considered in the next chapter.

In 1816 a new Collector in Rangpur reversed his predecessor's findings and upheld the Bhutanese claims to most of Maraghat except for a few areas and two years later Babu Kishen Kant Bose, when Collector, had bamboo posts set up to mark at least this part of the frontier.

Until now British official policy had been to favour the Bhutanese wherever possible without alienating the rulers of Cooch Behar and violating the spirit, if not the letter of the treaty. This had been in keeping also with the policy of the Court of Directors. But times were changing: British rule was extending across the sub-continent and the Company was now a major political force. With the conclusion of the first Burmese war in 1826 the Burmese withdrew from Assam which the British occupied in 1828. As they were no longer threatened from the East the British did not feel so obliged to keep the Bhutanese frontier peaceful at all costs. Nor did the overland trade with China through Bhutan seem so attractive as it had done before expansion in India had opened up new markets. There was less reason to mollify the Bhutanese and at the same time there was greater cause for friction as the withdrawal of the Burmese from Assam meant that the British frontier with Bhutan had been greatly increased to include the seven Assam duars which now bordered territory that was British in all but name. There were eighteen duars occupying a long narrow strip of land 220 miles long and 10 – 20 miles broad. During the period of Assamese rule the Bhutanese had occupied the Assam

George Bogle wearing formal Bhutanese clothes presented to him
by the Deb Raja, detail from an oil painting by Tilly Kettle, *c*.1775.

"View between Murichom and Choka", aquatint by William Daniell after Samuel Davis, 1813.

"Murichom to Choka", watercolour by Samuel Davis, 1783.

One of Chomolhari's eastern glaciers (White, 1906).

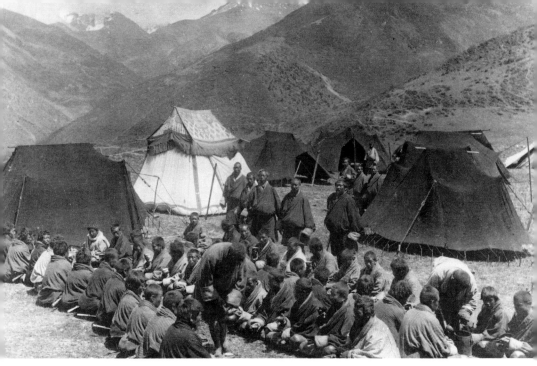

Bhutanese army on northern border (White, 1906).

Fortified cantilever bridge north of Drugyel Dzong (White, 1906).

Drugyel Dzong (White, 1905).

The Drugyel armoury (Hyslop, 1907).

Interior courtyard of Drugyel Dzong with stacked wooden shingles ready for reroofing (White, 1905).

Map of Bhutan showing the disputed Duars (House of Commons, 1865).

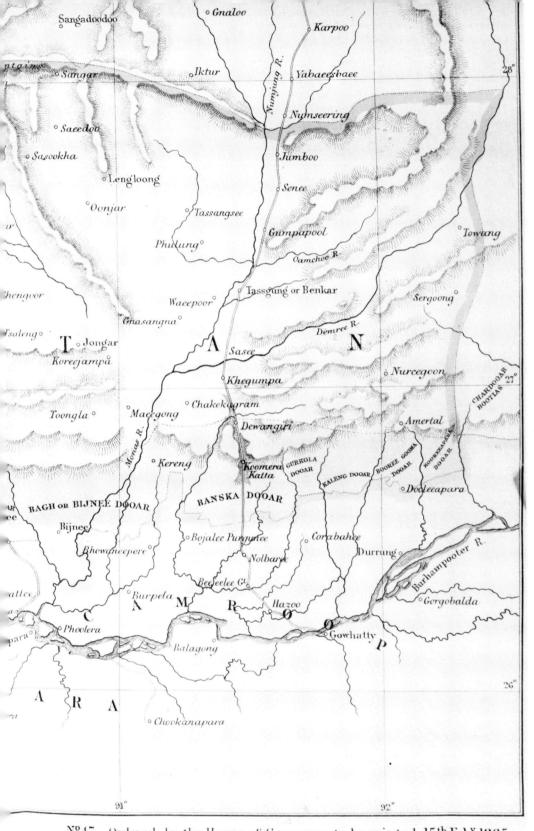

Sangadoodoo

Gnaloo

Karpoo

Sangar

Iktur

Yabaeesbaee

Saeedoo

Nunseering

Numjung R.

Sasookha

Jumboo

Lengloong

Senee

Oonjar

Tassangsee

Gumpapool

Towang

Phulung

Oamchoo R.

T   Jongar

A   Tassong or Benkar

Sergoong

hengoor

Waeepoor

Demree R.

Gnasangna

N

Tsaleng

Sasee

Nurcegoon

Koreejampa

Khegumpa

CHARDOOAR BOOTIAS

27°

Toongla

Macegong

Chakekagram

Amertal

Monas R.

Dewanguri

Kereng

Koomera Katta

GURKOLA DOOAR

KALENG DOOAR

BOOREE DOOAR

GOOMA

KOOREEAPARA DOOAR

Dooleeapara

BAGH or BIJNEE DOOAR

BANSKA DOOAR

Bijnee

Bojalee Purgunee

Corabahee

Bhowaneepore

Durrung

Burhampooter R.

Nolbaree

Burpeta

Beeeelee Gt

Hazoo

C   A   M   R   O   O   Gorgobalda

Phoolera

Balagong

Gowhatty

P

A   R   A

26°

Chookanapara

91°

92°

Paro Rimpung Dzong (White, 1905).

Paro Dzong with Ta Dzong above and bridge below (White, 1905).

Paro Dzong destroyed by fire, November 1906, with Ugyen Dorji and John Claude White (Hyslop, 1907).

Tashichodzong, Thimphu (White, 1905).

Tashichodzong, Thimphu (White, 1905).

Tashichodzong, Thimphu, watercolour by Samuel Davis, 1783.

Tashichodzong, Thimphu, watercolour by Samuel Davis, 1783.

Punakha Dzong, watercolour by Samuel Davis 1783.

Punakha Dzong (White, 1906).

John Claude White entering Punakha, 15th December 1907 (Hyslop, 1907).

Wangdiphodrung Dzong, watercolour by Samuel Davis, 1783

duars but had acknowledged Assamese sovereignty by paying an annual tribute of yak tails, ponies, musk, gold dust, blankets, and various other items including a certain amount of hard cash. Bhutanese Pönlops were in charge of administration but their subordinate officials, who paid a heavy price for their offices, in their turn saw to it that they were suitably rewarded by the taxes extracted from the people.

The land of the duars had a rich, black fertile soil, much of it vegetable mould washed by many rivers, and was capable of producing almost any crop, particularly cotton. There were 11 Bengal and 7 Assam duars of which 3 had a peculiar form of alternating tenure. They were virtually depopulated as a result of so much raiding and the custom of Bhutanese officials of retaining what crops there were for their own use. Many of them were inhabited by people called Mechis and Kacharis, some of whom had become virtual slaves to their Bhutanese overlords.

After the treaty of Ava and the withdrawal of the Burmese from Assam the British took over the existing arrangements. Consequently they now controlled the Assam duars, including two Darrang duars and five others for which they received tribute from the Bhutanese. This led to considerable resentment as the agents employed by the British substituted inferior articles. Consequently at the subsequent auction, held by the British to raise their cash value, they actually fetched less than the assessed value of the tribute so that arrears accumulated which were never paid.

In 1828 there was more frontier skirmishing when the Dzongpön of Doompa attacked a frontier post killing a native officer and some sepoys of the Company's forces, carrying off captives whom he refused to release and there were counter attacks by the troops of the 'Sebundy Corps' which had been raised for service on the north east frontier. The Buriguma duar was occupied and not returned until 1834 in accordance with a new policy of temporary occupation in order to deprive the Bhutanese of the agricultural benefits of the land. The handful of British officers who served on this frontier were by no means all agreed on this policy and Captain Adam White considered that Bhutanese complaints of police actions which had led to the raid in 1828 were justified as a great deal of looted property was found in their possession.

In 1834 Major J. Robertson, the Agent for the north east frontier, recommended that there should be a peaceful settlement of all differences to be effected by sending an envoy to Bhutan but this was not accepted by the Bhutanese.

In 1835 a detachment of Assam light infantry was sent to Bijni in order to force the release of several captives after a Bhutanese raid on Nogong. A fortified stockade was stormed and nine people were released. In the same year following a raid from Kalling duar troops of the Assam Sebundy corps fought another action and forced the return of the twelve people.

The situation deteriorated still further the following year when
Captain A. Bogle (no relation to George Bogle) led eighty men of the
Sebundy Corps to negotiate with the Dewangiri 'Raja' (so called, but
in reality a lesser official) about the surrender of criminals. When he
refused to comply with Bogle's demands the duar was annexed. Captain
F. Jenkins, then Agent for the north east frontier, laid down four conditions for the return of this land: the extradition of criminals, compensation
for losses, fines to be imposed and an agreement that there should be no
more raids. The 'Raja' handed over twenty offenders but refused to
agree to the extradition of village officials or to sign an agreement. Bogle
favoured permanent annexation but at that time Jenkins was more
inclined to see the force of the Bhutanese case although later he came to
think that the only way to stop outrages was to annexe all the duars
outright. Meanwhile the 'Raja' followed up his refusal to sign an agreement by attacking Bogle's eighty men with six hundred Bhutanese formed
into five companies armed with bows and arrows, matchlocks, swords
and spears, carrying shields and wearing shining helmets. He also had
a small force of about twenty men on horseback. The battle began with
the Bhutanese opening fire on Bogle's elephant but the better training
and firepower of the Company's troops won the day. The Raja fled, a
number of minor officials surrendered and a large number of wanted
men were handed over. Jenkins now wished to withdraw. The government of Bengal was even more anxious not to become further involved
in concessions of territory which might not be supported by the directors
in London and told him that no more attacks should be made by the
Company's troops. However, when it was realised how successful Bogle
had been they were forced by the nature of their victory to retain the
land for the time being.

The following year four Zingaps arrived in Gauhati with letters from
both the Dharma and the Deb Rajas and the Tongsa Pönlops asking for
the return of the duar because of the shortage of grain arising from its
loss. An agreement was signed by which both sides undertook to put
down dacoity (brigandage) to give up harbouring criminals, to return
them when requested; and if this was not done to permit the police to
follow them across the border. It was also agreed that arrears of tribute
should be paid. The agreement was never ratified by the Bhutanese
leaders, probably because a number of the clauses, especially those
concerning the police, would inevitably favour the British. However the
signing of the agreement by the Zingaps gave the Company an honourable justification for withdrawing at a time when war in Afghanistan and
the danger of war with China inhibited any wish for further military
operations.

Meanwhile the old border area with Cooch Behar continued to present
as many difficulties as the new one with Assam. Not only were a number

of British officers aware that the Bhutanese often had just as good a case as the Cooch Beharis but they were also reluctant to respond to calls for aid as they were aware that the Burmese and the Gurkha wars had both originated in response to frontier incidents. An attempt was made to settle boundary disputes by despatching Ensign T. Brodie to survey the whole of the frontier with the Bengal duars but his recommendation for the erection of masonry pillars was never carried out, mainly because of British insistence that the cost should be shared. As a result of the survey it was agreed that certain areas should go to Cooch Behar and others to Bhutan but Brodie agreed with Jenkins that the Raja of Cooch Behar had been largely to blame for most of the incidents on this frontier.

In 1837 there was an incident typical of the confused and inter-related identities of border inhabitants when a father and son who were revenue farmers in three Bhutanese districts as well as in the two British administered areas of Patgram and Baikunthpore refused to return to Bhutan to answer charges of extortion and the British authorities refused to extradite them on the doubtful grounds that 'political offenders or revenue defaulters ought not to be given up to another state'. There had now been so many vexatious incidents along the whole frontier that it was decided to send another mission to Bhutan.

CHAPTER FOUR
1837–1838 The Pemberton Mission

A major reason for sending another mission was that there had been a breakdown of communication with the government of Bhutan. No letters appeared to be getting past the subordinate officials of the frontier. Later it transpired that they had all been intercepted by the Deb Raja who had not passed them on to the Dharma Raja. There was also felt to be a need for much greater intelligence on conditions in Bhutan and despite the fullness of previous reports there were still a number of areas on which further information was sought.

The mission included Captain R. Boileau Pemberton of the 44th Native Infantry, Ensign M.T. Blake of the 46th N.I. and Dr. W.M. Griffith, an assistant surgeon on the Madras establishment who was to be botanist as well as medical officer and twenty seven soldiers of the Assam Sebundy Corps under a Gurkha subadar ('native officer') and about ninety assorted camp followers: servants, grooms and others.

It was decided not to go from Buxa Duar, approaching from the south west as Bogle and Turner had done or from the south like Kishen Kant Bose as this would add nothing to what was already known about the geography of the country. Instead it was decided to go by the Banksa duar and to head as far over to the east as possible without exciting suspicions. Information about the mission was sent to the Deb Raja but as no reply was received after a long delay it was decided to press on and the mission set out on 21st December 1837.

Once across the Nao Nuddee the fields of luxuriant rice on the British side gave way to dense reeds and grassy jungles as far as the foothills from whence they kept on until they reached Dewangiri on 23rd January. Whilst there, attempts were made by the Bhutanese to pursuade them to return to the border and re-enter by the usual Buxa Duar route. A rebellion had broken out headed by a Pönlop whose brother controlled the district through which the mission would have to pass if they took the direct route to Punakha. The Zingaps sent to escort them, having failed to make them go to Buxa Duar; now advised a long detour because of the the unrest. Pemberton wondered if there were other reasons and if they were suspected of undertaking a reconnaissnce prior to a British invasion. The Bhutanese may well have had some cause to think this but in any case were justified in trying to keep foreigners away from an area of civil strife. Pemberton seems to have been unreasonably suspicious right from the beginning which did not make for an auspicious start. On the other hand the route ultimately followed was so rugged that it may well have been selected in order to show the British what terrible terrain it would be for military operations and so deter them from planning invasion. Their journey of 250 miles (described in Dr. Griffith's report) took sixty eight days although there were only twenty six actual marches. Delays accounted for the rest of the time.

The mission left Gauhati in Assam on the 21st of December and ten days later had reached the first Bhutanese village just over the border. From there they had a fairly uneventful trek through low lying country until approaching Dewangiri at 2,100 feet after a steep ascent on the last part of the journey. There they had to spend over a month kicking their heels awaiting permission from the Deb Raja to continue. However, they were received by the Subha in a very friendly manner and liked the people they met who were 'fine specimens of human build'.

At last their permit came through and they left on 23rd of January, after being given scarves by the Subha, and by the next day had reached a height of 7000 feet. At about 4000 the vegetation had changed from wooded grassy hills to steeper hills dotted with rhododendron bushes and similar species. They climbed up steep and rugged paths along ridges clothed with trees covered with pendulous mosses and lichens. At one stage they had to wind round a huge eminence, the peak always towering several hundred feet above them as they made their way cautiously along narrow rocky paths overhanging deep precipices. At Khagumpa, after covering only eleven miles they saw a solitary pine tree.

The next day they descended gradually through a forest of oaks until coming on to a dry open ridge covered with rhododendrons, continuing their descent until reaching a stream bed and then once more starting to toil laboriously uphill. They halted at a village called Sasee where they rested for five days before continuing on the 28th. The next few days followed the same pattern, ascending and descending across the grain of the many ridges that lay across their path. On the 31st they passed a temple at 8000 feet north of Bulphee where the country had now become downland fringed with cultivation, mostly rice and wheat with a few villages and picturesque temples to be seen.

On February 1st they reached the Dumree Nudee, climbing up the far side to reach the village of Tashigang, situated on precipitous spur at 3100 feet with rivers on either side, known to Griffith and the others as 'the Gibraltar of Bhutan'. It contained the Subha's large square house, 'decorated in the usual manner', a few poor houses crowded together and defence works consisting of round towers connected by a wall to the village. They were lodged in the Subha's guest house half a mile up the torrents where, as it was an 'open house', they suffered from furious gusts of wind sweeping up the ravine. A few days later they had an

interview with the Subha who arrived 'in all possible state', with thirty
armed followers preceded by a band 'which consisted of a shrill clarinet
and a guitar guiltless of sound, a gong and a bell, ponies, a Tartar dog,
gentlemen of the household, and priests, all in single file'. They met in
a small silken pavilion where they found the Subha to be polite and
obliging. After the interview, at the end of which they were presented
with scarves and strips of coarse blanket, they were entertained, whilst
chang and rice were circulated, with music and dancing women 'who only
differed from their compeers of India in being elderly, ugly, very dirty
and poorly dressed'. They were rather taken aback at the end to be asked
by the head priest to contribute at least a rupee. During this time they
learnt that the Deb had been deposed and heard of the consequent
disturbance but didn't allow the news to delay them and left on the 5th,
the day appointed for their departure by the Subha.

They continued through an even greater variety of scenery, along
precipitous paths decending to river beds and up steep ascents, passing
only a few inhabited villages and rather more deserted ones. On the 8th
February they were halted by a combination of snow and the late arrival
of their baggage following far behind. The whole country at the higher
levels was now snow-covered including the downs that they had crossed
days before, which were still in sight from high ground.

The area around Tashiyangtse which they reached on the 10th was very
attractive with large pine forests studding the snow covered hills. Surprisingly, although it felt cold, the thermometer did not fall below 34
degrees. Toiling on, they reached a height of 12,500 on 15th February,
the last 3000 feet of the ascent being through thick snow. From 10,000
feet upwards all the trees, including black pines, were covered with hoar
frost and icicles.

During the ensuing descent Griffith had the frightening experience of
being lost. He had stopped to urge on the coolies who had decided to
halt for the night in an empty hut but as they refused to go any further
he pressed on to join the others ahead and after proceeding for about
half an hour, 'slipping, sliding and falling in all imaginable directions'
and getting no answer to his shouts, he returned with great difficulty to
join the collies for the night, overtaking his companions the next day.

From the 18th of February they followed the course of the river
Koorsee for much of the way until reaching Langlung where, 'as it was
the residence of a Subha, we suffered the usual inconvenience'. The
interview with this very young official was conducted with much less state
than at Tashigang but he behaved 'very civilly and without any pretension
. . . dancing girls more than ordinarily hideous were in attendance'. They
left on 23rd of February 'after the usual annoyances about coolies and
ponies'. For the next few days their route took them along river beds,
through woods of oak and rhododendron and past villages and temples.

On 26th they began an ascent through heavy snow, along a path 'built up the faces of sheer precipices'. At 12,300 they crossed the Rudongla pass consisting of 'a gap between two rocks barely wide enough to admit a loaded pony' where one of the rocks was inscribed with 'Om Mani Padme Hum'. The descent was very steep and the followers, who had wanted to remain in a ruined log hut, had to be exhorted to keep trudging on but cheered up once through the snow.

Griffith noted the variety of vegetation during the ascent: oaks, rhododendrons and bamboos almost up to 11,000 and thereafter black fir, alpine pines, polyganums, a species of Bhudra and many other alpine forms. During the descent, however, all he could see were three species of pine, the black fir pinus Smithianus, a larch-like species, and pinus excelsia.

Bumthang, a village of 'immoderate filth', at 8,700 feet, he rather surprisingly considered to be nevertheless 'the most desirable spot we yet had met with'. In the valley wheat was cultivated and 'the tillage was better than any we had seen, the heads kept clean and actually treated with manure, though not of the best quality'.

From thence they went on to Bjakar whose Subha was absent at Tongsa. His 'castle', a long irregular straggling building, on a hill 500 feet above the plain, was sometimes used by the Tongsa Pönlop in the hot weather, when the Subha had to take himself off elsewhere. Leaving on the 4th of March they climbed to over 10,000 feet, soon coming on snow again, seeing few villages or cultivation until approaching Tongsa where there were fields of barley.

Griffith didn't think much of Tongsa which, 'although the second, or at any rate the third place in Bootan, is as miserable a place as anybody would wish to see . . . wretchedly set in a very narrow ravine drained by a petty stream'. In the nearby fields barley alternated with rice and in the garden almonds and pears were in blossom. 'Our reception', he wrote, 'was by no means agreeable. I was roared at most insolently to dismount while descending to the castle. Our followers were constantly annoyed and in fact we got no peace until we had an interview with the Pillo (sic) on the 15th'. Despite considerable pressure Pemberton refused to see the ex-Pönlop separately even though a stoppage of supplies was threatened, as it had already been arrange that he should attend the interview with his nephew, the current Pönlop.

They were received with a good deal of state: 'The attendants were very numerous and mostly well dressed but the effects of this were lessened by the admission of an indiscrimate mob . . . We were not admitted, however, into the presence without undergoing the ordeals which the low impertinence of many orientals imposed on those who wish access to them'. Griffith preferred the old Pönlop, 'the most aristocratic personage we saw in Bhutan', to the new one, 'a mean looking bull-necked individual'. During the interview 'a novel part of the ceremony consisted in the 'stirring up of a large can of tea and the general recital of prayers over it, after which a ladle full was handed to the Pillos (sic) who dipped their forefinger in it and so tested it'. The meeting passed off well: and afterwards several 'less ceremonious and friendly meetings took place'.

Their last interview on March 22nd was occupied mainly in hearing the Pönlop list the presents he required the British to give him. Griffith was glad to leave Tongsa where it had started raining, their lodging had not proved to be waterproof and where they had been annoyed with 'a profusion of rats, bugs and fleas'.

The next day they came to a temple 'in a most romantic spot', on a patch of fine sward in a gorge of the ravine, the sides of which were covered with beautiful cedar pines; the background was formed by lofty mountains covered with heavy snow. The continued through 'pictur-esque glades' to Chendebji, 'the prettiest place we saw in Bhutan', where there were fine oaks and two specimens of weeping cypress.

They reached Punakha on the 1st of April, having followed the valley of the Pochu. Griffith was as disappointed as he had been at Tongsa, 'I saw a miserable place promising little comfort as respects accommodation and one glance at the surrounding country satisfied me that little was to be obtained in any branch of natural history; for a narrow, utterly barren valley, hemmed in between barren hills, in which no arboreous vegetation was to be seen, except at considerable elevation, gave no great promise of botanical successs'. The quarters allocated to the mission fulfilled his gloomy foreboding. They were housed in a former stable block in a square enclosure surrounded by low mud walls; and above the stables small recesses, not much larger than coffins, had been made for their lodgings. Later, Captain Pemberton insisted on renting better accommodation in the village where two thirds of the houses were 'completely ruinous'. The neighbouring villages also bore 'the stamp of poverty and the marks of oppression'. Griffith was not even impressed by the magnificent dzong which was so admired by later travellers. He thought it to be 'too uniform and too heavy to be imposing'. He regarded the climate of Punakha with equal distaste for although the temperature in April and May only varied between 64 and 83 Fahrenheit the valley was something of dust bowl in the path of powerful winds.

On the 9th May after the failure of the mission to induce the Deb Raja to accept a treaty they left Punakha without regret, and in some haste to avoid a diplomatic impasse, having refused to see the old Deb or to accompany the new one on his own forthcoming journey, .either action being liable to be regarded as support. They followed the course of the Pochu Mochu for much of the way until they started climbing and spent the night at Telagong where they were lodged in the dzong held by the followers of the old Deb.

They reached Woolakha on the 16th and continued past 'rather fine wheat cultivation' and on through woods of oak and yew, emerging onto an open sward on the summit of a ridge with beautiful rhododendron, birch and juniper woods. During this march they saw gooseberries at 9,000 feet and in other places there were euphorbias, primroses, saxifrage, clematis, anemones and ranunculus; and near the summit a genuine larch. They were able to have a good view of the old dzong at Simtokha at one stage. Following the course of the 'Teembo' (Thimphu) river they saw roses in profusion and luxuriant crops of barley. Chipcha turned out to be a delightful place with variegated scenery and a pleasant climate which they left with regret, descending by a precipitous path to a torrent 800 feet below: and then following a southerly course they passed Punagga where Turner had camped. Their route took them along a bad road 'scarcely passable for ponies but through splendid scenery' in the height of spring luxuriance. Keeping to the course of the 'Teembo' they returned once more to Murichom.

From there they went on to Buxa and from thence to Koolta and Cooch Behar whose richly cultivated state was in striking contrast to the 'absolutely desolate state of that belonging to Bhutan', meaning presumably the adjacent lowlands; for even Griffith had been impressed by some of the cultivation seen on higher ground.

In his journal Dr. Griffith was more informative about the route than Pemberton who gave only a brief outline as a preface to sectional reports on various aspects of the country, starting with a geographical description and going on to describe under separate heads the government and its officers, the priesthood, revenues, military resources, agriculture, live stock, wild life, manufacture, commerce, religious and social life and architecture. The document closed with a section on political relationships to which was annexed a copy of the proposed treaty submitted to the Deb Raja who had refused to accept it.

Pemberton's observations on climate and vegetation were made with the help of 'two excellent barometers' and his appendix included tables of distances of various townships from Dewangiri, a list of places showing their height, local cultivation, vegetation and geology with remarks noted against each entry such as: 'heavy snow', 'good village' (whatever this might mean), 'residence of a Doompha'. His comments on the geography of Bhutan and its 'Alpine valleys' where the main population centres were located would be endorsed by modern travellers: 'With the exception of the duars', he wrote 'the whole of Bhutan territory presents a succession of the most lofty and rugged mountains on the surface of the globe: separated only by narrow beds of roaring torrents which rush over huge boulders of primitive rock with resistless violence: and the paths most generally frequented are formed at an elevation varying from 2 to 7,000 feet above the level of the sea; while the mural ridges above them frequently rise to an altitude of from 12 to 20,000. The consequence is that the traveller appears to be shut out on every side from the rest of the world and it is only when winding round some spur from the minor ranges that he obtains an occasional glimpse of the more distant peaks and ridges which bound the view of the deep dell at his feet where some restless river is urging its way to the sea . . . This general character of extreme ruggedness is hardly at all interrupted save by some geological basins between the retiring flanks of the ranges and to which, for want of a more appropriate term, the name of Alpine valleys must be given.'

Pemberton estimated the valley at Tashichodzong to be 7271 feet and Punakha 3739 which accord fairly well with modern maps. Of the rivers he wrote: 'The largest are the Monas (Manas) which flows under the walls of Tassgong (Tashigang) the Patchoo Matchoo (Pochu and Mochu) at whose confluence stands the winter castle of Poonakha (Punakha), of the Deb and Dharma Raja, the Tchinchu (Chinchu) which skirts the walls of Tashichodzong, the summer residence of the same functionaries, the Toonshsa which enters the plains from Lakee (Lukee) duar, the Manchee, by that of Cheemerchee (Chamurchi): and the Durla, by the celebrated pass of Dalimkotta (Dalingcote)'.

The location of roads was determined, then as now, by the geographical features of mountain and valley. Pemberton thought that the easiest road to the capital from the Eastern frontier was to follow the river bed to Dewangiri and to go from there to Punakha, skirting the left bank of the Pochu river. The most direct route to or from Tashichodzong was the one taken by the mission on their return journey although an ascent in the reverse direction would have presented almost insuperable problems for ponies and pack animals: hence the easier route taken by the annual Rangpur caravan of merchants travelling from Tibet through Bhutan as well as the earlier British missions, along the right bank of the Chinchu river through the territory of the Paro Pönlop.

Amongst the most interesting sections of Pemberton's report was his description of the government of the country and the status of the Deb Raja. According to the law he should only hold office for three years after being selected from amongst the principal officers of state; but, according to Pemberton, this was 'a dead letter in practice'. The incumbent at that time was a person originally 'in a very humble rank of life'. He had led a rebellion to make himself Deb, and although successful, there was still civil war raging in parts of the country, which was only suspended during the mission's residence in the captial. Of the Deb himself Pemberton wrote that he was 'about forty years of age, of rather dark complexion, mild manners and pleasing address' and that the 'exceptionable' aspects of his conduct only arose from 'his extremely precarious situation'. The obvious inference, that the Bhutanese were reluctant to receive a foreign mission during a civil war in which the ruler's position was still precarious, does not seem to have occurred to either Pemberton or Griffith.

The Dharma Raja was described as being 'like his great prototype of Lhasa' and 'supposed to be Buddh himself, clothed in the human form, and by successive transmigrations from one corporeal frame to another, to escape the ordinary lot of humanity: on the death, or temporary withdrawal of the Dhurma from the sublunary scene of his existence his office remains vacant for a twelvemonth, during which time the senior Gylong, or priest, regulates the religious observances of the country. The first appearance of the Dhurma is supposed to be indicated by the refusal of his mother's milk and an evident preference for that of a cow. He is also supposed to be able to articulate a few words distinctly and to convey his meaning by certain intellegible signs. The intelligence of these miraculous manifestations of precocious intellect is conveyed to the Court, and a deputation composed of some of the principal priests proceeds to the spot where the young Dhurma is said to have appeared, conveying with them all those articles which in his former state of existence he had been in the habit of using. These are spread before him, mingled with a number of others purposely made to resemble them, with the innocent intention to test the fallibility of the re-nate God. As might have been anticipated, the infant always proves victorious in this contest of skill; the priests delare their conviction he is their former spiritual head and he is conveyed with great ceremony to the palace of Punakh, at which place all installations must be made, either in the rank of Dharma or Deb, to give them validity'.

Pemberton was impressed by the Dharma Raja, a child of nine with 'a fair complexion' and flowing black hair, 'neatly and elegantly attired in silk with a pointed embroidered cap; the extreme neatness and cleanliness of his dress presented a very remarkable contrast to the filth which peered through the half worn silken dresses of the motley group after him'. He very sensibly allowed 'an aged priest concealed behind the throne to dictate remarks which avowedly emanated from himself'.

He thought that Turner had been mistaken in considering that the secular and spiritual authority were united in the Deb Raja and that it was probable that his mission had arrived during the interregnum following the death of a Dharma Raja when the Deb would be more in evidence.

He described in some detail the mechanism of government and the personalities of the current office holders. There were two councils: the senior one included twelve gelongs whose main function was to exercise spiritual control but tended at times to acquire secular authority; and was supposed to have been responsible for some of the power contests with which the country had been plagued. The other council, under the Deb Raja, who seldom presided, consisted of six principal officers of state of whom the senior, the Lam Zimpön, was supposed to represent the interests of the Dharma Raja, but was usually a nominee of the Deb. The Paro and

Tongsa Pönlops were also entitled to seats. Under the Paro Pönlop were six Subhas, so called by the Muslim rulers of Bengal with whom they had been in contact, but more properly termed Zimpöns. Of these the Hartoom, Done and Buxa Zimpöns were in charge of duars adjoining British or Cooch Behar territory. Under them came the Doompahs in charge of the villages. The Tongsa Pönlop also had six Subhas under him. There was also another grade of official, between Subha and Doompah called Chang Doompah, of which the Dewangiri 'Raja', so called, was one. Others whom the British had encountered included the Daka Pönlop and the Cheerung Subha.

The Zingaps, who were the usual emissaries sent to deal with British officers in India, were an even lower grade, and fairly numerous. The lowest of all were called Gurpas, assistants to the senior Zingaps, 'an office', according to Pemberton, 'which is eagerly sought after as it affords opportunities for oppression, plunder and gain, of which these functionaries avail themselves with quite as much sagacity and as little remorse as the native public officers in Bengal.' He failed to mention any evidence for this extreme condemnation and was even more critical of the Zingaps themselves, of whom he wrote: 'It is principally against the inhabitants of the duars that the rapacity of the Booteah Zeenkaff (sic) is principally exercised: his own countrymen have as little as himself to give but the plains produce those articles of luxury and commerce which cannot be extracted from the bare mountains; and the powerless government he serves is unable to check his excess. The arrival of a party of Zeenkaffs in the duars on any pretext, is a calamity against which the oppressed inhabitants earnestly pray . . . fowls, pigs, goats, rice, clothes and tobacco are all placed under contribution . . . '

As most of the British officers who served on the eastern frontier throughout the 19th century wrote on much the same lines it is probably fair to assume that, in the absence of firm central government with whom communication was tenuous even when there was no civil war going on, the local officials did much as they pleased; and as the duars were so much wealthier than other areas, they provided a natural target for personal gain.

Although the authority of the Pönlops and Zimpöns was absolute, nevertheless Pemberton thought that the constituted government would be perfectly just and effective if it were fairly administered; but the lack of continuity of officers, the absence of fixed salaries, the evasion of punishment for offences by payment of fines and the uncertainties of office all contributed to the rapid accumulation of private wealth. National prosperity was hampered by a system whereby all a man's goods were forfeited to the state on his death. There was thus little incentive for hard work when sons could not reap and build on the rewards of their fathers' industry. This accounted for the many deserted houses and villages seen by this and some of the other missions.

Pemberton's view that Bhutan could have supported a population ten times larger is absurd in view of geographical factors. It was an exaggeration also to ascribe the lack of old people to the legalisation of prostitution and the custom of polyandry, strongest in the areas bordering Tibet; to the consequent excesses of indulgence and to the related tradition of monastic celibacy, not only for priests but also for all aspirants to high secular office. Pemberton wrote prudishly of 'a total deprivation of morals and an utter disregard to the observations of those obligations of mutual fidelity . . . post-nuptial chastity is held in as little esteem as virgin purity . . .'

He was equally shocked by the priesthood 'which exercises so prominent and injurious an influence on the country, either by the indulgence of a spirit of intrigue, both moral and political, or as the authors of customs which have been shown to produce a state of the deepest demoralisation that no account of Bhutan would be complete without them'. The monks spent their days more in 'listless idleness' than in prayer or instructional duties in the villages. They formed such an élite that every Bhutanese parent with an eligible son tried to enter him for the priesthood by paying a fee of 100 rupees to the Deb and Dharma Rajas. The boy was then provided with food and clothing and remained in a monastery for two to six years, after which he could either continue as a monk or enter the public service, remaining in the monastery if he wished. No doubt, as in all closed societies, there were problems of moral behaviour but Pemberton's extreme views probably reflect more accurately the Protestant ethic of 19th century Britain than the true state of Bhutanese religious society.

The Dharma Raja was head of the priesthood, under whom came the Lama Tripa who occupied the position during the interregnum, another Lama, who was the Dharma's spiritual teacher and the Lama Khenpo, who was the visible head of the hierarchy.

Pemberton thought that reform of the system was inevitable because of the priests' immorality and 'secret indulgence in forbidden pleasures' and also because this increasingly large number of drones could not for much longer be supported by a comparatively small population of workers who had to contribute the necessary supplies of grain, fowls, pigs, kids, sheep and bullocks to the monasteries. Very little revenue apparently of any other sort passed to the central government except for the contribution of the duars, about 40,000 rupees a year, of which government officers were supposed to receive a portion. In effect, though, most of this was also paid in kind. 'A government', wrote Pemberton, 'which is conducted on such principles can do little more than preserve itself for total dissolution: the real power of the state is vested in the two haughty barons of Paro and Tongsa, within whose jurisdiction are comprised nearly three fourths of the whole country and population. The Deb holds his precarious tenure of office at their pleasure . . . '

Although some of Pemberton's value judgements have about as much validity as those of, say, an intelligent young Chinese from an advanced civilisation, introduced into late medieval Britain, beholding the power of secular priests and monastic orders, the wealth of monasteries, the demands of tithes and the venality of some of the magistrates and sheriffs, nevertheless his more factual and less moralist observations added considerably to the sum of knowledge of Bhutan at that time. He gave, for example, useful information about the coinage in current use. The coin known as a 'debe' rupee, nominally half the value of an East India Company rupee, was made by using the Narainee rupee dies of the Raja of Cooch Behar, captured during the invasion of his territory as described by Kishen Kant Bose; but as the degree of purity of the metal depended on the honesty of the Subhas in whose dzongs the coins were minted, leading to a great deal of variation, they were largely rejected by the inhabitants of the plain and in those duars where Narainee rupees still circulated although these were becoming increasingly scarce as the Bhutanese remelted and alloyed them to make more 'debe' rupees.

Pemberton did not think much of Bhutan's military resources and considered that although Kishen Kant Bose's estimate of 10,000 men capable of bearing arms could be about right, the inadequacy of supplies would limit any force to 5 or 6,000 in any one place. The only standing army consisted of about 200 guards at the largest dzongs, augmented to 3 or 400 on state occasions. To raise a larger force it would be necessary to overcome the jealousy between the Tongsa and Paro Pönlops.

He thought better of Bhutanese agriculture, especially the methods of terracing and the full use made of the more favoured areas. He saw barley, buckwheat and hemp at over 4,300 feet above sea level, the latter also at over 5,000; wheat at an estimated height of 9,400, as well as sugarcane, castor oil plants, betel vines and orange trees. There was not much use of manure, however, apart from the spreading of decayed leaves and vegetable matter, and very limited rotation of crops. The only implements observed were hoes and ploughs drawn by a couple of oxen; but, like almost all the visitors to Bhutan, Pemberton was much impressed by the system of irrigation and the great ingenuity displayed over the carriage of water. Large black cattle and smaller red animals were encountered, although not in large numbers. Very few goats or sheep were seen and only two herds of yak. These were jet black, browsing on the edges of snow at a height of 11,000.

Like his predecessors he also thought highly of the Tangun ponies, which were only 11 or 12 hands, with thick bushy manes and tails, large heads, heavy shoulders and broad chests, and had tremendous powers of endurance. They were not usually ridden downhill and their main use was to carry their riders up the many steep ascents. Bhutanese saddles were therefore made for that purpose rising about seven inches above the seat at each extremity in order to give maximum support. They rarely had to go at more than a walk because of the nature of the country: and for uphill work runners held the animal on each side by a leather thong, moving in short rushes a few yards at a time, pausing in between for man and beast to get their breath back. When an important official went on journeys the runners pressed firmly against his back, so that he had to make no muscular effort to retain his seat. Ponies were used almost exclusively by senior officials although mules were regarded even more highly for riding and some were as big as 14 hands. They were usually a cross between a Bhutanese pony and Tibetan donkey. The latter were used almost exclusively for the carriage of salt, threading their way over rocky paths and over the mountains by instinct and without any form of guidance.

Turning from livestock and agriculture to manufacture and commerce, Pemberton described the former as being limited to the manufacture of blankets, coarse cotton cloth, cooking pots, wooden bowls, swords, copper cauldrons, paper and poorly tanned leather; and the production of butter and ghee (clarified butter), mostly for local consumption. Trade was confined to Bengal and Tibet, the Bhutanese acting to some extent as middlemen, obtaining broadcloth, coral, white cloth, cambric and elephants from Bengal, via the duars, in exchange for Tibetan flowered silks, musk, rock salt, tea, coloured blankets, gold and silver. The Bhutanese caravans usually arrived at Rangpur in February and March and returned in May and June.

The Bhutanese traders no longer paid any tax and the expenses of the caravans, stables and housing, were paid by the British. However, by Pemberton's time this trade had begun to wither away, partly because the trade with Tibet had declined since the establishment of the Gorkha dynasty in Nepal and the consequent Chinese occupation of Lhasa, closing Tibet to the inhabitants of India. Even the Bhutanese now needed passports to get there and were restricted to a few main routes. Most of the trade with Assam was carried on, not by Bhutanese but by Tibetans from the south of the country, about four hundred of whom, in several groups, had been passed by the mission between Dewangiri and Tashichodzong, on their way to Assam. Sometimes as many as two thousand used to congregate in Dewangiri before descending to the plains, accompanied by officials of the Dewangiri 'Raja'.

Pemberton's conclusions about Bhutanese social life were, as might have been expected, much more critical than those of Bogle, Turner or Kishen Kant Bose: 'Every element of deterioration', he wrote, 'is comprised in their government, both secular and spiritual. Their energies are paralysed by the insecurity of property, their morals are degraded, their numbers reduced by the unnatural system of polyandry and the extensive prevalence of monastic institutes, alike unfavourable to the creation of domestic sources of happiness and a feeling of love for country or desire for improvement.' Although he admitted that there were 'some redeeming traits of character' and that he had seen 'some touching instances of filial and parental respect' he considered that he had never before encountered a race 'so wholly degraded in morals'.

Nothing could be in greater contrast to the views expressed by Bogle half a century before or those held by John Claude White sixty years later, or for that matter by today's traveller to Bhutan. As Dr. Griffith very largely agreed with the sentiments of his chief it must be concluded that although he and Pemberton were perhaps representative of the morality of their age, class and race at that time, and although they themselves may not have had the same benign characteristics as Bogle or White, there must be other factors. The general state of tension on the borders and the exasperation felt and expressed by most of the British officials in the frontier regions at the apparent impotence of local Bhutanese officials to stop the increase of cross-border raiding, may have contributed to a state of mind that was not well disposed towards the Bhutanese in the first place. Possibly also the semi-permanent state of civil war had had its effect on the character of the Bhutanese people themselves who were not inclined to view with any great favour an uninvited mission that refused even to follow the prescribed route and was seen as a military reconnaissance party.

According to Pemberton the most menial work was done by the descendants of Bengali and Assamese prisoners carried off from the plains and made to marry Bhutanese partners. A number of applications were made to him by Assamese captives for their release but as they had been captured in most cases before British rule in Assam and he had no legal right to seek their liberation, he was only successful in one instance. In fact, manumission for this slave class only occurred in the 1950's.

He devoted a mere paragraph to religious observances, which shows that he had not appreciated the all-pervading part played by religion in Bhutanese life. He thought that the whole ceremonial of Buddhist services were 'a curious compound of Romish, Buddhist and Hindu worship'.

His descriptions of Bhutanese costume, which complement those of other travellers, are more interesting although even here he could not refrain from criticism: 'The dresses of the priests invariably consist of a garnet coloured garment thrown loosely over the left shoulder, leaving the right arm bare and which exhibits generally a power of muscle better adapted to grapple with difficulties in the field than turning leaves in a cloister. The garments of the upper classes consist of a long loose robe which wraps round the body and is secured in its position by a leather belt round the waist. Among the higher orders the robe is generally made of Chinese flowered silks, the favourite colours being red and yellow. Over the robe in the winter a large shawl of black satin or silk is generally thrown, and when seated, the person wearing it wraps it round the knees and feet so effectively as to conceal them from view. A legging of red broad cloth is attached to a shoe made of buffalo hide; and no Bootea ever travels during the winter without protecting his legs and feet against the effects of snow by putting these boots on and they are secured by a garter tied under the knee. A cap of fur or coarse broad cloth, or blanket, completes the habilment; and the only variation observable is the substitution of a cloth for a woollen robe during the summer months of the heat. The habits of all classes are most disgustingly filthy and the man must be endowed with more than an ordinary share of nerve who would willingly interpose any member of their society between the wind and his nobility'. Presumably this is meant to be facetious but even so it displays a narrow intolerance that makes all Pemberton's value judgements suspect.

He was very impressed by the decorative appearance of Bhutanese houses. The ground floor was often occupied by livestock and the upper floors were reached up a flight of steps through a door turning on a wooden pivot, fastened by a wooden latch. The light filtering through wooden shutters was inadequate except on the south aspect where the projecting wooden balconies were the occupants' favourite haunts. In winter their imperfectly fitting shutters let in the cold outer air whilst most of the smoke from the domestic fire was unable to escape. The fireplaces were made of solid masonry raised two feet from the ground with circular openings for cooking utensils and an aperture for the fire below. The second floor was reached by a ladder constructed of a single piece of timber with notches cut for steps; but as these were of inadequate breadth, descent became a hazardous enterprise for foreigners. This floor was divided into several compartments, 'all equally remarkable for smoke and soot'. Occasionally there was a third floor; and the roof consisted of a flat terrace of well beaten earth which was itself covered by a 'pent' roof formed of fir planks laid horizontally across timbers kept down by stones. Inevitably, Pemberton was critical of this form of fastening 'which came adrift in high winds when the stones rolled off followed by the fir planks'; and considered that this afforded proof of Bhutanese indolence. Yet this custom has stood the test of time and is still prevalent in the rural areas. Houses were built of stones or earth and the earth walls, formed by pressing moistened earth between boards, were so strong that Pemberton found he could use them as rifle butts. Bullets fired at eighty yards were flattened but the earth was hardly indented.

He described the customary diet of the upper classes as consisting of rice boiled in large copper cauldrons, goats, pork, and beef, although not much attention was paid to the quality or cleanliness. The priests and principal officers dined together in the dzong and drank large draughts of chang made from fermented rice handed round in brass ornamented buffalo horns. 'On all religious festivals, feasting and drinking are carried to excess, the effects of which sometimes incapacitates those who have been engaged in them two or three days for any employment: and I experienced on more than one occasion the inconvenience of a carousal which had disqualified the Deb and his ministers from seeing very clearly the questions submitted for their consideration'. However, he did at least concede that the Bhutanese were never quarrelsome in their cups. The ordinary people had a diet 'which is the most miserable it is possible to conceive; they are restricted to the refuse of wretched crops of unripe wheat and barley, and their food consists generally of cakes made from these grains, very imperfectly ground. Before commencing a journey the cakes are prepared and thrust into the bosom of their robes, with a little salt, some chillies and a few onions or radishes. They deposit their loads at the summit and foot of every steep ascent and descent and solace themselves with the contents of the recess in the front of their loose robes. This is followed by copious libations of chang from the horn; and there is little prospect of the journey being speedily terminated until the bottom of the horn has been seen.'

Pemberton was surprised that the Bhutanese were not better at archery considering the amount of time spent on it. The mark was usually a piece of V-shaped wood, about eight inches by seven, placed in a reclining position 120 yards from the firing point, at which 'the arrow is shot at a greater degree of elevation than appears necessary'. However he did at least admit that he only attended a single tournament. The competitors had been mostly six foot tall with 'stalwart Herculean frames, but wanting, apparently the plastic elasticity of limb which is so conspicious in the tribes further East'. He was rather more impressed by Bhutanese skill at quoits, in which a stone, serving as a quoit, was thrown with great accuracy at a slanting stick thirty yards away having first been laid flat on the hand and then projected by a rotary motion. He also praised the Bhutanese for being good sportsmen, 'quarrels seldom or never occurring and their hilarity being unaccompanied with that boisterous rudeness which characterises the festivities of most of the savage tribes around them'.

They were also honest and equable despite being 'indolent to an extreme degree, totally wanting in energy, illiterate, immoral and victims of the most unqualified superstition'.

'Their virtues are their own', he wrote, 'and their vices are the natural and inevitable consequence of the form of government under which they live and the brutalising influence of the faith they profess . . . ' The higher classes were 'shameless beggars, liars of the first magnitude, whose most solemnly pledged words were violated without the slightest hesitation, who entered into engagements which they had not the most distant intention of fulfilling . . . exhibiting in their conduct a rare compound of official pride and presumption and the low cunning of needy mediocrity;

and yet preserving at the same time a mild deportment and speaking generally in a remarkably low tone of voice'. Although he had, in the course of his duties, 'met a few native officers of the different courts of inter and ultra gangetic India' who provided exceptions to the 'generally condemnatory judgement' he would have pronounced on the remainder, he failed to discover one in Bhutan 'entitled to the slightest degree of confidence in either word or deed'.

The last part of Pemberton's report included sections on Bhutan's political relations with her neighbours. The country had once been ruled by Tibet on behalf of the Chinese whose ultimate withdrawal was in return for the payment of an annual tribute and recognition of the Emperor's secular and the Dalai Lama's spiritual authority. Considerable deference was paid to 'the supposed views' of both. Few Bhutanese, however, had ever been to Lhasa, although rather more visited Tashilhunpo in the three snow-free months. Once a year messengers arrived bearing the Imperial mandate (whose provisions were described by Bose) addressed to the Dharma and Deb Rajas and their senior officers, written on fine cambric in large letters with twenty one pieces of gold as a mark of respect to the Dharma Raja. The reply was sent by messengers accompanied by twenty three coolies bearing loads of fine rice, silk and cloth, all from Assam. In return the Chinese sent flowered silk and scarves, coral, gold and silver. Three Bhutanese lamas were always in attendance on the Dalai Lama, regarded as an elder brother by the Dharma Raja who sent him annual presents, receiving in return silk from China, chowries (yaks' tails) and gold leaf for temples and palaces.

The Chinese had only once in recent years interfered in Bhutan's incessant internal turmoil, when in 1830 the Tongsa Pönlop rebelled against a Deb who had hung on to power for nine years instead of the statutory three and two Chinese officers and a detachment of troops were said to have supported the rebellion. They were reputed to have effected a compromise by arranging the temporary abdication of the Deb, who then resumed office five years later after the Pönlop's death. He had been deposed by the Deb whom Pemberton met and was now once again in a state of rebellion, occupying Tashichodzong, preventing the court from going there in the summer months. During the mission's visit negotiations were going on to allow the Dharma Raja and the priests to make their annual summer migration as the Bhutanese preferred to patch up some sort of inconclusive agreement based on the 'status quo' rather than call in the Tibetans or Chinese, for whose powers they had considerable respect.

Bhutan's political relations with Nepal arose from the assistance given to Sikhim when the Gorkha army invaded its territory in 1788. In a few months the Goorkhas were forced to retire but as soon as the Bhutanese withdrew their help they advanced again and captured much of Sikhim.

The Chinese then sent a force which defeated the Gorkhas and made them accept Chinese overlordship. From then until 1813 when the British invaded Nepal and the Gorkhas, despite their enormous successes elsewhere, left Bhutan to its own devices, out of a healthy fear of Chinese reaction on the one hand and of the British presence in Sikhim on the other. Thus, for the first time for years, the Bhutanese had a secure frontier. However, in 1815 the Nepalese invited the Chinese to send an army through Bhutan to attack the British in Bengal, in order to force them to withdraw from Nepal. The Chinese declined and Bhutan was spared.

There was little contact with Sikhim except for some minor trading; and the only other country with which there could conceivably have been some minimal vicarious contact was Russia as there were supposed to be Russian agents in Tibet. Several merchants from Lhasa whom Pemberton met in Bhutan, described foreigners similar to the British in dress, appearance and manners; who sat at tables in the same way, writing and reading books. He considered that these people could have been behind the Nepalese aggressive attitude and its consequences for Bhutan. In reality, however, they were more likely to have been only inoffensive Armenian traders.

He ended his report with some observations on Anglo-Bhutanese relations. He was critical of Hastings' return of the duars to the Bhutanese, who largely depended on them economically; especially as, in his view, they had been 'justly forfeited'. He also criticised the agreements made with Bhutan after the British occupations of Assam in 1828. He considered that the Bhutanese had been given title to land extorted from the Assam princes and that Britain had been unnecessarily lenient. In his view, concessions in the interest of amicable relations were only rewarded by repeated aggression and the murder and abduction of British-Indian subjects, the refusal to pay tribute or, until force was used, to make reparations. He thought that nothing would be done to fulfil the hope of the British government in India that once the central authority was made aware by the mission of their distant underlings' behaviour, they would take action. The constant internecine struggles for supremacy were such that the central government's writ didn't extend very far and the rulers dared not enter into any engagements that might clash with the supposed interests of a Pönlop or Zimpön.

During his discussions with the Deb, Pemberton had quoted chapter and verse for the misconduct of Bhutanese subordinate rulers and, in order to settle outstanding problems a draft treaty was prepared. This appeared to have the concurrence of the Deb and his ministers who, both in private and in public, admitted that its 'provisions were unobjectionable . . . but kept evading and postponing ratification'. Despite this the Deb continued to admit that he had no valid objection, that the treaty would remove many causes of dissatisfaction, that the Paro Pönlop and the other senior governors agreed with him, but that he dared not sign for fear of the Tongsa Pönlop.

Pemberton commented, 'With such a government it is sufficiently evident that negotiation is utterly hopeless. Its nominal Head is powerless and the real authority of the country is vested in the two barons of Tongsa and Paro who divide it between them'. However, despite his preference for ultimate British control over all the Bengal and Assam duars, he did not recommend such a drastic policy in the first instance as the Bhutanese economy was too dependent on the wealth and trade of the duars. He recommended instead that as the Tongsa Pönlop was mainly to blame his territory should be made to suffer by the resumption of British rule over the Assam duars only and that this distinction should be forcefully pointed out to the Bhutanese. However, he thought that the mere threat and consequent effect on the economy would be sufficient to make the Bhutanese government accede to any terms for the restoration of the duars. He also suggested that if the opening of communication with Tibet was still considered desirable the British would be justified in refusing to treat with anyone other than the authorities in Lhasa. If the duars were threatened the Bhutanese would try to enlist Tibetan support as they had done in 1782 and the way would then be open for direct Anglo-Tibetan contact which the Bhutanese had always hitherto tried to prevent but would now realise to be in their own interests.

If direct contact with Tibet proved impossible however, Pemberton advocated the use of force to annexe the duars and for the British to dictate terms and not restore them until all tributes and debts were paid and captives returned. On the other hand he did not favour their permanent retention, which would lead, not only to constant attacks on the whole frontier by men suddenly reduced to extreme distress but also to an inevitable British invasion of the hinterland in order to defeat the leaders, effectively ending all hope of profitable contracts with Tibet and China; and leading to further Nepalese aggression. Nor did he recommend the continuance of the tribute currently paid by the Bhutanese for the duars which caused them great dissatisfaction and brought the British only a trifling revenue: a nominal quit rent in acknowledgement would be sufficient.

Pemberton proposed the appointment of a permanent British Resident in Bhutan on the grounds that if even the presence of a temporary mission was sufficient to cause the suspension of hostilities during its stay a permanent British presence would have a more lasting effect. Although on the only occasion when the possibility was raised with the Deb it was flatly rejected, he thought it could have been insisted on as one of the conditions for the return of the duars if they were annexed. A Resident would also be able to counteract any unfriendly external influences and his presence would be a check to internal misrule in the duars and prevent local acts of aggression. The Chinese would not like such an appointment but would accept a *fait accompli*.

There was, however, no mention of this possibility in the treaty submitted to the Deb Raja on 25 April 1838 but never ratified. It included clauses permitting free intercourse and trade between Bhutan and British India and for extradition arrangements which were, however, far from being mutual. Under these proposals British-Indian subjects who committed offences in the duars were to be handed over to the British authorities as well as Bhutanese who offended against British Indians: but Bhutanese who had complaints against inhabitants of British territories would have to take them to the Company's magistrates. Tribute was to be paid in cash, not kind (contradicting the views expressed in the report). Current arrears were to be annulled but any future arrears of more than a year would result in annexation until the balance had been paid. There was to be joint participation in boundary demarcation and Bhutanese agents were to be stationed in Assam and Bengal to facilitate communication between the Company and the Bhutanese government.

Finally, Pemberton acknowledged the help provided by Ensign Blake who surveyed and prepared a map of the route and by Dr. Griffith who compiled a botanical collection, undertook necessary medical services and kept a journal of the mission's experiences.

Griffith's views on the people and customs of Bhutan reflected those of the mission's leader with whose trials, resulting from 'constant intrigues', he sympathised, especially when the Deb's 'Bengal Secretary' regularly changed the time and location of meetings which, more often than not, were then postponed. He thought the priests 'a most pernicious class' and blamed the prevalence of celibacy for the preponderance of women in certain districts as well as for the nationally low population. With the single exception of the Subha of Dewangiri, 'a gentlemanly unassuming man', he was not impressed by the ruling class to whom he could not 'attribute the possession of a single good quality . . . They are utter strangers to the truth'. To the 'lower orders', however, he was 'disposed to give credit for much cheerfulness'. In general he considered the Bhutanese to lack courage, to be 'great boasters but a small performer' whose military qualities were despised by the Gurkha Subadar of the escort. Their 'ideas of religion appear to be confused', their women were used as slaves, the men were 'excessively idle', spending their days drinking chang and arrack. Both sexes, 'in all their habits', were 'inexpressibly filthy . . . strangers towards changing clothes'. He disliked the disorderly arrangements for meetings and the begging for presents when these did take place.

He too opposed the return of the duars on the grounds that the Bhutanese had learnt nothing from their defeat in 1836 and the loss of the duars. 'By the plan of allowing barbarians to hold court in the plains, the inhabitants of those plains lose a portion of their most fertile soil . . . The Bhutan government has been invariably treated with great liberality by the greatest power in the East and how has it requited it? It has requited it by the rejection of a treaty which would only be productive of an advantage to them, by shuffling mendacity, by tampering with British subjects and by inconsiderate conduct to a British mission . . . in short they showed themselves to be ignorant, greedy barbarians . . . ' Small wonder perhaps that he had few Bhutanese patients (mostly suffering from venereal diseases).

So ended a mission that yielded nothing of any political value: merely a body of additional information on Bhutan for which too high a price had been paid by way of bad relations between the mission and its reluctant hosts; a legacy of anger and irritation on the Bhutanese side and lack of sympathy on the British. Pemberton had, by his manner and choice of route, given the impression of leading a military reconnaissance; and although his descriptions of uncontentious matters were more comprehensive than those of any other report, his intemperate comments on Bhutanese life and customs reflect unfavourably on the value of his judgement on anything. He was not a good choice for such a difficult mission and was hardly in the mould of the sympathetic soldier-diplomats and administrators, such as Malcolm, Munro, Elphinstone and the Lawrences, that British rule in India was already producing. Yet he was no 'mere' barrack room soldier floundering in a novel world of diplomacy; nor was he new to the problems of the north east frontier. He had already completed eighteen years of service when he went to Bhutan, including survey and exploration work on the frontier, in Sylhet, Cachar, Manipur, Khasia and Assam. He had also seen active service in Manipur where he was mainly responsible for establishing the authority of Raja Gambir Singh. He died in India only two years after his return from Bhutan, at the age of forty two.

Neither of his two companions reached fifty, which was not unusual for British officers in the East at that time, when home leave to a temperate climate was infrequent and many of them served for as long as fifteen or twenty years without going home. Ensign Blake lived the longest, being killed at the age of forty eight when, as a major commanding the 2nd Gwalior infantry, he died trying to prevent his regiment from joining the mutiny in 1857. Dr. Griffith who became Professor of Botany at Calcutta Medical College was only thirty five when he died in Malacca in 1845. A graduate of University College London, and M.R.C.S. he had not been long in the Madras medical service before going on to a mission of exploration in Assam, returning via Ava and Rangoon, which preceded his joining Pemberton. After returning from Bhutan he went the following year to the Hindu Kush which he crossed, exploring and collecting plants of which he contributed a number to various institutes as well as publishing two volumes of notes on plants in Bhutan, Afghanistan and neighbouring countries and several scientific papers.

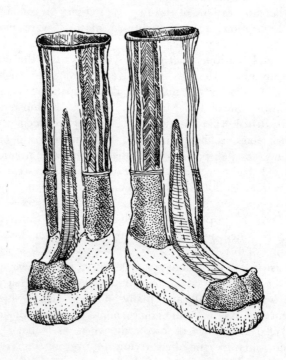

CHAPTER FIVE

1838–1864: The Humilation of Ashley Eden

Over the next ten years or so there were a number of serious incidents, including 12 cases of abduction in 1839 alone. Only a few however could be blamed entirely on the Bhutanese, such as the occasion when two girls and two elephants with forty head of cattle were taken away; but in other instances much of the blame lay with the British–Indian side. One of the main causes of friction was the British complaint that tribute due to them as the successors to the Assamese rulers, in return for the Bhutanese occupation of the Assam duars, was always in arrears; but this was only partly due to the rapacity of the Bhutanese tax farmers. The main reason was the British refusal to accept Bhutanese currency and their insistence on payment in Narainee rupees. As these were valued more highly than Bhutanese equivalents the net result was a demand for considerably more in real terms than the agreed sum. This was quite contrary to the custom of the Assam Kings from whom the tribute had been taken over; as was the other British custom of auctioning the goods that had been received in part payment. As the local officials invariably substituted inferior articles before they reached the auction, the sums obtained were deemed to be insufficient when the articles did not fetch the appropriate price and the shortfall was regarded by the British as arrears.

Meanwhile within Bhutan the insurrection continued and letters were received from both the Deb and Dharma Rajas complaining that their country was being devasted. The Deb claimant had made himself a secure stronghold by taking the dzong of Wangdiphodrung.

Colonel Jenkins recommended that an attempt should be made to persuade the Bhutanese to give the British control over all the duars, 'in the distracted state of the hill country' and that if diplomacy failed force should be used. The Governor General declined to adopt this policy but instead sent an admonition and warning 'that it would be his painful duty to occupy the duars if the state of anarchy continued and the Company's frontier areas suffered'. He did not, however, support Jenkins' proposal to send a British envoy to discuss the possible take-over of the duars. 'Fruitless missions of this kind', he wrote, 'only tend to aggravate our embarrassment and are not creditable to the British power'.

The constant border feuding led to a strengthening of military preparedness by retaining the Shan militia after the end of the Burma war and increasing the strength of the Assam Light Infantry and the Assam

Sebundy Corps and other levies. On 27th March 1840 the government in Calcutta asserted its right to annexe the Assam duars on the grounds that the Bhutanese had not fulfilled their obligations, although stating that compensation would be paid; and in November the two Darrang duars of Nalling and Buriguma were annexed, despite the government's initial reluctance to take such a step with the Afghan war on their north western frontier still in progress. The capture of the girls, cattle and elephants, led to the retention of these two duars the following year instead of being restored. In 1841, however, the Dharma Raja wrote to request their return on the grounds that the State of Bhutan was no longer in turmoil and suggested that a member of Pemberton's mission should return in order to check this for himself. In 1843, instead of returning them, the British agreed to pay 10,000 rupees annually for them. The Bhutanese were not happy with this and over the next ten years regularly asked for their return and never accepted the British case. There was undoubtedly some truth in Jenkins' contention; and indeed some of the chiefs in the duars welcomed and assisted in the annexation. Nevertheless it was a period of imperial expansion and this sort of action would never have been acceptable to the Company earlier in the century. It had also by now become apparent that the Assam duars were a fertile area for tea planting on a large scale. Jenkins himself came to revise his views on annexation and wrote some years later 'if we possess the duars, the source of their subsistence, the Bhutanese government would in a short time become entirely dependent on us'.

Although after 1851 the Bhutanese ceased making formal requests for the return of those duars that had already been annexed they never fully accepted the situation and always contended that the compensation offered was less than the annual income derived from the land. However, although still not accepting the justice of the deal they did finally agree to receive, in 1846, the sum of 10,000 rupees as arrears of payment for the previous three years, as well as the 10,000 for that year. This sum was paid annually by the British until the war of 1864 but Jenkins' recommendation for its increase was not agreed by the government in Calcutta. Despite this and the government's prevention of Bhutanese attempts to enlist the aid of the Nepalese, the local British administration in the border area, which was nearly always favourably inclined towards the Bhutanese, managed to set up markets where the Bhutanese could obtain supplies of products from the duars.

Meanwhile there was no lessening of frontier incidents. In 1845 seven people were abducted by followers of the Dewangiri 'Raja' as a result of which the Banska duar was occupied until they were returned and much the same sort of incident occurred again in 1850 when refugees from Bhutan were carried back across the border. Five years later the Dewangiri 'Raja' was held responsible for a number of criminal acts within British territory and when the Tongsa Pönlop refused to pay a sum double the value of the property removed by his subordinate's henchmen he was told that in future the value would be deducted from the compensation and that any further outrages would lead to annexation of the Bengal duars, the threat of which proved effective.

The Bengal duars continued to present almost as many problems as those in Assam. In 1840 some Bhutanese were ejected from Khutagghat on the grounds that it belonged to the Raja of Bijni but shortly afterwards it was re-occupied by 80 or 90 armed men including Sikhs and other Indians serving with the Bhutanese. At the subsequent enquiry the Raja's claim was upheld after the boundary had been surveyed; but later requests for British assistance by the Bijni and Sidli Rajas were not agreed.

In another dispute, in the Maraghat area a decision was given in favour of Bhutan by Dr. A.D. Campbell, the Superintendent of Darjeeling from 1840 to 1862, who was to prove very sympathetic towards the Bhutanese. He was told to inquire into the problems of the Bengal duars from the river Teesta in the west to the river Manas in the east, a distance of about 200 miles. As a result he found that in the majority of cases the Bhutanese were not the main offenders. In 1842 he and the magistrate in Rangpur decided that although the Bhutanese Durga Deva was a major cause of trouble the Baikunthar Zemindar's son on the Indian side was as much to blame. They also considered that the Bhutanese were not hostile to the British government, only to British subjects who invaded their land. The Durga Deva who held land on both sides of the border and was able to escape to either at will, was made to agree not to cross into Bhutanese territory without express permission. It was stipulated that armed British subjects should not cross into Bhutan and the Bhutanese were asked to make a similar edict. Meanwhile the Fallacottah district was taken over again by the British and 800 rupees a year were to be paid for it.

In this, as in other disputed areas such as Chaklakhati which was awarded to Cooch Behar in 1848, the fundamental cause of all the trouble was the lack of permanent boundary marks. They were frequently recommended and the frontier was reconnoitred in order to establish the boundary before erecting posts but nothing much ever happened. This was partly due to the British government's insistence on Bhutanese representatives being present – a reasonable stipulation in view of past events – who were never sent, even when this condition had been agreed; but it may also have been partly due to Jenkins' views on the desirability of permanent annexation as the only way to preserve stability in a region whose economic potential was only now being realised. In the event only in a few disputed areas such as the Baikunthpur frontier was there any physical demarcation and that was only because of Dr. Campbell's insistence.

In 1850 a Bhutanese minor official raised some armed followers in British territory and pursued a vendetta against one of his superiors on the Bhutanese side for which he was arrested. The Government of British India however ordered his release on the dangerous grounds that no action could be taken to prosecute offences committed outside British borders. This was taken as a carte blanche by some of the criminal elements in British India to do as they pleased across the frontier. As always, there were rights and wrongs on both sides. Even the tolerant Dr. Campbell referred to a 'notorious absence of justice or system in the Bhotia mode of trial' and suggested that each side should be able to send prosecutors or witnesses to trials across the border. The Bhutanese did not trust the Raja of Cooch Behar to apply even handed justice but were prepared to allow the British to try criminal offenders. They refused to extradite offenders demanded by the Cooch Behar authorities who in turn rejected their demands which then led to the attempted imposition of rough justice by cross-border raiding.

Nevertheless, despite the continued feuding, the years of Campbell's administration provided an enlightened period of comparative peace on the frontier during which trade between Bhutan and the Company's land was encouraged. In 1850 however, Jenkins, now Agent to the Governor General, took personal responsibility for all policy issues towards Bhutan on both Assam and Bengal frontiers and a more aggressive policy was adopted. In fairness to Jenkins it should be said that few people had longer experience of the problems of the north east than he had and his views were the outcome of a long history of Bhutanese prevarication, the ease with which local Bhutanese officials could go their own ways without control from the central authority, and the realisation that the people of the duars would be economically better off under a stable British administration capable of exploiting the potential for tea plantations in the west; rice, wheat and millet in the central plains and timber in the east.

In 1854 a Bhutan government mission to the British Headquarters at Gauhati failed to obtain an increase in the amount of revenue and then went on to commit a number of robberies in the Banska duar on their way home, which didn't assist their case.

Jenkins reported 'further robberies and dacoties' and in April 1855 his assistant reported that on the night of the 12th 'a party of about forty Booteahs plundered a resident of the whole of his property, amounting it is said, to between 7 and 800 rupees'. Less than two months later Jenkins heard from the officiating magistrate at Kamroop to say that written confessions from captured robbers had implicated the Dewangiri 'Raja'. Shortly after this it was learnt that he had been replaced but was fortifying a position near the frontier and that he and his brother the Tongsa Pönlop were both in opposition to the Deb Raja, himself a usurper. His deposition was confirmed by the Tongsa Subha who wrote to complain of Jenkins' writing over his head direct to the Deb Raja. Although he likened the relations between the Company and the government of Bhutan to 'the friendship between the lotus and the sun and the moon' he accused Jenkins of evasiveness which 'is not the practice with us Booteahs' – echoing Pemberton's criticism in reverse!

Jenkins was accused by the Tongsa Subha of having taken possession of the duars 'without any fault of ours' but it transpired that the real cause of his anger was that the Deb Raja had made him pay the fines imposed by the Company for various acts of plunder. He demanded that Jenkins should not only return Bhutanese who had been captured but should also pay half the fines himself. In a later letter he wrote 'you have taken possession of the Darma Raja's duars' (not the Deb Raja's) and enjoy their revenue and making false statements appear true . . . '

In January 1856 the Secretary of the Government of India wrote to the Secretary of the Government of Bengal supporting Jenkins' refusal to pay anything and commenting: 'However unwilling the government may be to bring about a hostile collision, some effectual means must be used to put a stop to the aggressions of the Booteahs and to shield our ryots (peasants) . . . ' Jenkins was therefore authorised 'by His Lordship in Council' to refuse to comply with the Subha's demands and to point out 'the extremely unbecoming tone of his letters' and to demand an apology. If a satisfactory reply was not received the Bengal duars were to be occupied. Nevertheless when a few months later the acting Agent threatened to withhold payment of revenue for the Assam duars unless offenders else-where were surrendered, the Government of India considered that he had gone too far, that this line should not be pursued, and that the officers near the frontier should do nothing to provoke hostility. He was also held to have exceeded his instructions in informing the Tongsa Pönlop that unless he apologised for the disrespect shown to the Agent, means would be taken to cripple his authority, the value of plundered property deducted from revenue and all payment withheld until all offenders were surrendered.

The Government of Bengal, the intermediary between the frontier officers and the Government of India, was at times equally critical of its servants as in the case of one Arung Singh. Although still holding office in Bhutanese territory he had been allowed by Jenkins to settle on the British side of the border: and when he was captured the Secretary of the Government of Bengal, in reporting the incident, considered that Jenkins had been at fault. Surprisingly, though, on this occassion the Government of India did not agree with the Bengal Government's advocacy of a softer line in view of Jenkins' 'injudiciousness' and insisted that offenders be punished and apologies demanded, and the Bhutanese informed that if 'atonement is not made for this new aggression the Government of India will hold itself free to take permanent possession of the Bengal duars'.

In the event this was not immediately necessary as the Agent reported apologies from both Dharma and Deb Rajas, the Tongsa Pönlop and the Dewangiri 'Raja'; and in return the Governor General agreed that provided full satisfaction was given for the abduction of Arung Singh the revenue should be raised to 12,000 rupees. Despite this the Deb Raja's response was evasive and further incidents were reported including the capture of a merchant who had gone to Myganoree to trade, and the abduction of two men and their wives from Cooch Behar.

In 1880 after a further series of incidents, the Assam revenue was withheld. The Raja of Cooch Behar again invoked the treaty in asking for British assistance. There were reports of a Bhutanese raid into Sikhim and even of a proposed attack on Darjeeling as a force of armed men was reported to be preparing to cross the River Teesta. Bhutanese frontier officials were increasingly becoming a law unto themselves and the Bengal administrative report of 1862 stated that 'there is reason for suspecting that they (the rents paid by the British) had never been remitted to the Deb Raja' . . . 'it is probable that the revenue of Ambaree Fallacottah is annually appropriated by the Dalimkote Soubah (sic)'.

On 20th January 1857 a Government of India letter to Bengal had stated plaintively 'We are not sure in whose hands the chief authority rests or whether there is any effective chief authority, that there appeared to be two Deb Rajas, that the Tongsa Pönlop was virtually independent and that, in truth, considering that Bhutan is a neighbouring state, that the country has a government of some sort and established rulers and that our intercourse with the people is constant and on the whole not unfriendly, our knowledge of its condition is curiously imperfect'.

Agreement was given for the frontier to be reinforced although there was still no desire to take military action and the Secretary to the Government of India wrote, 'the Governor General in Council would still avoid if possible not only a collision with the Bootias but the incumbrance of an additional charge of territory, which although productive, is described as formidably unhealthy to native as well as to European troops'. It was again suggested that the revenue of the Assam duars be withheld 'The answer will depend upon the degree to which the government of the Eastern duars is independent to that of the Western duars . . . it is not certain that the withholding of money conceded from the revenues of the districts under the Tongsa Pillo (sic) would be a matter of concern to his fellow governors further west . . .'

It was decided not to take any further action in view of the death of the Deb Raja, a usurper whose rule had been challenged, and the appointment of a successor who had the Dharma Raja's support, which increased the possibility of effective control over the frontier.

The only action suggested by the Government of India was that if force proved necessary the tract of country known as Ambaree Fallacottah on the Indian side of the river Teesta, ceded to the Bhutanese seventy years before, should be seized as it would put no incumbrance upon the Government of India. However, the outbreak of the Indian mutiny in the summer of 1857 ensured that no action be taken.

In 1859 the Bengal government submitted a list of thirty three cases of alleged aggression in the previous two years in which forty five people had been carried off, and Colonel Jenkins was authorised to take over Ambaree Fallocottah. The response of the Government of India was to censure him for exceeding his instructions as he had told the Bhutanese that the annexation was to be permanent and that more land would be seized if demands were not complied with; and he had not written to the Deb Raja as instructed. As so frequently happened with frontier officers his actions were disapproved of but not disavowed. Jenkins continued to recommend annexation as a policy, whilst giving the Bhutanese a share of revenue, as the only way to secure their vested interest in a stable frontier; but this did not find favour either with the Government of India in Calcutta or in London.

Several British officers also thought that there was not much to choose between both sides, in regard to frontier incidents and shortly before the Eden mission left the officiating Agent wrote, 'I am inclined to think that the Booteas may have a good deal to say and that in some cases they may have justice on their side'. He repeated a story told by 'a very respectable looking old gentleman', whose lands were just inside Bhutan, who had paid a stealthy visit to report how dacoits from Cooch Behar had carried off fifty of his buffaloes. They were chased by his retainers, one of whom caught a robber but, was, in turn, captured by the Cooch Behar authorities and imprisoned. However, the old man did confirm that Bhutan was in a chaotic state with no Dharma Raja until a new incarnation had been found. Several Deb Rajas had been murdered in quick succession and the Tongsa Pönlop was in the ascendant. Consequently, the officiating Agent, recommended the annexation of the Bengal duars but thought that if that was not acceptable a mission should be sent to Bhutan. 'It is most unreasonable' he wrote, 'to expect any satisfaction from the Deb Raja and though for some purpose it may be a useful fiction to assume that we are in correspondence with him, nothing short of our having a European functionary stationed at the court of the Deb could give assurance of communications reaching him.' In forwarding this the Lieutenant Governor of Bengal proposed instead that a non-European Agent should be located at the court of Bhutan, but the Government of India decided that this time a mission should be sent. Messages were sent to the Deb and Dharma Rajas informing them of this proposal and inquiring after routes.

The messengers returned in October having had 'a fair reception' but the Deb Raja's reply was evasive. He was prepared to talk about the

Assam duars but wanted payment of the Ambaree Fallacottah rents and complained of aggression from Cooch Behar. This seemed reasonable enough; the Agent thought it to be 'not unfounded' and recommended that no further action should be taken until the arrival of the Zingaps whom the Deb promised to send in order to settle all disputes. The Lieutenant Governor of Bengal still thought that the mission should go but the reply from the Government of India stated, 'On the whole His Excellency in Council thinks the better course will be to await the Bhutanese messengers and hear what they have got to say, the more so that the Officiating Commissioner of Assam admits that the faults are by no means all on one side.' However, as the Zingaps never arrived and even the usual messengers who came at that time of year to receive the Bhutanese share of the revenue of the Assam duars, were of inferior rank and knew nothing about the Zingaps, it was agreed that the mission should go, and letters were sent to that effect.

The instructions to its leader, The Honourable Ashley Eden, were to 'explain clearly and distinctly but in a friendly and conciliatory spirit . . . ' why Ambaree Fallacottah had been occupied and that it would only be for as long as the Bhutan government did not comply with the request to restore captives and property. If the Bhutanese showed any desire to see justice done the British government would, whilst retaining the land, pay a sum of 2000 rupees on condition of good behaviour. He was to find out the details of any alleged atrocities committed by British Indian subjects and to make arrangements for their extradition but warned in this connection to 'bear in mind that from the inequality of the state of civilisation and the administration of justice in the British possessions and in Bhutan, there can be no system of strict reciprocity between the two governments.' He had also to explain the position of the protected states of Sikhim and Cooch Behar and British obligations towards them in case of aggression, to obtain permission for the stationing of an agent in the country and to secure arrangements for free commerce if this seemed feasible in the light of the mission's reception. He was to inform himself all about the country and to draw up a treaty for joint signature. A draft had been compiled for him to take as a guideline.

He was given 10,000 rupees for the purchase of presents and had to furnish a detailed list and account for expenditure on return although given discretion in minor financial matters.

On 10th November Eden wrote from Darjeeling to both Deb and Dharma Rajas and asked to be met at the frontier by the Subha of Daling-cote who should have coolies ready. If he did not comply it would be considered a breach of friendship; hardly the most tactful way to start a mission to a foreign country. Shortly after this he learnt that the whole country was in a state of anarchy with a full scale rebellion in progress. Messengers were received from the Dzongpön indicating that the delay in

making arrangements was solely due to this but hinting that he was prepared to help, even in the absence of official assent from his superiors, if
a suitable present was given. Eden was then given permission to go ahead
by the Bengal government, in view of the news that the rebellion appeared
to have been successful, as the new Deb Raja might wish to strengthen his
position by cultivating an understanding with the British.

Accompanied by the Dewan, or prime minister, of Sikhim, Cheeboo
Lama, Dr. Benjamin Simpson, Captain Henry Haversham Godwin-Austen
the second-in-command of the mission, Captain W.H. Lance and the
escort, Eden left Darjeeling on the 4th January. There were problems
right from the start for the coolies were unwilling to go without more
direct encouragement from the Bhutanese. In this they showed more
political acumen than their masters. Only thirty miles into their journey,
when the Teesta river was reached, many of them returned home. However, Cheeboo Lama came to the rescue and lent his own men. They then
faced the problem of crossing the river, which was ninety yards wide,
extremely rapid and full of dangerous boulders. They managed to get
across with difficulty by constructing bamboo rafts and ferrying their
stores over. Once over the river they started climbing and at 3,733 feet
reached Kalimpong which, although just inside the Bhutanese border, was
quite well cultivated. According to Eden the inhabitants were very pleased
to see them, praised the British administration in whose areas most of
them had relatives and decried their own rulers.

At a monastery he visited just over the border he reported that the
people dared not sell their oranges which had been earmarked for the
lamas. These tales may well have been true but Eden was receptive to
any adverse comments about Bhutan. From the tenor of his report and
the descriptive language used he seemed to have set out to be scornful of
his hosts and to look for abuses.

From the fort at Dhumsang where they arrived on the 9th they could
see on three sides, from their vantage point at 5000 feet, the snows of
Bhutan, Sikhim and Nepal as well as parts of Tibet. The officer in
charge of the fort, 'a dirty looking man, little better than a coolie',
refused to let them look inside which is hardly surprising when they had
given no notice of their arrival and there had been no permission from
his own government. On the 11th they reached Labal at 6,620 and then
began their descent down a steep aand difficult road to a river bed where
they were met by 'ponies and mules and musicians' sent by the Dzongpön
of Dalingcote. From there on they had an uncomfortable ride sitting on
unaccustomed high Tartar saddles on figety mules.

They camped at Ambiok on a level plain immediately below the fort,
where they had marched to the accompaniment of silver flageolets and
brass cymbals. Apart from the fort there were only six or seven houses in
Dalingcote and so far they had seen few villages on the Bhutanese side

of the frontier. Whilst in camp they learnt that any villager selling provisions to them would be fined as the Dzongpön had the monopoly,
buying rice cheaply in order to sell at an exhorbitant price, especially to
the mission who were made to pay in advance.

On the 14th they were visited by the Dzongpön, accompanied by 'a
large and disorderly following'. There were about two hundred people
including standard bearers, musicians, led ponies, mules and soldiers,
who stopped every twenty yards and gave loud shouts, apparently in
imitation of a pack of jackals, whilst the Dzongpön put his head down
and shook himself in the saddle, explaining afterwards that it was an old
custom, the reason for which he had no idea. He was 'a fat, uncouth,
boorish, ignorant man' who assumed airs of great dignity for a time until
given brandy when he began to boast of his powers of consumption.
Finally he had to be forcibly removed after four or five hours. Later,
after another bout of drinking he tried to stop the flogging of recaptured
coolies who had deserted after taking their pay. Again he had to be
forcibly ejected.

As it proved impossible to get sufficient supplies Eden sent Captain
Godwin-Austen to Jalpaiguri to buy rice and later travelled 16 of the 40
to 50 miles himself, in order to inspect the road. They passed land
sparsely populated by people called Mechis in country on which Eden
commented 'under any other government the whole tract would be one
vast rice field for it is not unhealthy, like our Terai . . . ' It abounded
with herds of elephant and rhino who, surpringly, did not molest the
travellers or their pack animals. According to Eden, the Mechis complained bitterly of the oppression of the Booteahs for whom they evidently
entertained feelings of deep hatred. They were constantly employed
carrying up rice to the fort and received no sort of remuneration for
their services. Their only hope apparently was for the British to annexe
their territory and according to Eden they welcomed the mission with
delight.

The mission's camp site at Ambiok was on the very finest soil and yet
not a village was to be seen. 'Where under good government' wrote
Eden, 'there would have been a large standing bazaar, where there would
have been cotton fields, tea fields, timber depots and countless acres of
rice, not a human habitation was to be seen.'

After a few days a letter was received from the Deb Raja, 'as usual
evasive and undecided', instructing Eden to say what he had come for to
the Dzongpön of Dalingcote who would then make arrangements for a
meeting with the Deb. He was now friendly enough but afraid to let the
mission continue until more definite orders than these were received.
Eden therefore wrote to the Deb to ask for a more positive reply, saying
that the demands would have to be enforced in some other way if he did
not assent to discuss them amicably – hardly the right approach for a

mission wishing to be welcomed by a ruler whose position was endangered by civil war.

The Dzongpön himself complained of the government and the lack of reply to his repeated letters about the mission and said that the Deb's object in being so evasive was to make him the scapegoat for anything that might befall.

The mission was also held up by the refusal of the Sikhimese and Nepalese coolies to go any further as they had noted the lack of warmth in the reception and were deserting in large numbers; and as the Dzongpön was also making difficulties about procuring more men they had to remain where they were for the time being. The problem was that although a godown of rice had been set up at Ambiok there was still insufficient as each coolie required nearly a maund (just over 82lbs) of rice carried on another coolie's head.

The Dzongpön was in an awkward situation as he was himself in revolt against his superior, the Paro Pönlop, who would think he had invited the British in to support his cause. Reluctantly however he at length agreed to assist, in return for payment, by agreeing to look after a depot of stores and keeping open the line of communication with the plains. He also gave a little help in the end over finding some more coolies. Eden therefore decided to press on despite everything, taking only half the escort, about fifty Sikhs and a few sappers; a rash decision in view of the state of the country. All the tents were left behind.

Before leaving they stopped at the fort, a thousand feet higher than their camp. This time the Dzongpön's manner was very different, refusing to sit down even in Eden's presence and personally serving refreshments. They were shown over the fort, which Eden inevitably called 'a miserable building'. The Dzongpön lived over the gateway and the rest of the dzong was inhabited by monks with space also to house soldiers and peasants from the duars when they brought their tribute; as well as a residence for women, as wives of senior officials were not allowed to live under the same roof or eat with their husbands. Like his predecessors, Eden was critical about the position of women who were treated like servants and 'live entirely with the lowest menials of the forts and are pushed, hustled and abused by all the followers and hangers on of the officials'.

He went into some detail as to how the fort could once again be captured as it had been by Captain Jones in 1774 and gave details of a likely line of assault and approach routes. The following year British and Indian soldiers were to curse Eden's amateurish military forecasts.

Surprisingly, none of the inhabitants had ever heard that the British had once captured their fort. Eden considered that although the garrison was nominally about two hundred men they could probably muster no more than seventy. Nevertheless, just before the mission's arrival they had managed to repel a seige by the forces of the Paro Pönlop.

The first night's halt was in an unhealthy malarial place, a feeding ground for elephants. The next day they passed through a thick forest before crossing the Nurcho and later pitching camp by the bank of the Mochu. They had seen no people all day.

From there they continued through an area depopulated by the former Dzongpön's oppression, to Sipchoo where they were unable to get any more coolies. Eden was faced with a difficult choice. He could either press on despite objections of the local official who told him not to do so without the awaited permission from the Deb, jettisoning more baggage and reducing the escort even more, or he could return to India. To await permission could be a lengthy business with steadily dwindling supplies, only to be met, in all probability, with further evasion if not outright refusal. However, as he had not encountered any hostility, only boorish incivility and great indifference on the part of the authorities, who nevertheless expressed their desire to cultivate friendship with the British government, and great friendliness from the ordinary people, he decided to go on. He remembered that the Pemberton mission had received similar treatment but had been allowed to leave the country unharmed. He reckoned that if he were to withdraw the Bhutanese would make capital out of it, saying that they had planned a fine reception for him at Punakha. He also recollected that the Government of Bengal had not advocated delaying his departure just because no arrangements had been made for his reception in Bhutan and would probably not approve of his turning back. He decided therefore to regard the treatment he had received as 'the natural insouciance of the Booteahs'. He argued that although there was a risk he was probably no worse off with only fifteen men than with fifty and determined therefore to press on with fifteen Sikhs, and ten Sebundy sappers for road clearing, leaving all the other troops and expendable followers at Sipchoo. It was a brave choice but, in the event it proved to be the wrong one.

On the 2nd February they reach Saigon, where more coolies deserted before they began climbing the next day towards the top of the pass, plodding for much of the time through knee deep snow. They halted 'in a miserable place' at eight and a half thousand feet. 'The snow was deep and a more wretched place for a bivouac in the open air could scarcely be conceived'. Nevertheless they managed to keep their fires going all night.

On the fourth day they reached the top of the pass at 10,000 feet and began a 2000 foot descent. 'The men were thoroughly exhausted and despondent: and nothing but the fear of again crossing the snow prevented the great majority of our coolies running off and leaving us alone in the jungle . . . '

Spirits rose after they had had a day's rest and then reached the bank of the Am-Mochu, 'a very beautiful river, deep, very rapid and broad; it is full of enormous boulders which make the river one continuous line of white sparkling foam . . . If the country had been in any hands but those of the Booteahs, a road into Tibet would have been thrown across this valley'.

On the 6th they began climbing again, passing some hill villages for the first time, dropping down to a small stream before ascending once again to Sangle, a pretty little hamlet of some four or five houses, where the villagers were friendly and apparently anxious to come under British rule. They flocked round the camp with presents of eggs, chickens and milk. Around the village were neatly cultivated fields of barley, buckwheat, millet and turnips. The Dzongpön was sent for and arrived with 'the usual noise and display'. He proved to be the son of a Bengali slave who did not look like a Bhutanese. He had orginally been sent to supersede the Dzongpön of Dalingcote who had proved immovable and was then directed to take over at Sangle where the same thing had happened as his predecessor was still there. He had received no orders about the mission and could therefore give no assistance. He could not obtain coolies and he would not allow the villagers to help. In this situation he could hardly be blamed for playing safe.

As most of the Nepalese coolies were suffering from frostbite incurred when crossing the pass, Eden purchased hides and woollen cloth, despite the Dzongpön's attitude, and instructed the coolies to make themselves boots patterned on those worn by the Bhutanese. He now realised the impossibility of ever bringing up the rear party and sent orders to return to Darjeeling but to leave behind the store of rice and the Governor General's presents. He also sent orders for a guard to be placed over the depot at Dalingcote and arranged for a system of runners between the two base areas and himself. During their stay at Sangle, Dr. Simpson removed an enormous tumour covering most of his mouth, from a miller who lived by the waterside. Thereafter his reputation spread before him and wherever they went people asked for the famous doctor and he was kept very busy. 'Their chief diseases' according to Eden, were 'precisely what one might expect from a people at once so filthy and so immoral; and there seemed to be scarely a person in the country, male or female, who was not suffering more or less in this respect'.

On the 9th February they left Sangle, passing the fort, described inevitably as a wretched place, a little building of rubble and stone situated in a most lovely position. Outside it there was a prayer cylinder, turned by a water wheel, containing the usual words 'om mani padme hum' written thousands of times. They were hospitably entertained at a monastery where Eden noted with supercilious amusement how 'careful the more superstitious of the coolies and Bhuddist servants' were to pass the stone walls of the temple precinct on the same side as the inscriptions.

The dropped down to the river Soochu, crossed over a wooden bridge and climbed up the opposite side of the valley by steep zig zags passing a superb waterfall where the water fell from a great height and 'scattered like rain'. At the top of the hill a group of villagers met them, paying the usual compliment to 'persons of distinction' of setting fire to little heaps of wormwood as they passed. According to Eden they took it for granted that the visitors' objective was to assume control of the country and 'abused their own government'.

They halted at Saybee, a very fine little village with some cultivation and good houses where they heard that Zingaps had arrived from the court with written orders to send them back. When Eden sent for them they only came rather reluctantly under threat of punishment. It transpired that in fact one letter was addressed to the Dzongpön of Dalingcote with orders to turn the mission back, but that if he was unsuccessful in this he should at least ensure that they went via the Samchi and to arrange supplies. He was also threatened with execution for having allowed the British to cross the frontier in the first place. Eden thought this proved that his fears had been quite justified, to judge by the harsh tone of the letter, which was not meant for the British to see. A second letter also addressed to the Dzongpön was the one intended for Eden. This professed friendship for the British and instructed him to settle all outstanding disputes. The poor Zingaps, who had exceeded their instructions by showing Eden both letters, were now understandably anxious that he should comply with the order to turn round and start again, re-entering the county by the Samchi road. Eden was not prepared to do this and in the end the Zingaps helped him on his way, supplying fodder for the horses. On February the 15th they set off again towards Punakha regretting that they could not respond to the villagers' plea to take them back to Darjeeling.

Once again a steep descent was followed by a stiff climb towards the pass over the Taig Onlah mountain. They halted at 9000 feet where there was still only a sprinkling of snow and saw a magnificent herd of yaks that had been driven down from the top of the pass. The next day the snow became thicker as they trudged upwards and the country began to change. The rhododendrons, magnolias, oaks and chestnut trees of the lower slopes gave way to clumps of pines. This happened so suddenly 'a chain pulled across the mountain side would have divided one class from the other'. They enjoyed going through a pine forest with beautiful grassy glades where 'the effect of the snow and icicles on the leaves of the pines was very magnificent'. That evening they pitched camp at nearly 12,000 feet with the thermometer registering -3 degrees Fahrenheit. They made fires using branches of juniper and pine and Eden noted with surprise that in a camp of 'some two hundred persons' including Sikhs and Bengalis, none suffered from the cold. The remarkable thing is that a twice truncated mission should still have been so large. Personal servants, coolies and other followers inseparable from travel on the Indian sub-continent in those days and the retainers of Cheeboo Lama, must have accounted for most as there were now only twenty five soldiers and four British officers.

The following day they reached the top of the pass at 12,150 and saw the usual cairn of stones supporting poles from which fluttered prayer flags to which passing travellers had attached small strips of coloured cotton to ensure safe journeys. None of the coolies would cross until Cheeboo Lama had added some yellow and red chintz to the other flags.

Descending the other side of the pass the snow was even deeper and to add to their difficulties they had to cross the same stream no less than ten times by little wooden bridges. The men had great difficulty making a road through the snow and in walking on sheets of ice with large packs on their backs. At several places they saw waterfalls that had frozen with twenty foot icicles. At last they descended far enough to enter very lovely park-like scenery in the Ha valley and camped beside the bank of the Ha chu. A few miles before halting they had joined the Paro road which seemed to be well used and in good repair.

They left on the 12th and marched through the valley following the line of the river, along a good level road, past some 'fine villages' with substantial three storeyed houses. Many of them had, however, been burnt down and many others had been abandoned because of the civil war. Others had been left unoccupied as their owners habitually spent the winters at Samchi. 'The Booteah', wrote Eden, 'thanks to the cupidity of those under whom he lives, has no property except his homestead and a few cattle and therefore leaves his home without fear of robbery'. The compensatory virtues of such a system do not seem to have struck him.

They were now in an area of magnificent scenery, of snowy peaks on either side and the high peaks of the Tibetan frontier in front. On the sides of the valley were grassy slopes dotted with clumps of pine trees and between them, in the centre of a wide, flat plain, flowed the clear waters of the Hachu about sixty yards wide. Beside the river banks were fields, neatly fenced with stone walls and irrigated by system of channels, ter-races and revetments. In the distance below the snow line were large flocks of black sheep, yaks and grazing cattle.

At Ha Tampia they were met by a large crowd of people from neigh-bouring villages, most of whom had a thick deposit of pine soot on their faces as their houses had no chimneys and, according to Eden, they never washed. The next day they met the Dzongpön, a very fine and 'well mannered old man', who made them welcome. They also met his mother-in-law, wife of the Paro Ponlöp, who assured them of her husband's welcome.

The following day there was a very heavy fall of snow and the Dzongpön, with his wife and children, all came to ensure that they were not suffering unduly, bringing straw and fir poles to make huts for the coolies. That day also Captain Godwin-Austen, who had stayed with the rear party, joined up with them, having experienced a dreadful time getting off the pass through breast deep snow. Two men who lagged behind were found to be dead.

The weather cleared on the 17th February but they were still unable to depart because of the depth of the snow although, with the temperature now fallen again, they were able to explore the immediate locality. Close to the camp was a medicinal spring where baths, heated by throwing hot stones into the water, were used by sufferers from rheumatism and skin diseases. The dzong was 'a pretty little four storeyed building' and nearby was a monastery and a temple. Although the people of this valley, the richest inhabitants of the country, had the reputation of being lawless the mission found them to be more civil, obliging and less given to falsehood than the people of the country generally.

On hearing that a deputation from the Deb was on its way to 'stop or delay' him and not wanting to remain in Ha engaging in protracted correspondence Eden decided to get going again saying nothing of his intentions to the Dzongpön – a somewhat ungrateful return for his hospitality. At daybreak therefore Captain Godwin-Austen and Dr. Simpson set off with Cheeboo Lama's servants and twenty strong men, reinforcements sent by the ruler of Sikhim, in order to make a path through the snow hoping to reach the village the other side of the pass by the afternoon. After they had left, the Dzongpön arrived to protest, saying that he had orders to detain the mission until the messengers arrived. However when he learnt that half the mission had already gone he accepted the situation and sent guides and sepoys to go with Eden's party, in return for a present and Eden's promise not to tell the Deb that he had been assisted. At three o'clock they overtook the advance party whose progress had naturally been much slower. At this point the snow, already three foot, began to get deeper: up to six foot for a time, then eight foot, so that the horses and mules were sinking over their backs. At six o'clock they reached the top of the Cheulah pass at twelve and half thousand feet.

Godwin-Austen and Simpson kept on with their party but Eden and Lance remained to collect up the rear party and see them over as some of the coolies were trying to lie down and go to sleep in conditions from which they would never wake. At last they started their descent, thinking their troubles to be over, but although the snow had cleared at the top of the pass it became deeper the further downhill they went and men and horses were sinking to their necks. They had to go in single file as there was a steep bank on one side and a precipice on the other. Consequently any delay caused by one man or animal held up the whole column. As evening drew on the coolies became frightened and some just wanted to lie down and die. As a halt would have meant death for everyone the

British officers drove them on, although they made painful progress, no more than a quarter of a mile an hour, plodding wearily through the snow under a bright moon. At eleven they reached a forest where Eden allowed the coolies to bivouac provided that they were in gangs of a dozen or more with one man in charge of each party to see that they kept close together and that their fires burnt all night. Eden went on ahead with an advance party, horses and mules still sinking at every step. One of his ponies went over the side of the mountain but they kept going until at last at one in the morning they arrived at a village in a state of exhaustion after marching through deep snow continuously for fifteen hours.

The advance element of the deputation sent to halt the mission was also in the village having given up the attempt to go up the pass. It was pitch dark and in great confusion the two groups milled around in the small hours until the deputation withdrew.

The next morning the coolies arrived with all their loads intact and even Eden's pony had been recovered by 'the indefatigable' interpreter from the Darjeeling court who went back to look for it. Later on in the morning the main body of the deputation arrived, making themselves, according to Eden, 'exceedingly offensive, ejecting many of our people from the shelter they had taken in the houses', their servants trying to carry off the mission's cooking utensils. They delivered the Deb Raja's letter, saying that they had orders to accompany Eden back to the frontier where they were to re-arrange the frontier boundaries and resume control of the Assam duars. Only after that would the mission's other demands be considered; and if the Zingaps thought it necessary Eden would then be allowed to go on to Punakha to see the Deb and Dharma Rajas. Eden refused to comply and although one of the messengers was 'exceedingly overbearing' in his language and manner they eventually agreed to the mission continuing and even undertook to go ahead to make preparations for its reception.

Although the letter from the Deb was of the usual negative and evasive character Eden thought that it hardly constituted a downright refusal to allow them to proceed although strong preference was expressed for settlement of disputes at the frontier, a not unreasonable attitude in view of the fact that the Deb had his hands full with the civil war, despite a temporary lull in physical conflict. Eden, however, chose to read into it a level of deviousness that may or may not have been justified, writing: 'their policy was to compel me by passive resistance and long discouragement to return to our own territory and then to say they had been perfectly ready to receive me and settle all disputes amicably but that I had returned without any sufficient pretext'.

The messengers set off ahead and Eden followed a day later. They were again met on the road by the Zingaps requesting them to halt a few miles short of Paro as the Pönlop wanted to receive them with great honour. Eden assented and did not therefore reach Paro until the 22nd February when they discovered that in fact no arrangements had been made. No one had been sent to receive the mission or to tell them where to pitch camp. Each camp site he then proposed was objected to on the grounds of 'its being sacred to some wood sprite or river demon or some equally frivolous excuse'. After being kept standing on a sandy plain for over two hours they were at length permitted to camp at one of the places first suggested where 'a few oranges and pieces of Tibetan bread were presented on the part of the Penloo (sic) but none of the usual ceremonies of friendship were observed'.

The next day the Pönlop, together with his stepfather, the former holder of the office, sent for Cheeboo Lama and at first threatened him and 'abused him for bringing the British into the country'. He then changed his tack and said that although the mission could undoubtedly achieve much good the Deb's orders were that they should not proceed. He would get in touch with the Deb again and in the meantime they were to stay there. They would be made comfortable and accorded respectful treatment. Finally he said that there was no real point in going on to Punakha as the Deb had no authority and he was the ruler of west Bhutan and the proper person to deal with.

Although Eden agreed to remain pending an approach to the Deb the attitude of the authorities continued to be unfriendly. They were stopped when they tried to go out and told to stay in camp until further orders. 'Their sepoys crowded round us', wrote Eden, 'stealing everything they could lay hands on, jeering at our coolies and followers, calling them slaves and drawing their knives on them on the slightest rejoinder being made'. Villagers who sold provisions or had any contact with the mission were punished.

When Eden heard that the messengers to the Deb, who should by then have returned, had not even set out, he threatened either to go on regardless or to return to Darjeeling. This produced a changee of attitude, the messengers were sent off and when Eden met the Pönlop he was told that the previous unfriendly course had been advised by his stepfather, who continued to interfere although he had voluntarily abdicated. However, a number of informants told him that this was not the case and that it was only an excuse for 'getting out of a false position'. Nevertheless there were fewer annoyances from this time onwards. He had a friendly meeting with the former Pönlop at which it became apparent that the abdication had merely been a political expedient and that the stepson was just a puppet. At a subsequent meeting the old man explained that although for the sake of appearances hostilities had been suspended during the mission's stay in the country, he did not recognise the authority of the present government as the Tongsa Pönlop, having forcibly dethroned the former Deb, had usurped power. The present Deb and

Dharma Rajas were both his puppets and the leading officials were incompetent. The Tongsa Pönlop's chief adviser was a Hindu called Padsha Raja by the Bhutanese. He had arrived shortly after the Indian mutiny announcing that he bore 'the seals of the Kings of Delhi, Lahore and Nepaul' and proposing that the Bhutanese should join in a general war to drive the British out of India. When his overtures had been rejected he joined the rebellion against the former Deb, was taken prisoner by the Paro Pönlop but had escaped and was now with the Tongsa Pönlop.

Even Eden was impressed by the magnificence of the dzong at Paro. He described the seven storeyed tower, surmounted by a copper cupola, the granaries on the lower of the five floors, the ornamented gateway, the Tibetan mastiffs and the huge prayer cylinder, turned by a crank that rang a bell each time. He also reported on the military aspects, noting that if shot was directed anywhere lower than the verandahs it would only enter the store rooms and be stopped by the inpenetrable rock into which they were built, the entrance to the dzong being on a level with the third floor. Although the walls, which sloped from base to top, were very thick they were made of rubble and would soon crumble to pieces if the framework of the windows was knocked away.

Most of the inhabitants were monks and officials but Eden was also interested to note that there was a garrison of 250 sepoys, nominally 400, who were villagers bound to serve for seven years unless they could purchase their discharge for seven rupees. This was very rarely done for although they received no pay they had free food and clothing 'and a general licence (sic) to plunder and extort from the rest of the inhabitants of the country'. Although most were 'insolent . . . beyond all conception there were a few exceptions, two or three quiet, intelligent men who abused their employer in hearty terms and gave us much information about the country, expressing a strong hope that we should take it'. Their side arms consisted of long knives in handsome silver scabbards, the hilts usually covered with lizard skin. They had no knowledge of drill and much of their work consisted of repairing and building forts and shoring up river banks which they did extremely well.

The bridge into the dzong, made of large pine beams built into each bank, had a stone tower with a guard at each end under the command of the warden of the bridge. An even more important piece of military intelligence was that any attacking force obtaining control of the six small outpost forts above the main building would have little difficulty in capturing the dzong itself. The Bhutanese recognised this and none of their officers was trusted to live there.

The other side of the river from the dzong was an area that had once been an attractive garden with pear trees and a fine specimen of 'cypresses funebris'. Opposite this level area, used by monks and soldiers as a recreation ground, was a little dark blue temple dedicated to the tutelary deity of prisoners.

Eden described the Pönlop's stateroom as being 'of great size', the beams richly painted in blue, orange and gold, with Chinese dragons much in evidence. The roof was supported by carved arches and everywhere were suspended bows, quivers, polished iron helmets, swords, matchlocks and coats of mail. There were also Chinese lanterns, flags and silk scarves that had been consecrated by the 'Grand Lama' of Tibet, arranged with the most perfect taste.

According to his guest, 'the former Pönlop usually lounged away the day on a little platform built into the recess of a large bow window which commands a magnificent view down the valley'. Each time he had visitors a vase of burning scented wood was placed before him. Eden thought that this was because 'the great ambition of the chieftains in all these Buddhist countries is to keep up a sort of dreamy mysticism around them'. Although he 'managed that we should only have a hazy and silent interview in a cloud of smoke on our first visit, he was of far too cordial and inquiring disposition to keep up these ceremonies longer than was necessary'. On later visits he turned his people out of the room, dispensed with ceremony and 'talked in a most unreserved manner, refreshing himself the while with the most copious draughts of chong (sic) a very fair substitute for whiskey, distilled from barley and rice mixed'. He was 'physically completely worn out with every kind of debauchery of every description' and like most men in authority in Bhutan, he was, according to Eden 'seldom in a state to be seen after two o'clock in the afternoon'. Nevertheless, he was 'by far the most intelligent man we met within the country' and after the first misunderstanding treated the British with 'the greatest friendship and kindness'. He depicted the unscrupulous character of some of the leading officials and especially the Tongsa Pönlop 'with the greatest fidelity and unreserve'. Despite his virtues Eden doubted if he would allow any sense of right or wrong stand in the way of his own interests as he had the reputation of having done as much violence as any one else in his day. He was also 'a singularly childish old man and would amuse himself for hours with a mechanical toy or musical box'. This seems a rather ingenuous judgement on an elderly gentleman of enquiring mind. He begged to be given one of these toys on the grounds that he might as well have it as everything the mission had would be taken 'by guile or violence in Punakha'.

Eden, the son of a bishop, commented prudishly: 'Like all his countrymen he was absolutely without shame and his conversation was marked by an absence of modesty and an amount of indecency that would have disgraced the most uncivilised barbarian in the world'. Despite this his favourite daughter, the wife of the Dzongpön of Ha, was often present at interviews and had considerable influence over him. This, said Eden was the only instance we ever met of a woman being treated with the slightest respect or consideration in Bhutan'.

The Pönlop *de jure* was a very different stamp of a man. 'He was the son of a previous Pönlop to whom the ex-Pönlop had been chief officer and had, on his master's death, succeeded not only to his office but also, according to custom, to his wife and children as well. These included the young man whom he placed in the seat of power. He was so well connected, being related also to the Dzongpön of Wangdiphodrung and the other leading officials, that this had seemed a prudent insurance policy to the older man when hard pressed during the rebellion, trusting in his stepson's connections to save Paro from being attacked. He himself retained all real authority in his own hands allowing the young man only the outward trappings of power, occupying the state rooms in the middle of the tower of the central quadrangle. The young Pönlop had little to say for himself except to beg for presents and was apparently very unpopular with the leading people.

At this time the town of Paro had about thirty good three-storeyed houses. Every evening several hundred people gathered in the market square but there was little for sale except walnuts, peas and radishes. No one was allowed to enter the market with their head covered or on horseback and Eden had an altercation with the official in charge as he refused to dismount.

North east of the dzong was the road leading straight up the valley to Phari, an important commercial town in Tibet. It was a level grassy track all the way up to the pass below Chomolhari, a distance of only two days march by a fully laden porter and was the way by which Turner had entered Tibet. Eden commented that Paro was therefore so situated as to be one of the largest cities of the East, situated in a level and fertile plain richly cultivated with rice, wheat and barley on the lower slopes. It had easy access not only to Tibet but also to the plains in the south. It could have been an *entrepôt* between Tibet, Tartary, China and India and yet no Tibetan ever crossed the frontier and there was no trade.

One day Eden rode ten miles to the confluence of the Chinchu and Pochu (or Thimphu) rivers along a level grassy ride beside the river which was lined with an avenue of weeping willows. Both sides of the river were straddled with pretty villages, mostly belonging to officials and sepoys of the dzong as the whole garrison returned to their homes every evening. There were six or seven hundred houses altogether in the valley, all of them with three or four storeys. Cattle were numerous and the whole valley wore an air of prosperity that would have been threatened when the river flooded had it not been for some very ingenious water engineering with numerous embankments and revetments. Even whilst praising this ingenuity Eden could not refrain from his customary sarcasm, this time, for once, at the expense of people other than the Bhutanese. 'In controlling the action of these rivers', he wrote 'the

Bhooteas show greater foresight, ingenuity and public spirit than is usual with Orientals.'

The soil in this area was heavily charged with iron and there were some iron mines two days journey from Paro. The Bhutanese were also well versed in methods of burning charcoal. All round the Paro valley were hills on the top of which were monasteries; and on a bleak hill to the north was the famous Tiger's nest (Taktsang) which Cheeboo Lama and most of the Sikhimese were able to visit. This did not appeal to the British officers who did, however, go to the races, held just before the great annual festival. These were not at all Eden's idea of horse races as the ponies were flogged into a gallop whilst their riders ran along beside them holding on to their manes before vaulting into their saddles.

On March 10th, tired of waiting for any answer from the Deb, and with the old Pönlop's support, the party left Paro. Later they learnt that he had refused to obey instructions from the Deb to seize Cheeboo Lama and send the others home.

They ascended to the top of a pass at over 11,000 feet before starting a gradual descent through smooth grass and scattered pine forests filled with all sorts of game. They camped at eight and a half thousand near a large prayer cylinder and an empty dzong. Many of the inhabitants of this place were Bengalis who had long since forgotten their place of origin. Here at last they met messengers from the government, who turned out to be the same ones whom they had encountered before. They came with orders for the mission to turn back to Paro but were empowered to listen to Eden's views and, if necessary, send for more senior officers to treat with him. He decided, however, that this was just a cover-up and that their sole object was to indulge in delaying tactics and that he would turn back only if he received unequivocal instructions from the Deb to go back to India coupled with a flat refusal to see the mission.

It is surprising that someone of his experience should not have realised that it was customary in the diplomacy of the time to hedge one's bets and prepare for all eventualities but never to give a hostage to fortune in the shape of over-precise instructions that could subsequently be used as ammunition for criticism if things went wrong. Eden continued to ask for the impossible instead of trying to comprehend the position of the Deb, with his country in the throes of civil unrest, his own legality far from certain and two powerful Pönlops at daggers drawn. It should have been obvious that the Deb was in no position to ratify a treaty about distant frontiers over which he had little control. On the other hand Eden was probably justified in going on to Punakha having got this far; for to withdraw at that stage would have been to get the worst of all worlds. By going on he could at least say that he had reached the seat of government before deciding that nothing could be achieved and making an early withdrawal without loss of face. The messengers naturally insisted that the Deb had never actually refused to see Eden and said that if he was not prepared to return to Paro he had better keep on his way to Punakha, although they refused to accompany the mission and went on to Paro to fine the Pönlop for allowing the British into his territory.

Instead of taking Turner's route over the crest of the hills to Tashicho-dzong they followed the bank of the river valley until it joined the Chinchu. Here they joined the Buxa Duar road and the route followed by Turner and Pemberton. They halted at Chalmafee, a large village where the Punakha and Tashichodzong roads met, only two miles from Tashichodzong itself, which could be seen from where they pitched their tents under two enormous cypress trees. As in most of the other villages in the area many of the inhabitants were Bengali slaves, many of whom had been born there. They could be seen in the gaps in the forest hewing wood and collecting pine leaves used for manure for their masters.

The following day they reached Simtokha dzong, the oldest in the country, then being occupied by the former Deb who had been removed from power at the start of the rebellion. He declined even to see Cheeboo Lama as he did not want to be accused of helping the mission. From Simtokha they climbed to a pass from where they could see the whole of the Punakha valley and in the distance the snows of Tibet. They halted just above the village of Telegong 'a place chiefly inhabited by Gylongs (sic) or monks, who had as usual taken great care of themselves'. There were some fine houses with much carving and ornamental work and the area was well cultivated with mustard, barley, wheat, chillies and 'excellent turnips'.

On 15th March they descended into a valley, crossed a little river by a wooden bridge and had an easy march through open country at about 5000 feet. Arriving at the outskirts of Punakha they could see no sign of any welcome although messengers had been sent ahead to report their imminent arrival. Only when in sight of the dzong was a message received and this was merely to forbid them to approach by the road under the main gate of the dzong and requiring them to enter by a back road entailing 'a precipitous descent'.

They were left kicking their heels for several days receiving only a little 'inferior rice' from the Punakha Dzongpön and a demand for the surrender of two Bhutanese subjects who had attached themselves to the mission with which Eden reluctantly felt he had to comply.

During this period of enforced inactivity they had time to look at their surroundings. Eden thought that the dzong was not a patch on Paro and was 'a shabby, straggling, mean, tumbledown pile, very dirty and ill-kempt'. Just as Bogle and Turner had done at Tashichodzong, he watched the lamas go for their daily bathe, counting only two hundred and seventy five of them and being sceptical of there being two thousand in the dzong, as he had been told. He also thought that the two bridges at the entrance of the dzong, across the Pochu and Mochu rivers, were very inferior to those at Paro and commented that 'if troops ever enter the country and have to cross bridges of this particular construction, care must be taken that the men do not keep step, for this causes a strain which many of the bridges would not bear'.

The garden that Turner had admired no longer existed: 'Everything about the place is gone to ruin and decay during the great internal struggles for the place which have for so many years convulsed the country.' Near the dzong there were a few houses intact and a fair number in ruins. Eden thought that the dzong itself was militarily indefensible as it was commanded by a height above the west bank. One round of shell would set the place ablaze and if the bridges were held and a force posted to the north, none of the garrison could escape.

The valley in which the dzong was situated was full of iron but not nearly so fertile as Paro, and there was no shade as all the trees had been felled for firewood.

On 17th March the members of the mission were summoned by the Amlah, the Council of State, to meet them at a house near the dzong. They had to pass through a 'disorderly crowd of sepoys and servants who were extremely insolent' and several stones and pieces of wood were thrown at them. They were kept 'standing out on the plain in the burning sun, exposed to the jeers and impertinence of several hundred persons' before meeting the council, consisting of the Dzongpöns of Tashichodzong and Punakha, The Shung Drönyer and Deb Zimpons, the Deb Raja's chief officer and chief secretary respectively, and the Tongsa Pönlop who had appointed himself chief to the Dharma Raja so that he was by then all powerful. Although, by rights, only an extraordinary member of the council, 'he occupied the seat of honour and took upon himself the office of spokesman', monopolising the proceedings. 'Although this first visit was one of mere formality none of the customary friendly ceremonies were observed', wrote Eden; and whilst the other council members, who played no part in subsequent proceedings, were perfectly civil, the Tongsa Pönlop was extremely supercilious. He did however make the sensible suggestion that, in view of the language difficulties, Cheeboo Lama should visit him daily with Eden's proposals and that Cheeboo could then acquaint the mission with the Amlah's response. Eden agreed and on returning to his quarters sent Cheeboo Lama back with the entire draft treaty. By doing this he made the fundamental mistake of showing his hand at the outset instead of first sounding out reactions and, if it seemed appropriate, replacing the first two and most controversial articles with softer alternatives, as he had been empowered to do if necessary. Instead of insisting that the Bhutanese had to restore all property, and give up all captured British, Sikhimese and Cooch Behari subjects within six months, the alternative merely proposed that they 'should use their utmost endeavours' to that end. Instead of the British agreeing to withdraw from Ambaree Fallacottah only when all property and captives had been freed, and on condition that the Bhutanese gave 'prompt and full redress' for any future crimes committed against British, Sikhimese and Cooch Behari subjects, the alternative proposal was for the British to continue to occupy the area but to pay rent on the same conditions of justice for offenders. Had Eden, in the light of his hostile reception, presented the alternatives, after some discussion, thus appearing to be amenable to argument, it is just possible, although hardly probable, that the Bhutanese would have accepted the treaty as the other articles were far less contentious. Under these the British agreed to inquire into crimes alleged to have been committed by British subjects against the Bhutanese and to return any Bhutanese taking refuge in British territory who were accused of major crimes in Bhutan. Disputes with the rulers of Sikhim and Cooch Behar were to be referred to the British government for arbitration. If the British were to appoint an Agent in Bhutan he and any special envoys would be received and treated with due honour. Finally there should be 'free trade and commerce between the two governments'.

Over the next two days Cheeboo Lama discussed the articles of the treaty with the Tongsa Pönlop who appeared only to object to the possible stationing of an Agent and free trade, neither of which were insuparable obstacles. This seemed to augur quite well for a comparatively successful outcome. These hopes received a setback when, on 20th March, after complaining of the delay, Eden was at last granted interviews with the Deb and Dharma Rajas of which he wrote 'every opportunity was taken of treating us with indignity'. Whereas previous missions had been received in the dzong and were permitted to remain seated Eden and his officers were 'hustled into a tent a few feet square' and 'jostled by a mob' all around them. From there they were taken to another tent inside which the members of the Amlah were already seated. As there was no room for anyone else, the mission had to sit on mats outside in the sun. Their servants were forbidden to bring their chairs and they were told that they had to accept the custom of the country. Eden decided to submit to this, in the belief that they were about to sign the treaty and that his poor treatment arose from ignorance rather than malice. He also agreed to hand over the Governor General's letters to the Tongsa Pönlop despite his initial insistence on handing them to the Deb and Dharma Rajas in person.

Eden and his colleagues were then 'pushed through the crowd to a little canopy in which the Deb was sitting' and made 'to stand outside with uncovered heads in the sun'. The Deb seemed frightened and hardly spoke but the Tongsa Pönlop said that he would conduct the business on his behalf. They were then 'pushed rudely to one side to make way for the Deb' and after a short delay followed him to another little canopy in which a boy of about eighteen was seated'. This was the Dharma Raja who never uttered a word and once again the Pönlop proclaimed his authority to conduct all business. They were then taken back to the first tent being jeered at by the Bhutanese soldiery pressing against the side of the tent. As they had been forbidden to take their escort there was little they could do to protect themselves. After an hour of this they were returned to the Amlah where, after reading the first two articles, the Tongsa Pönlop insisted that a new clause should be added to the effect that the Assam duars should be handed back to the Bhutanese immediately. If that were done, he announced, all the rest would be acceptable but if not there was no point in any further discussion.

Eden was completely taken aback, not only by this new proposal, but also by the 'overbearing manner' of the Pönlop. He explained that the Assam duars had been taken over many years before because of crimes committed by the Bhutanese and had been a closed issue for twenty years, that regular compensation had been paid and that no Bhutanese official had raised the issue for a very long time. He also said that he had no authority to discuss the subject, the only land right problem he was empowered to raise being that of Ambaree Fallacottah. Nevertheless, although he thought it would do the Bhutanese more harm than good to raise an issue that had been dead for so long, he was prepared to take back to the Governor General any letter the Tongsa Pönlop wished to write on the subject. He was, however, quite sure that the Assam duars would never be returned and that the Bhutanese would do better to take steps to prevent any further loss of land arising from 'a refusal to comply with the moderate and just demands of our government', compliance with which 'would be immediately followed by the release of the tract now under attachment'.

The Tongsa Pönlop's response was to crumple up the treaty and declare: "Then we will have war; you are nobody; you have no authority from the Governor General. We didn't want Ambaree Fallacottah; and as to the demands of the government of India a chupprassi (orderly or messenger) might have been sent to settle them. I will have nothing more to do with you; go".

Eden replied, addressing the other members of the council, that despite all the obstacles put in his way he had come to secure a friendly understanding and although he had done all in his power to bring it about, he now saw it was hopeless and would return to India to report this to the Governor General.

The British then returned to their camp and were preparing to leave as there seemed little point in lingering after such a meeting, when messengers arrived from some of the other members of the council entreating them to postpone their departure, deploring the actions of the Tongsa Pönlop and stating their support for the draft treaty. They also said that the return of the Assam duars was not required as the Tongsa Pönlop had appropriated all the revenue from them and had paid nothing to the Deb and Dharma Rajas for three years. They were sure that if the mission remained the Tongsa Pönlop's views would be resisted and all would be settled amicably; but that if they departed there would be disturbances, reinforcing a message already received from the Tongsa Pönlop that their departure would be resisted by force.

Eden agreed to stay a little longer on condition that the Assam duars were not referred to again and that the Tongsa Pönlop should be excluded from further interviews. He also wrote a letter addressed to the government of Bhutan to say that he had been about to return because of the Tongsa Pönlop's refusal to negotiate unless the Assam duars were returned. He hoped that the response would be public dissent from the Tongsa Pönlop's attitude now that other members of the council had expressed contrary views. The only response was for the Tongsa Pönlop to query the need for any written communication.

On the 22nd Eden was invited to another meeting, to be attended by the two council members previously absent, the chief judge and the Dzongpön of Wangdiphodrung, the main supporter of the Tongsa Pönlop who, it was said, would not himself be present.

Once again they had to pass through a 'disorderly crowd' and had a few more stones thrown at them despite an agreement that this should not happen again. This time however they were allowed to be seated and had taken their seats with the council members when they were astounded to see the Tongsa Pönlop march in and place himself at their head, despite all the assurances they had been given. The draft of the treaty was read out and once again exception was only taken to the same two articles as before. Eden was told that if he would abandon these the rest could be accepted. As it was by now quite obvious that no Agent would be safe and that there were few prospects for trade in the present state of the country he was prepared to comply and agreed to have an amended treaty copied and translated, together with lists of captured British subjects and stolen property within two days.

They returned to camp and set about this considerable task with all possible speed. Whilst this was going on Eden received several messages accusing him of delay from the Tongsa Pönlop, whose Hindu adviser was often seen in the camp attempting to bribe the escort, whose Jemadar reported each instance to Eden. The man called himself General Nundanun Singh, said to have been a grandson of the great Ranjit Singh, and spent much of his time abusing the British government. He even tried to claim that some of the Sikhs of the escort were Bhutanese subjects.

On the 24th tents were brought across to the mission's side of the river and the British officers were taken to one of them where they passed an hour whilst the Amlah amused themselves examining the arms of the escort, joking with their own sepoys and the rest of the crowd who had gathered. However, despite this appearance of unfriendliness or at least disinterest by people who had sent him encouraging messages, Eden assumed that as a new treaty had actually been called for the nature of the reception was due only to ignorance. His initial fears were allayed when they were shown into the Amlah's tent and engaged in friendly conversation whilst rice and tea were served.

The terms of the revised treaty were then read out but after the first two articles the Tongsa Pönlop stated that the Assam Duars should be given to him as soon as the treaty had been signed and that all the revenue collected since their date of resumption, calculated at 3000 rupees, be paid to to him. Eden was astonished but, looking at the Amlah for support, found them all, except the Dzongpön of Wangidphodrung, pretending not to know what was happening and 'talking in a trivial, childish way to the other officers of the mission'. Eden, calling on them to listen, repeated all his former remarks and also complained of his treatment: that he had been urged to postpone his departure and to prepare an apparently agreed treaty with great haste, only to find that, after all, nothing had been agreed. All the time he was speaking 'the Amlah were laughing and talking . . . and did not pay the slightest attention to what was passing'. The Tongsa Pönlop said that they had never agreed to any treaty, only that the draft should be copied; that he would never assent to anything until the Assam duars were returned and that although Eden should never have gone to Bhutan in the first place, now that he was there he should see to it that the only matter of real interest could be settled.

The officers were then told to go to another tent 'in a more public position and surrounded by an immense crowd where the manner and tone of the Tongsa Penlow (sic) and the Angdu Forung Jungpen (sic) became every moment more offensive. The Penlow took up a large piece of wet dough and began rubbing my face with it,' wrote Eden. 'He pulled my hair and slapped me on the back and generally conducted himself with very great insolence. On my showing signs of impatience or remonstrating he smiled and deprecated my anger, pretending that it was the familiarity of friendship, much to the amusement of the large assemblage of bystanders'. The Dzongpön of Wangdiphdrung went even further, telling Dr. Simpson to eat some pan he had been chewing and when he refused throwing it in his face where it remained as the Doctor refused to wipe it off, in order to emphasise the insult. Next, the Cheeboo Lama's watch, given him by the Governor General, was wrenched off its ribbon round his neck and passed to one of the Amlah.

However, when they saw the officers consulting together and looking round for the escort, the Bhutanese realised they had gone too far; the watch was returned and Dr. Simpson was asked to wipe off the stain which he still declined to do. Eden appealed to the other members of the

Amlah but most· pretended not hear him whilst others said they agreed with the Tongsa Pönlop. The British were then permitted to go, the Tongsa Pönlop shouting after them "I want nothing but the Assam duars and if I don't get them it is better to have war than a treaty; I will write to the Governor General".

It was too late to get away that night as they had not prepared enough supplies for such a hurried departure but Eden intended to leave the next day, March 25th, if he could do so unmolested. The next morning they heard from the chief judge who had always been friendly, asking to see Cheeboo Lama, who set out to keep the meeting but was turned back by the Tongsa Pönlop's sepoys. The British realised that they had no support as the rest of the Amlah had proved to be broken reeds. They continued to profess friendship but appeared to be more interested in receiving presents than giving any assistance.

Cheeboo Lama was then sent for by the Dzongpön of Tashichodzong who presented a paper proposing that the Government of India should return the Assam duars, pay compensation of 3000 rupees a year for the period since they had been taken over and deliver up runaway slaves who had taken refuge in British territory. Eden retained the letter, assuming it to be the one that the Tongsa Pönlop had threatened to send to the Governor General, and then requested supplies and a passport for the mission's return. Instead he received a message to the effect that the paper was a treaty for him to sign and affix his seal. Eden replied that his signature on such a document would be worthless and that he would instead pass on the requests to the Governor General. Cheeboo Lama warned him that they should now be on their guard and that the Amlah was becoming more abusive and disposed to violence: and indeed when he received Eden's reply the Tongsa Pönlop threatened to imprison him with Cheeboo Lama, confined to the stocks in the dzong. The Dzongpön of Wangdiphodrung was even more ferocious and was overhead by Cheeboo Lama saying that it would be best to kill all the officers of the mission.

Eden decided to stall for time, pleading with some truth, that he was suffering from fever caused by the long exposure to the sun endured by the mission during the interviews. Cheeboo Lama was sent for again and told that Eden would be imprisoned until someone came vested with authority to hand over the duars. He agreed to bring an answer the next morning and then, before returning to the camp he took soundings of friendly Bhutanese who confirmed that the threats of imprisonment were not bluff.

The British officers set about arming as many as possible of their followers before starting a long discussion on what to do. It was obvious that there was no chance of securing a friendly treaty and that their only course was to try and get back to British territory without causing embarrassment to their government. They could not stay where they were without supplies and Bhutanese guards had now been posted all round to prevent contact with villagers. Their mail had been stopped although they had been able to send out occasional letters by special messengers under various pretexts. Their escort of fifteen Sikhs could not long have resisted the hundreds of armed men all around them. They had only three options open to them: to allow the Bhutanese to detain Eden and Cheeboo Lama on condition that the others were allowed to withdraw safely: to escape by night: or to sign the paper. The first was impossible because no relieving force could be sent at that season when the rivers would soon be swollen and malaria would be rampant in the valleys. Even if troops were sent the Bhutanese would threaten to kill the hostages unless they withdrew. The second alternative seemed at first to be the most attractive but although the British officers, Cheeboo Lama and the escort might have managed to escape there remained 150 coolies, of whom some were sick, who could never have got away swiftly, and to whom they had an obligation. They would also have had great difficulty feeding so many and protecting their line of march. The only viable course, however repugnant, was to sign the treaty, especially as under the circumstances any engagement entered into was clearly not binding on the British government. It was agreed there-fore that Eden should sign but if, despite that, there was then any attempt to detain them they would try to steal away at night despite all the difficulties.

Eden determined, however, to make one final effort to obtain leave to depart without signing the paper. The following day, therefore, Cheeboo Lama took a message saying that it served no purpose for Eden to sign the paper as, apart from his lack of authority to sign away the Assam duars, he could not undertake that the British government would return runaway slaves as the status of slavery was not recognised under British law. Cheeboo Lama could not sign on behalf of Sikhim and Cooch Behar as demanded by the Bhutanese as he was not there in a representative capacity. The Tongsa Pönlop refused to accept any of these arguments, abused Cheeboo Lama and insisted that he should return at once with Eden's agreement.

Further resistance was useless and Eden agreed to sign. The next day when a fair copy was produced it was found that a number of changes had been made. The demand for 3000 rupees had been omitted but new paragraphs had been added to the effect that if the British ever again encroached on Bhutanese territory they were to submit to punishment by the combined powers of Bhutan, Sikkim and Cooch Behar acting together and that all duars were to be returned. As there seemed to be little object in pointing out the differences between two equally worthless treaties which would only give them an importance they didn't warrant, and as there was no clause binding Eden to obtain the Governor General's ratification he agreed to sign. He was not allowed to do so in his own tent prior to an immediate departure as the Bhutanese were aware that the Governor General's presents were due to arrive that day. A message from the Tongsa Pönlop referred to a long list of cloth and articles listed in the Governor General's letter to the Deb and accused Eden of appropriating some of the goods and engineering the delay, although, in fact, this had been due to Bhutanese local officials refusing to provide coolies. Eden was sure that the Tongsa Pönlop could not really have been aware of the contents of the letter as it had been written in English and the Pönlop had refused to allow Cheeboo Lama to translate.

Later that day as soon as the presents arrived the Amlah demanded to receive them. Fearing that the camp would be plundered if he withheld them, Eden promised to give them out as soon as he had received supplies and proper arrangements had been made for the mission's departure. The Bhutanese then agreed to meet on the 27th for the treaty to be signed and for the mission to be free to leave the following day. The supplies began to arrive and some of the presents were distributed although Eden retained the guns and small articles of jewellery that could be concealed. The Tongsa Pönlop professed great scorn for the gifts, referring to some beautiful pearl earrings as 'glass ornaments set in brass' describing the gifts as of 'imitation or inferior manufacture'. Nevertheless, according to Eden, all the most valuable articles were taken off to his own house instead of to the treasury.

At the meeting on the 27th the Amlah, having received their presents, treated the mission, who were allowed to be seated on a dais, with greater civility and the customary ceremonies were observed for the first time. No one was permitted to press against them, they were received in a house instead of tents, were addressed courteously and were not exposed to any insults. Nevertheless the Hindu 'general' was on the verandah and was frequently consulted by the Tongsa Pönlop.

The day after the meeting several members of the Amlah came to the camp and insisted on entering the hut where Eden, who was feeling ill, was resting. They posed a number of questions on which they had been briefed by the 'general' about the relative powers of the Kings of Lahore and Delhi and the British. In the end Eden had to call in the Sikh escort to prevent pilfering. It later transpired that they had been sent by the Tongsa Pönlop to see if there was anything in the camp worth plundering, in which case he was planning a night raid. Fortunately everything had been hidden before the party arrived.

On 29th March they were taken to the Amlah's tent where Eden and Cheeboo Lama were each made to sign two copies of the treaty although no Bhutanese signed. The seal of a former Dharma Raja had already been affixed to one of the copies but no signing or sealing took place in the mission's presence. Eden added the words 'under compulsion' after his signature, just in case a copy should arrive in Assam before he was able to get there himself. He refused to sign a third copy for the Tongsa Pönlop and was supported for once by the Amlah who agreed that the Pönlop was not entitled to one.

They were then taken to the tents of the Deb and Dharma Rajas where white scarves were placed round their necks. By custom this should have been done at the first meeting. They were then told that a demon would be put on the heads of all present and that if any Bhutanese were injured it would take revenge. 'A large wooden fur headed demon was then carried round and everyone near the tent received a knock from it.'

As soon as the British left the meeting the Tongsa Pönlop set off for his own territory with a large procession, accompanied by the 'general' in robes of honour riding a pony next to his chief. As soon as they had gone the mission began to strike camp but were prevented from doing so by Bhutanese sepoys who said they could not leave until the Dzongpön of Wangdiphodrung, who had gone back to his own district, had returned to Punakha. Eden flatly refused to comply and when the soldiers started to become violent offered to go to the dzong and explain that he was too ill to remain in such a hot climate and that if anything happened to him the Amlah would be held responsible. The whole mission then brushed past the Bhutanese guards and took up a better defensive position on the road further up the hill. A message was received from one of the Amlah urging the British to leave and take no notice of his colleagues and Eden sent the others on with orders to halt a few miles further on. Meanwhile he remained with the Sikhs until Cheeboo Lama, for whose safety he was concerned, returned. He did not arrive until late that night, having been detained by violent arguing amongst members of the Amlah who were divided as to whether or not to let the mission go. He had been told that he would be detained until Eden returned but the chief judge managed to get him away on the pretext of giving him dinner. The judge expressed regret for the conduct of the Tongsa Pönlop who was apparently the only person to want the Assam duars, from the compensation for which he had been the only one to benefit.

Later still that night some Bhutanese officers with seven or eight men turned up to forbid any move until the Dzongpön of Wangdiphodrung arrived. Eden refused to wait any longer saying that by their conduct the Bhutanese had shown they attached no importance to treaties signed that morning. However, on being told that the Dzongpön had something of great importance to communicate he agreed to wait on the road for six hours the next day until the Dzongpön came up by a cross country road to join him. At the same time he sent a message to the others telling them to get over the pass before dark. At about eleven the next morning word was received from the Dzongpön insisting that Eden should return and threatening his capture before he reached Paro if he tried to escape. By this time Eden had had enough and gave orders to move. When the Bhutanese stated their intention of taking Cheeboo Lama prisoner he told them they would be resisted. This sign of firmness unsettled them and they suggested that Eden should write to the Dzongpön saying that he had waited for him on the road but could delay no longer although assuring the Pönlop that had he been there he would have taken leave of him properly. Armed with this, presumably to safeguard themselves, and with a present of money, the Bhutanese officers left, saying that they would delay their return and subsequent report of the mission's departure, until the British had got clean away.

They managed to get across the pass before dark and halted on the other side. Even so, during the night a Zingap arrived to demand the surrender of Cheeboo Lama, keeping 'the whole camp awake for some hours with his vociferations'. However, when threatened, he became civil, and as with all Bhutanese approaches to the mission if Eden's account is to be believed, showed that he had come prepared with two cards to play. He had been instructed by one of the Amlah first to try intimidation, but if this was not successful to give the mission a passport to take them through the next valley with injunctions to remember who had been friendly towards them. He also handed over a white scarf from the chief judge with a request that his friendship should not go unremembered. A good deal of hedging of bets seemed to be going on at this stage as the more perceptive of the Bhutanese realised that they had not seen the last of the British.

They set out again by moonlight and by forced marching managed to reach Paro on the morning of April 1st. The former Pönlop was 'friendly and attentive'. He had heard all about the proceedings of the Amlah and told Eden that if there had been any violence he would have marched to the rescue. Eden was inclined to believe him 'for he was a far-seeing and shrewd old man'. The Tongsa Pönlop 'had been his enemy for years' and he did not recognise the authority of the current Deb. The young Pönlop tended to be importunate and tried to obtain possession of some of the mission's effects. Eden was also suspicious of him as he was a relative of the Dzongpön of Wangdiphodrung.

They found everyone at Paro preparing for an immediate revolution and after a vain attempt to obtain the release of some Bengalis who claimed British protection, with whom the Pönlop refused to part, they left on 2nd April on the final stage of their journey home.

Their only difficulty was in the crossing of the Taugun pass where the snow was still four or five feet deep. The mules and ponies sank up to their girths and several of the poor creatures had to be abandoned. At the pass they were overtaken by a messenger from the ex-Paro Pönlop to say that the insurrection had started and that he had left with his men to help the ex-Deb who had already had a hostile meeting with the Dzongpön of Tashichodzong. His plan, which Eden called 'characteristic of the Booteahs', was to offer to arbitrate, get a foot in the dzong and then take possession of it.

When they reached Dalingcote they learnt that the next phase of the ex-Paro Pönlop's plan was to shut the Tongsa Pönlop out of his own dzong for which he would have the Amlah's support. Meanwhile the Tongsa Pönlop's own plan was to place his brother at Tongsa and make himself Deb. Eden wrote 'These internal commotions are the normal condition of the country . . . it will at once be seen how futile it is to expect that under any circumstances a strong and stable government can ever be established.'

As they approached the frontier they began to receive their mail which had been held up on the orders of the Tongsa Pönlop almost from the start of their journey. They reached British territory fifteen days after leaving Punakha although it had taken them two and a half months to get there. Remarkably, their only casualties had been the two coolies who had died of cold and exhaustion crossing the pass.

In concluding his subsequent report Eden wrote: 'It may at first sight seem to be a matter of regret that a friendly mission should ever have been sent to Bhutan, but from what I have seen of the government of that country, I am satisfied that it will in the end prove to have been the best course which could have been adopted. We have for so many years borne patiently the outrages committed by these people on our territory that they had learnt to treat our power with contempt: we know that there is in point of fact no government in the country, and that it is quite impossible that there can ever be a government there sufficiently strong to warrant an expectation that they will ever become good neighbours. We were formerly restrained from avenging the insults offered to us by a doubt of the complicity of the higher authorities; we know that they are the instigators and promoters of every act of lawlessness and aggression on our frontier, and that all British subjects captured on these occasions are kept as slaves in their forts and residences . . . the friendship of this government has been deliberately rejected and we have no option as to the course which we must pursue'.

The report included a number of appendices mostly covering aspects already described by previous missions: on Bhutan's history, the nature of its government, titles and duties of officials, the roles of the Deb and Dharma Rajas, none of which had anything particularly perceptive or new to say. The conclusions reinforced those already closing the main report: that 'Bhutan really has no government of any sort, that it is parcelled out into two large and a number of smaller divisions for the possession of which unceasing struggles are carried on by a number of unscrupulous robber chiefs. There is no one man in the country who is capable of making his authority felt by another man . . . it is therefore futile to suppose that we can . . . secure the good neighbourhood of the Bhutanese . . . I imagine that there never was a country in which entire anarchy had prevailed for so many years . . . '

A few sections of the report were concerned with aspects of Bhutan that had only been briefly dealt with before. One of these was the revenue system, based, according to Eden, on the doctrine of 'might is right'. No one's possessions were their own and although the population was decreasing the level of taxation in grain remained as fixed many years before. For every milch cow a tax of six Narainee rupees and two seers (one seer equalled 3lbs.10oz) of butter had to be paid. Many owners therefore stayed near the frontier and smuggled ghee across in order to obtain money to bribe the Zingaps sent to take stock of the cattle. As there was little incentive to expand most people lived on a subsistence economy, only looking after the fields near their houses and buying any extra grain or rice so as not to attract the tax collector, and then smuggling it to Tibet or Sikhim. The crops were excellent, especially the turnips, and the terracing and irrigation were very ingenious, water being brought long distances through stone aqueducts. The houses were, in Eden's view, 'better than many small houses in England,' built of rubble stone and clay or empisé clay, many consisting of three and even four storeys. The floors were neatly boarded with deal and the joinery work on doors, windows and panelling was of a high standard. He differed from Pemberton, in thinking that the system of placing large stones on the roof to prevent it from blowing off was effective, especially as a Bhutanese house was also protected by the floor of the store room, immediately below the roof, usually made of beaten earth. Most houses had farm yards and out-houses as well as a space for pigs underneath.

Eden thought that the civil wars were the major cause of the decline of the population which he estimated to be about 79,000. 'For miles', he wrote, 'not a trace of a village was to be seen where there were unmistakable signs of the land having once been cultivated and terraced'. At first he thought that the Bhutanese practised a form of shifting cultivation but learnt that wherever possible they stayed on the same fields and only left when forced by circumstances. Another reason for the decreasing population, in his opinion, was the people's 'gross immorality and filthy habits' without specifying their nature except to refer to 'withdrawal from the agricultural villages of a great majority of the able bodied men of the country who idle away their existence either in the dreary indolence of celibacy or who find it pleasanter to form one of the bands of bravoes by whom every official is surrounded, than to earn their bread by honest labour'. Yet the potential was enormous, with excellent irrigation, 'villages more like a clump of European farms than anything that is to be seen in any part of India' and a plough whose share dug deeper than

than those in use elswhere. 'If they were only able to enjoy a few years of tranquillity and feel assured that they would be permitted to keep the profits of their own labour the Bhutanese would probably be surpassed by the inhabitants of no Oriental country as agriculturists. From the great elevation and climate there is scarely any crop which might not be produced with facility . . . It is one of the parts of India in which, in my opinion, European colonisation could be practically carried on . . . '

The judicial system appeared to be non existent: 'Where there are no rights of property and the hereditary system is unknown, there is no need of civil law and where crime is the only claim to distinction and honour, there can clearly be no criminal law . . . No one dares to complain of an offence for if the person charged pays a sufficient bribe he is sure of obtaining his revenge by having his accuser heavily fined and probably robbed of all his possessions . . . The only resemblance to laws are those relating to etiquette . . . '

In this and in most respects, Eden judged Bhutan by the yardstick of Victorian England, then approaching the height of its power, and regarded by some as the epitome of all that was best and worth emulating. This was not a view ever held by the best of British administrators, certainly not those of an earlier generation in India or, as a whole, by the Indian Civil Service later in the century. Many of them would have realised, as Major-General Sir John Malcolm had done earlier in the century, that it was essential to retain intact and even raise the prestige of local rulers, customs and laws. Indeed, he wrote that his subordinate British administrators should have 'the sincere humility of heart that always belongs to true knowledge' and that they should be more attentive to the respect they gave to the inhabitants of the country than to the deference received. Eden's views on Bhutanese law was due solely to the lack of resemblance, to English law and he failed to realise the extent to which it was based on Buddhist theology.

His comments on the religion of the country were superficial and scathing: 'The Bhutanese nominally profess the Buddhist religion which they brought with them from Thibet (sic). In point of fact their religious exercises are merely confined to the propitiation of evil spirits and genii and the mechanical recital of a few sacred sentences . . . ' The educated lamas who had been to Tibet 'have the greatest contempt for their own people and country and only remain in Bhutan for the livelihood they obtain by painting and decorating – art which they acquire at Lhasa'.

Rather surprisingly, despite Dr. Simpson's good work, Eden approved of the Bhutanese medical system of exorcism administered by the lamas: 'disease is attributed to evil spirits having taken possession of the patient's body, the Lama reads incantations, drums are beaten and guns fired until the spirit makes a retreat. Little models of animals are made in flour and butter; and the evil spirit is implored to enter these models which are then burnt. This treatment is probably as successful as some other more civilised and modern systems which are mainly dependent on the faith and confidence of the patient'.

On the whole though, he thought 'the Lamas are an idle good for nothing illiterate set of men; education is gradually dying out amongst them and they are entirely ignorant as a rule of the tenets they teach. They are under vows of celibacy and perpetual chastity and are, as a natural consequence, the most sensual and immoral specimens of the most immoral race in the world . . . The form of worship in the temples bears a strong resemblance to the rites of the Roman Catholic church' (of which presumably, as the son of an Anglican bishop, Eden would have been almost as critical). 'Incense is burnt, holy water sprinkled, bells rung, beads counted and candles lit on the altar . . . the offerings presented by the people generally consist of large lumps of butter made up into various shapes . . . the villagers keep the Lamas well supplied with food; and the best land, gardens and fruit trees are here as elsewhere generally to be found in the possession of the priests'.

Turning his splenetic attention to more secular matters, he described Bhutan's trade as having been considerably reduced. The Rangpur trade had almost entirely ceased, there was very little contact with Darjeeling and trade with Tibet was minimal. 'In truth', he wrote, 'The Booteahs now have nothing to give in exchange for the commodities of other countries. They frequent the bazaars of Phari in Tibet but they are, from their turbulent, quarrelsome, careless habits, looked on with great disfavour by the Tibetans . . . ' Tibetan traders were now afraid to cross Bhutan and could no longer obtain the tobacco and indigo they used to buy at Rangpur.

In common with Pemberton and Griffith, Eden preferred the lower to the higher classes. 'They seemed intelligent, tolerably honest and, all things considered, not very untruthful', although 'immoral and indecent in their habits to an extent which almost surpasses belief'. Physically, he found them very fine, including some extremely tall men, although not as stalwart as Tibetans and Sikhimese which he thought was possibly due to 'their immorality and drunken habits'. The higher classes 'have their mouths perpetually filled with betel, a disgusting stimulant', and the occupation of the duars, by denying them their supply of betel would 'soon bring them to reason'.

Eden wrote quite interestingly about the eating and drinking habits of the Bhutanese, who lived on meat, chiefly pork, with turnips, rice and barley meal. Their tea came from China in the form of bricks, cut up when required into leaves which were placed in a large hollow bamboo into which hot water was poured, followed by boiling water, salt and a little crude soda. The bamboo was then covered and for ten minutes the tea was churned by stick placed through a hole in the cover. It was then poured into large tea pots, many of which were finely ornamented silver vessels: and from these poured into little china or wooden cups without handles. As many as twenty of these could be drunk by a person at a sitting, with a little parched barley meal, rice or Indian corn thrown into each cup. He found it 'unquestionably a very nourishing diet. A cup or two of such tea is most invigorating after great exhaustion or cold'.

More than any of the other British travellers, partly no doubt because of the route he took, Eden emphasised the prevalence of wild animals. Elephants kept his camp in a state of constant alarm near Sipchoo, tigers were common near the river Teesta and leopards plentiful in the Ha valley. Deer were abundant and included some very large animals; and musk deer were seen in the snows. Wild hogs were met at great heights, barking deer on every hillside and bears in the Ha, Punakha and Paro valleys. White rhino abounded in the duars. The Bhutanese did not shoot animals (they were no sportsmen according to Eden) as it would offend the deities of the woods and valleys and bring down rain when not required.

There was also a section on botany, compiled for him by the superintendent of the botanical gardens in Calcutta from whence Dr. Griffith's extensive collections had been sent to London where they were examined and classified by Sir William Hooker at Kew and distributed in 1862. The botanical gardens in Calcutta had now received some of them back from Kew including certain specimens that were 'quite new to science'.

Turning from the domestic habits of the Bhutanese and the flora and fauna of their country and other non controversial matters to the political and military outlook, Eden resumed his customary antagonism towards the country. Consciously or otherwise, he might have thought that the blacker he painted the picture the greater might be his justification for ignominious failure; but to do him justice, his views seem to have been formed from the very beginning. Certainly almost everything he wrote was designed to show the advantages to be gained both by the British and the Bhutanese from annexation. 'From their unscrupulous and marauding habits', he wrote, 'the Bootanese are on bad terms with every one of their neighbours. The Sikkimese look upon the Booteahs as unscrupulous robbers'. The Towang (Tawang) Raja, a Lama subordinate to Lhasa, who rules in the east, was in 'a state of chronic feud' with them, retaining a force of five hundred armed lamas to protect the people of south east Tibet from the raids of the Tongsa Pönlop. For the past few years the Tibetans had made the Bhutanese deliver their annual tribute at the frontier, to avoid the maurauding habits of those Bhutanese who used to escort it to Lhasa. Eden considered that unless the Tibetan frontier was crossed the government of Lhasa would do nothing to stop a British invasion of Bhutan, especially as Tibet itself was at that time in a disturbed state. Such an invasion would, in his view, meet with little opposition, as the Bhutanese had no organised or disciplined force. The

Bhutanese had clumsy catapults 'which, after an immense deal of trouble, and the labours of twenty or thirty men, could throw stones about 180 yards'. Very few men were ever killed in Bhutanese battles, according to Eden, although many were wounded; and few men in authority did not have several scars and cuts on face and body. They admitted to him that they were 'the most despicable soldiers on the face of the earth'. The garrisons at Paro, Punakha and Tongsa consisted of about 1400 men of whom only 600 were armed with matchlocks. They had little ammunition and it took three men to fire a single matchlock. They had little confidence in their firearms and preferred their knives, bows and arrows although they were not very good archers. Poor Eden, almost all his views were shortly to be confounded. The British military officers who were to endure a difficult campaign over the next two years were to report on the extreme accuracy of Bhutanese archery.

Not only were most of his judgements on the military and political situation proved wrong, but so were his assessments of the Bhutanese leaders. He depicted the Tongsa Pönlop as a Machiavellian monster, the epitome of all villany: yet he turned out to be the only strong man in a country torn with perpetual civil war, who wanted to prevent the irrelevant intrusion of a foreign mission at that particular time; and his proposal that frontier quarrels should be settled nearer the seat of the problem had some justification. He showed considerable acumen in not wishing to risk confrontation with a great power if he could help it: hence the despatch of messengers at each stage with several possible cards to play, according to Eden's reactions. However when the mission actually managed to get themselves as far as Punakha he determined to make the most of it and get the best possible bargain for the country. His tactics were to isolate them, to unsettle them by studied contempt and difficult conditions and create the climate for a favourable treaty. Indeed the terms of the proposed treaty were not nearly so intolerable as Eden made out. They were not totally unacceptable, after some adjustment, with the exception of the proposed return of the Assam duars which was omitted from the final draft.

Eden failed to mention in his report, when taking exception to the clause requiring Britain to submit to punishment by Bhutan, Sikhim and Tibet if found guilty of aggrandisment, that in fact the four parties were to agree to unite in opposition against any one of their number that transgressed. The draft treaty was also quite fair in apportioning blame for frontier robberies on both sides and gave both the right of extradition: 'the Feringees (i.e. the British) will surrender such offenders to the Bhutanese and the Bhutanese will in like manner surrender all Feringees to the British'. Although there were never any 'Feringees' to be returned, and the victims or offenders were British-Indian subjects, only a minor adjustment of wording was needed to make this at least as acceptable as the alternative clause that Eden had been empowered to put forward if necessary. Even allowing for mistakes of translation by Cheebo Lama, who may have taken his own line when it served him, Eden does seem guilty of presenting everyone and everything in as unfavourable light as possible.

It is interesting to speculate on what might have happened if the Tongsa Pönlop had earlier accepted the mission's inability to include reference to the Assam duars and if Eden had shown himself willing to be more flexible on other issues as indeed his instructions permitted him to be, in which case the war might have been avoided and many lives saved. On the other hand, the Pönlop may well have decided from the beginning to humiliate the British for the sake of the domestic advantage this would give him as the leader who had bloodlessly routed the country's enemies. As to his personal characteristics, we only have Eden's word for his rapacity, told him by lesser men of the council who were busy trimming their sails for all eventualities.

In April Eden reported to the Secretary to the Government of India: 'It is with extreme regret that I have to record the entire failure of the mission . . . it is possible that judging after the fact, there will be some who will blame me for having pushed into the country after the cold reception by which I was met at the frontier . . . ' His anticipation of criticism proved well founded for in May of that year a summary of events in Bhutan, written by an Under Secretary at the India Office, showed that the conduct of the mission had not been well received in London. Its implicit criticism of Eden for not having informed the government either of his departure or of his progress was hardly merited in the difficult circumstances prevailing but more valid was the comment that he had left the presents behind although his instructions had been to open negotiations by delivering them. Even this however, could be excused, given the shortage of coolies. By far the most justified criticism was that he had shown his hand much too soon by handing over the draft treaty at the start of the proceedings although several of the clauses were alternative. He had not even been required to press some of them and as these were the very ones to which the Bhutanese had objected they could have been deleted without loss. Most important of all the comments was that he had failed to tell the Bhutanese that he was only signing the treaty under compulsion, a point that was made much of in subsequent correspondence from the government of Bhutan.

The Governor General concurred with the view held in London and wrote the next month to say 'In our opinion it would have been well had Mr. Eden given up his mission, particularly after he arrived in Paro . . . The point now is, however, not so much Mr. Eden's conduct as the proper policy which we ought to pursue. It is absolutely apparent that negotiations can be of no use . . . ' He supported the action of the

Lieutenant Governor of Bengal in withholding payment for the duars and strengthening police posts on the frontier; and agreed with the proposals to send two companies of Native Infantry to Cooch Behar and to take precautions in case Sikhim was threatened. He also considered that any future marauders should be chased back across the border at the discretion of the civil and military authorities, provided that careful inquiries were made and all evidence recorded. Punitive expeditions could be mounted not only to follow the raiders but also, in certain circumstances to attack and punish the chiefs who were behind them: 'There being no government in Bhutan to whom we can apply for redress our only remedy is to defend our territory the best way that circumstances will permit'. The Governor General reported that he had written to the Deb and Dharma Rajas repudiating Eden's agreement and informing them that nothing would be paid for the Assam duars and the Ambaree Fallacottah tract until all British-Indian subjects had been released.

Eden was understandably dispirited at his reception even though he had half expected it. He wrote, in his defence, not without justifiction, 'had I turned back, those who now blame me for going on would have been among the first to accuse me of display of want of spirit'. However he paid generous tribute to the work of Captains Godwin-Austen and Lance and to Dr. Simpson, who, in addition to his medical duties, also gave political assistance. Simpson went on to have a successful career, becoming Surgeon General, and being knighted with the order of K.C.I.E., dying in 1923 at the age of 92.

Henry Haversham Godwin-Austen who later achieved fame by having a mountain named after him, had already served in India for twelve years, had taken part in the second Burmese war and had served in operations in the Punjab, before joining the mission. He compiled a plane table section to accompany the official report, a table of boiling point observations and a survey report. He also included sections devoted to Bhutan's government, religion, education and trade, most of which repeat the information already provided by others from Bogle onwards. Of the Bhutanese he wrote: 'I cannot give much praise to the people of Bhutan for although among themselves they seem jovial and laugh and joke, and show at times great humour to strangers, they are over-bearing and rudely familiar . . . often coarsely obscene in their language and actions and this was not confined to the male sex . . . ' Godwin-Austen, who had transferred to the trigonometrical survey of India six years before going to Bhutan, later surveyed large tracts of the Himalayas, retiring as a Lieutenant Colonel in 1877, and a few years later becoming President of the Geographical Society section of the British Association. He contributed to several scientific journals and wrote *The Lands and Fresh Water Mollusca of British India*.

Lance, an officer of the Bengal Staffs Corps, formerly of the 98th

Foot, wrote a memorandum on points of military interest, with details of rivers, roads, agriculture, towns and houses, as well as more specifically military information, including an appreciation of the strength of the dzongs and possible tactics for attacking them. He did not rate the Bhutanese military capacity very highly and wrote of 'the cowardice of the natives'. In this he was to be proved wrong the following year when despite their absence of firearms which he had noted, 'except for a few miserable matchlocks' they were to prove a stubborn foe, as Lance, who served in that campaign, was to discover for himself. After some years he transferred to the civil administration and served in Assam. His most useful contribution to the prevailing knowledge of Bhutan was a vocabulary 'of certain useful words in the Booteah language'.

Despite the mission's failure, which was generally ascribed to his want of judgement, Eden also went on to have a successful career, no doubt helped by his family connections as a nephew of the Governor General, Lord Auckland. He resumed his post as Secretary to the government of Bengal, which he continued to hold for another seven years before becoming chief Commissioner for British Burma and finally Lieutenant Governor of Bengal where he was a great success and had a statue erected to him, by public subscription, in Calcutta. He was knighted, K.C.S.I., and on his return to Britain became a member of the Council of India until his death at the age of 56 in 1887.

Whether or not Eden should have continued his journey into Bhutan with a truncated mission, an escort too small to have any military deterrence and without the necessary presents for the accepted form of diplomcy, is a moot point. If he had possessed some of Bogle's good humour and if he had been prepared to temper some of the less essential clauses in the proposed treaty, he might have got away with it; but it is doubtful, given the internal situation in Bhutan. On the other hand, had he turned back he might well have come in for even greater criticism, for such are the ways of government.

A more interesting question is to consider why he and his officers formed such a low opinion of the Bhutanese. As already indicated, this was no doubt partly due, on the British side, to the more expansionist imperial attitude in which they had grown up. Since the beginning of the century there had been many policy fluctuations, the great period of expansion at the beginning of the century being followed by retrenchment and then again by a more consciously imperial policy after the mutiny; but the great men of the early years had not planned expansion for its own sake. It had come about in those days more in order to contain the French as a result of the power vacuum left by the Moghuls, the shifting alliances and changing fortunes of the Rajput princes, the Mahrattas, the rulers of the Carnatic and Hyderabad and the search for protection by a myriad of lesser princes. British administrators in the first quarter of the century were already talking even then of trusteeship, of rule in the interests of the native population, of preference for indirect influence through alliance and help to native princes, to direct rule, which accorded with the wishes, for different reasons, of the commercial directors of the Company. Now, however, a new spirit was abroad. There was a mood of intolerance of others, partly due to the horrors of the mutiny, partly to the evangelical spirit of the time which dismissed the claims of other religions; and there was a new type of man in the civil and military services, who lacked the close relationship with the people of the country that his predecesors had had. There were also now far more European women, whose husbands spent more time with them and less in the field or with their men in camp or barracks, whereas older generations of British in India had acquired wisdom and knowledge from their Indian mistresses. Nevertheless there were still great names in India and many more were to come though the newly formed Indian Civil Service but most of them cut their teeth in the Punjab or northern India and the North West frontier.

With the possible exceptions of Colonel Jenkins and Dr. Campbell the North East did not seem to attract men of the highest calibre until towards the end of the century when some of the best officers of the Indian Political Service were to serve there.

The Eden mission was composed of men who were the products of their own time, with the ideas and prejudices of the age, going into a country which even the most ardent supporter of the Bhutanese must admit was in a state of chaos, whose people had undoubtedly been at least equally responsible for a century of frontier brigandage. Consequently Eden and his companions were prepared to see the worst in everything in Bhutan. Nevertheless, there is so much corroboration between their reports and those of the Pemberton mission, on the nature of their reception and the incivility of the people they met, of prevarication, monastic greed, the role of women, that it is difficult to dismiss them all as exaggeration. The Bhutanese national character does seem to have changed in the century following the mission and especially since the unification of the country in the last quarter. This is not so surprising as it might seem, for the British character has seen some remarkable changes: from the zealous concern with religion that clouded the 17th century to the rational attitudes of the eighteenth and the evangelical zeal of the 19th. The literary archetype of the 18th century was very different from those of a later age and descriptions by foreign visitors of English people in the 16th century bear little relationship to those of the 19th. The characteristics of the rural population in both Britain and Bhutan probably changed comparatively little but, as far as it is possible to judge by literary and historical stereotypes, those of the ruling classes, subject to outside and unifying influences, may well have done so. Certainly today the

Bhutanese are the most hospitable of people, good humoured, realistic and more than ready to learn from others, retaining their traditional values and culture with no chauvinism towards others; and Bhutanese women are not only beautiful and, in many cases, most attractively turned out, but also have equality of opportunity. The contrast with the British reports of the 19th century is so great that the moral and spiritual changes arising from national unification must have been as significant as the physical progress made by the state of Bhutan under the great Ugyen Wangchuk and his successors.

CHAPTER SIX
1865–1885 War and Civil War

In September the Secretary to the Government of India, wrote to his opposite number in Bengal (presumably Eden had not yet resumed this post himself) to say: 'His Excellency in Council feels that, however much it is to be deplored, no option is left but to enforce the reasonable demands of the British government by active measures of coercion, taking care that these be limited to what may be absolutely indispensable to attain the objects in view'. Meanwhile, the Commissioner in Cooch Behar prepared an intelligence memorandum on the duars and the routes into Bhutan, including a detailed analysis of socio-economic factors; and preparations for the offensive now begun.

As so often happens, the military took a less sanguine view than the civilians of the problems to be surmounted and the size of the force required. Although an early military appreciation, based on Eden's views, reckoned that 2000 men would be an over-estimate, this view was not shared by the General Staff. The Quarter-Master General wrote from Simla to 'remind the planners that in 1772 the Bhutanese had put up a determined resistance at Chichacotta whose fortifications were said to be unchanged since then'; and passed on the comments of the Commander in Chief that the Bhutanese had the reputation of being experts in laying ambushes. He also wrote, 'Had the C. in C. been consulted on this essentially military question, His Excellency would have had the honour to submit different proposals for the composition of the force . . . H.E. would venture to observe that it is always dangerous to undervalue an enemy, especially mountaineers in their own . . . unknown country'. Another military appreciation referred at length to Dr. Griffith's report and the difficulties inherent in movement in the country around Dewangiri and elsewhere.

In October letters were sent from the Deb Raja and the Subha of Dalingcote to Cheeboo Lama who passed them on. They said that, if attacked, the Bhutanese would fight, as they felt fully justified in doing so, especially, as Eden had signed without protest the treaty of which the British now complained.

On 12th November 1865 a proclamation was issued from Fort William in Calcutta which referred to 'past outrages' and stated: 'The British Government, ever sincerely desirous of maintaining friendly relations with neighbouring states, and especially mindful of obligations imposed

on it by the treaty of 1774, has endeavoured from time to time by conciliatory remonstrance to induce the government of Bhutan to punish
the perpetrators of these crimes, to restore the plundered property, to
liberate the captives . . . ' Referring to the treatment of the Eden mission
it went on . . . 'This pacific overture was insolently rejected by the
government of Bootan. Not only were restitutions for the past and
security for the future refused but the British envoy was insulted in open
durbar and compelled, as the only means of ensuring the safe return of
the mission, to sign a document which the Government of India could
only instantly repudiate . . . ' It was then announced that the annual
payments for the Assam duars and Ambaree Fallacottah would never
again be paid and that both areas would be permanently annexed.

On receipt of an evasive reply in which the return of captives and
property was not agreed, the decision was taken to annex the Bengal
duars into the bargain and 'so much of the hill territory including the
forts of Dalingcot, Passaka (Buxa) and Dewangiri as may be necessary to
command the passes'.

Preparations now began for war. The Force Commander, Brigadier
General W.E. Mulcaster, was to command two right hand columns whose
objectives were the fort (dzong) at Dewangiri and Bishensingh whilst the
two left columns under Brigadier General H.F. Dunsford C.B. were to go
for Buxa Duar and Dalingcote, the former setting out from Cooch Behar
and the latter Jalpaiguri.

Only eight days after the proclamation had been issued and before a
reply had been received Major Macgregor (later Major General Sir
Charles) the Brigade Major to Brigadier Dunsford's column was able to
write: 'Everything is now ready for an advance along the whole line . . .
600 elephants and innumerable pack bullocks have been collected and
three months supplies have been stored at the bases'. Despite all this
preparedness he was critical of the plan to divide the force into two
groups with no means of contact between them which he thought was
'tempting Providence'. He was with the extreme left hand column whose
first task was to attack the fort at Dalingcote. After crossing the Teesta by a
'raft bridge of a peculiarly fragile and oscilating nature', they advanced, he
wrote, 'through the most dense grass and tree jungle I ever saw. . . nothing
but jungle and again jungle on all sides; no clearing to relieve the eye, all was
close and impenetrable jungle. . . ' The road to the fort at Dalingcote wound
up hill after hill affording the enemy wonderful opportunities which were
never taken for attacking the column so that Macgregor wrote 'I must con-
fess a most thorough contempt at our enemy was engendered in our minds'.

A few months later, after a number of setbacks, a very different view of
the Bhutanese was expressed by Colonel J.M. Adye Royal Artillery, writing
to Lt-Col R. Biddulph, Military Secretary in Madras: 'We have another
small war on our hands in Bhutan and the civilians have mismanaged it

just as they did the last (the government had reduced the size of the force recommended by the Commander in Chief) . . . the population has no military resources except the usual pluck of mountaineers . . . sending isolated columns into an impracticable country without roads and in entering the hills just far enough to get into difficulties is our playing the game in a way which gives the Bhuteers the advantage. Their only chance of success lies in the difficulty of their country and in their being able to concentrate against any column they choose'.

To oppose these hardy mountain people operating on their own ground the British force consisted almost entirely of Indian troops, of which much of the infantry were locally raised units. Six Armstrong mountain train guns and four 8 inch mortars were manned by British soldiers of the Royal Artillery, another six mountain guns were handled by Eurasian gunners. There were four squadrons of the 5th Bengal cavalry, and two of the 14th, four companies of sappers and miners; the 43rd Assam Light Infantry (later to become the 7th Gurkhas) two wings of the 11th Native Infantry, the 2nd Gurkhas, one wing of the 44th Native Infantry (30th Punjabis). In reserve were the 18th, and 12th Native Infantry, the 30th Punjab Regt. Assam local artillery, the 17th N.I. and 3 companies of the 80th regiment of foot (the Staffordshire Volunteers – later the South Staffordshire Regiment) the only British infantry, on the withdrawal of 3 companies of the 48th Foot (later Northamptonshire Regiment) to defend Darjeeling which it was thought the Bhutanese might attack.

On the 5th December the column on the extreme left began its attack on the fort at Dalingcote which Eden had described as a miserable building and which Captain Jones had succesfully captured in 1772 with only a few men. The assault was met with 'a smart fire of arrows, stones and matchlocks from a dense area of underwood' to which the attackers responded with 'a desultory fire which could have been of very little good' according Macgregor who was himself hit by an enemy bullet which passed through his helmet leaving a scalp wound. A British Officer of the Native Infantry had an arm pinned to his side by an arrow at much the same time. The advance, which had come to a temporary halt, resumed under a '. . . fire which was directed with considerable precision'. During this time the mortars were being man-handled by coolies up the steep and winding track which had proved to be impassable for the elephants. When at last they opened fire it resulted in the greatest single tragedy of the campaign as a mortar blew up, probably because of a defective fuse, killing three British officers and seven men.

The artillery now managed to get into position and opened fire making a small breach in the north east corner of the fort on which the sappers advanced and placed their powder kegs. It was left to a Gurkha soldier, with characteristic bravery, to set off the actual explosion. A storming

party charged into the resulting breach and the enemy bolted. The fort
had been taken but at quite a price.

Major Macgregor, whose first encounter with the Bhutanese had
caused him to revise his opinions, wrote 'We have been accustomed to
regard these Bhutias as a despicable, pusillanimous race, and yet we see
them with stones and arrows offering no contemptible defence to some
500 to 600 men with Armstrong guns and inflicting on them a loss of 58
killed and wounded . . . I doubt . . . if we could have lost many more men
if the enemy had been armed with muskets. The arrows are all sharp and
pointed and fly with great precision, having penetration enough to go
through a man's body'.

Further to the east an assault, also mounted by the left column, was
made on the stockade at Bala, of which Captain (later Colonel) A.H. Lewes,
adjutant of the 30th Punjabis, wrote a participant's account. His column
at first took the wrong road, providentially as it turned out as the correct
and more obvious route was heavily 'booby trapped' in the form of a line
of huge stones ready to be tipped over a cliff above. Even so, half a mile
from the summit they still encountered a hail of stones as well as arrows
and bullets. It was not till nearly sunset that the wall of the corner tower,
'pluckily defended by a few Bhooteas' was 'sufficiently hammered' for a
detachment of Lewes' regiment finally to reach the top of the hill where
some of them scrambled over the walls and others got in through a door
at the foot of the wall. He himself had a narrow shave, an arrow sticking
into the back of his neck until someone was able to remove it. He and
fifty men remained on the ridge all night in order to protect the guns
which had been manhandled up by the coolies; 'and a miserable sleepless
night it was', he wrote, 'with the intense cold and firing all round us'. On
searching the fort the next day he obtained 'a large silk banner . . . repre-
senting the great Lama with lots of figures worshipping round him and
below a sort of dragon figure'. This was almost certainly a Bhutanese
thanka, or prayer banner. Lewes, like Eden and Pemberton and their
officers found the Bhutanese 'very dirty, their womankind hideous'.

Two men of Lewes' regiment were killed in this action and twenty one
were wounded. A further twelve were wounded, mostly by arrows, when
he and a reconnaissance party of the advanced guard encountered the
enemy six hundred yards below their stockade at Chamurchi. That night
they fully expected to be attacked at any moment but instead the Bhutanese
spent much of the time shouting like jackals, partly in order to summon
more men by this signal, partly no doubt to unnerve their opponents.
During the next day Lewes and his men remained there whilst the Bhutanese
'kept dropping occasional bullets and arrows into our small camp . . .
four of these fell almost in one place and within a yard of the table we
were sitting at . . . '

The Bhutanese defences may have been inspired by a proclamation issued a fortnight before in the name of the Dharma Raja, probably drafted by the Tongsa Pönlop, which stated: 'The English do not cease attacking Bhutan and the people must now prepare for the attack of the English. They will now try to take the duars and after that they will attempt to proceed to take Punakha and deprive the inhabitants of Bhutan of the freedom they have enjoyed from time immemorial. It is the duty of the Pönlops and Dzongpöns to be firm in the faithfulness and love of freedom to protect Bhutan'.

The attack on Chamurchi was successfully carried out in the closing days of the year. Once again the advance had taken the form of a laborious slog up a very steep hill right up to its crest although the place itself was sited low down on a spur consisting only of a few houses and a monastery. 'The enemy' wrote Macgregor, 'had prepared this road in a manner that could have done credit to a European engineer. Every turn, every spot whence it was commanded was strongly barricaded'. The attack went in this time from the flanks and the rear instead of being a more costly frontal assault but even so five men were killed.

Lewes was with the left column in the final attack and after two hours of stiff climbing they reached a ridge where they could hear the Bhutanese talking above their heads. Unfortuntely 'although the men behaved awfully well and went the whole way up as silently as cats, the local dogs were alerted and started barking when we were at once saluted with a shower of arrows and some huge stones . . . '

At last the assault was ordered. 'The men gave a loud cheer and went in with a rush' . . . coming in for a 'regular fusillade of arrows' which killed two men and wounded three others, including Lewes' young Sikh orderly at his side. Lewes was again lucky as an arrow hit the tip of his boot and glanced off.

On reaching the stockade they saw the Bhutanese fleeing and took possession without further bloodshed. Lewes picked up a sword with a 'shark skin' handle (probably lizard). That evening he was one of the twenty seven officers who saw the New Year in together. The company included the Brigadier who reckoned, with some justification, that the campaign was now over as news from his other column further to the east was equally good. Setting out from Cooch Behar, they had taken Buxa Duar with little opposition.

Meanwhile the left of Mulcaster's two columns, consisting of 2000 men with 150 elephants, had experienced dreadful conditions hacking their way to Bishensingh, only to find that its sole inhabitant was an aged lama living in its single stone house. The extreme right, accompanied by Mulcaster himself had had a harder time of it but had also achieved its original objective. Dewangiri had been captured by Captain Macdonald and 50 native policemen after charging through a hail of arrows and stones, with the loss of one man killed. They took up their position on top of the hill when a solitary courageous Bhutanese leapt over the breastwork rushing at Macdonald with a spear before being shot dead by a policeman. The Bhutanese had been in greater strength at Dewangiri, a place where Pemberton had commented on many of the people being 'pure Bhoteas . . . fine specimens of human build'. On this occasion there had been about 5000 men of whom only 1500 were fighting men. The remainder were mostly porters for carrying away the wounded, coolies for the transport of provisions, servants and, surprisingly, musicians. Each fighting soldier was armed with a jingal (a traditional matchlock, used in Tibet as well as Bhutan) and in the fold of his belted toga-like garment carried a circular powder flask, 100 to 150 bullets, a supply of stones and some meat.

At the end of the year all the objectives had been achieved and the two right hand columns were already being reduced in strength, leaving only a holding force. Over on the left Major Macgregor set out on January 3rd to accompany his chief on a tour of the posts confidently expecting the arrival of an order to disband their forces as well. This came a few days later but fortunately there had not been too much reduction on the left when disaster struck.

At each of the fortified places taken and occupied by the four columns the Bhutanese had crept forward, establishing stockades within a commanding distance of the British forces, from which they were able to mount counter attacks on a reduced and unprepared enemy.

At Chamurchi on the extreme left the surrounding hills suddenly appeared to be 'crowded with Bhutias, of the vicinity of whom not a soul in our garrisons had the slightest idea'. As in the other places the stockades had been brought so close that arrows could be fired into the British encampments without their positions being seen, so dense was the undergrowth. Fortunately the threatened attack never transpired and the enemy withdrew.

At Buxa Duar the other left hand column which had hitherto been unopposed now came under very heavy attack and was gallantly defended by the outnumbered Gurkhas who were forced to withdraw when the supporting post at Bala pass was evacuated, after a disastrous action in which a British officer was killed. The day was only saved by the heroism of a native cavalry officer who, with his men, turned and beat off the pursuing Bhutanese.

The centre right column's position at Bishensingh held out despite being heavily attacked but also had to be evacuated because of the withdrawals elsewhere; but the greatest disaster was at Dewangiri. A warning letter had actually been received a week before but had been ignored as it was written in Tibetan which nobody could understand. Then on the 29th of January at five o'clock in the morning there was a noise in the camp like that of stampeding cattle, the sound made by the Bhutanese as they cut the tent ropes of the British force. This was followed by a general attack before proper defensive positions could be taken up. On the Bhutanese side it was led in person by the Tongsa Pönlop and on the British the counter attack was directed by Lt-Colonel R. Campbell who was suffering from a high fever when he charged at the head of the 43rd Native Infantry and the sappers, one of whose British officers was killed by a jingal bullet and another wounded. The attack was beaten off but left another four men killed and 31 wounded. For three days nothing happened but the Bhutanese were obviously still around. On the 3rd February they erected a stockade 600 yards away, just within jingal range, and cut off the water supply to the British camp, making it untenable. They also captured the Darangi pass, cutting them off from the plains, and a small force bringing supplies was forced to turn back. On the 5th therefore, at one in the morning, a withdrawal began in dead silence, covered by a few remaining pickets. Everything went wrong as the main column lost its way in the dark and secrecy was lost. The Bhutanese were alerted and some of the troops panicked. A purposeful and silent evacuation turned into a ghastly rout as men ran headlong away from the scene. The wounded were left behind and men of the 43rd Native Infantry refused to obey the order to help with the carriage of the guns. The twenty Eurasian gunners were unable to cope on their own and Captain D.E. Cockburn was forced to order them to be hurled down a ravine from whence they were subsequently retrieved by the enemy. He then formed a rearguard and beat off the pursuing Bhutanese.

After the action the Tongsa Pönlop sent a letter to the regrouped British force to enquire after the health of the Bhutanese prisoners and to say that all those captured by the Bhutanese were being well looked after, even sending a sum of money to cover the expense of a reply. He sent his compliments to the British officers hoping that they were as well as he was, but writing: 'You are wanting Dewangiri again but from whom did you receive permission to take possession of it when you first captured it? You will either have to fight with us or write a letter to the Dharma Raja if you are desirous to recover Dewangiri': a reasonable letter in the circumstances and especially so if the warning of the attack had come from him in the first place. It rather gives the lie to Eden's description of him.

After these losses there was a hurried call for reinforcements, one of whom wrote of the reaction to these disasters: Major C.J. Gough V.C., commanding the 5th Bengal cavalry which had been withdrawn from the campaign, as the thickly forested country, stiff with big game, had proved unsuitable for them, had returned with his men to the Indian border when, in February, he received orders to return to Bhutan. He was knocked up late one night by the magistrate at Jalpaiguri, saying 'The General is in a great state of anxiety about affairs along the frontier: the Bhooteas are in such force as to box up our troops and place them entirely on the defensive. Fears are entertained of their breaking through into the duars and pouncing upon Cooch Behar '.

'This is a most complete bouleversement of affairs', Gough wrote in his diary. Setting off back to Cooch Behar he commented adversely, like many another front line soldier before and since, on the incomprehensible ways of the staff. The orders and counter orders that he had received showed 'a great want of decision somewhere'. He had also heard from a friend in Calcutta that a council attended by the Governor General, the Commander in Chief and the Lieutenant Governor of Bengal had expressed 'unanimous disgust' at Eden's folly and want of discrimination in his report on Bhutan', presumably referrring to his comments on Bhutan's alleged military weakness.

Gough and his cavalry reconnoitred the roads to Chichacotta and Bala and reported that in each case there was plenty of open country suitable for cavalry. They passed through 'comfortable looking villages and very highly cultivated'. It was, he thought, 'the richest, best cultivated and most populated part of the duars I have yet seen and it is a great pity to leave so fine a country open to the Bhooteas to draw supplies from or to ravage as they please . . . '

It was during this march that he heard a story that 'a European artillery-man somehow wandered from the fort at Buxa close to the Bhootea stockade, the Booteas seeing him, beckoned him to come up, which he did and was entertained by them with tea and liquour (sic), treated kindly and allowed to go his ways'. Gough wrote in his diary 'good enemies if true', as indeed it probably was, corroborating what Turner and others had written of the Bhutanese attitude to war.

Meanwhile, new commanders had been appointed and Brigadier Generals J.M.F.F. Tytler C.B., and H. Tombs C.B., V.C., took command of the left and right pairs of columns respectively. On the left Brigadier Tytler spent ten days acquiring intelligence reports so that, in Major Macgregor's words, 'every foot of ground, every path was known and the position of every breastwork and every sentry ascertained before the counter attacks were begun'.

Both Gough and Lewes were present at the recapture of the Bala heights. The former described how a hundred men managed to get to the foot of the heights and from there up to Tazgong unobserved until an Armstrong gun was recklessly fired and their position given away. The Bhutanese rushed downhill in force and the advance guard was forced to retreat. During this action Major Macgregor was wounded in the hand. The two inch mortars and two Armstrong guns now opened up and the left detachment which had meanwhile climbed to a position above the Bhutanese right flank now swept down on their defences. They had had eleven hours hard toiling to reach their position up a very steep and difficult slope and without much water; but when the opportunity offered they made the most of it rushing the stockade and killing nearly sixty of the enemy.

Lewes was with the advance guard when the 'ill-timed shot' alerted the enemy who immediately resembled 'a hornets' nest, hurling their stings into their party in the shape of bullets, arrows and stones', wounding five men as well as Macgregor. Inside the fort he saw a gruesome sight and counted thirty six of the dead including 'a tremendous swell with a gold hilted sword and a silk head dress'.

He also took part in a successful re-occupation of Chamurchi on March 28th after a difficult march at the end of which the Bhutanese opened fire with matchlocks and jingals. Whilst the British gunners returned the fire Lewes and his men were able 'to snatch a mouthful of much needed grub' before advancing on the enemy position which they found to have been evacuated.

After the battle the Paro Pönlop sent letters to ask about the numbers of his dead and wounded. He accused the British of attacking whilst negotiations were in progress and when his men were performing religious observances. He may well have thought that an offer to talk about peace in itself constituted peace, or at least an armistice, but it is certain from their writings that none of the British officers on the spot knew anything about it.

At any rate Gough was now free to study the flora and fauna of the country under more peaceful conditions and wrote to his aunt: 'I declare that the orchids in this country beat conception', especially at Tazgong where the trees were covered with a profusion of flowers whose colours included scarlet, white, yellow, lilac and pink.

On the right a force of 1500 set off on 1st April to recapture Dewangiri, whose garrison was estimated by Tombs to be 3000, including a Tibetan contingent. The British advance guard consisted of a company of the British 55th regiment of foot (the Westmoreland, later Border regiment) a Eurasian battery of artillery and detachments of the 12th, 19th and 44th regiments of Native Infantry. They ascended the Durangal pass and the next day began their advance up the hill as the guns gave covering fire. One party trying to storm the defences on the right were driven off but the detachment in the centre were more successful. This time the Bhutanese panicked, offering little resistance as the infantry swarmed in. There was indiscriminate slaughter by some of the Native Infantry, especially by the Sikhs and Pathans, despite efforts to stop it by their British officers; and the 55th did what they could to succour the wounded. Nevertheless 120 Bhutanese, who had surrendered, were put to death in this shameful incident. Dewangari had been retaken solely for reasons of prestige as it was quite untenable. The few remaining buildings were destroyed and the force withdrew.

The later stages of the campaign were notable more for the appalling

losses from disease suffered by the British forces than for battle casualties
as there was now little fighting taking place. Gough's cavalry had seventy
men in hospital by the middle of April. His diary entry reads 'It is very
unfair to keep the troops out in this weather . . . What can account for
they ways and whims of men in authority when troops are very sick?' He
refused to send his men to take up an outlying position that no one had
bothered to occupy before when the troops were in good health. The
camp followers, who constituted an enormous tail in any army on the sub-
continent with its train of sweepers and water carriers and servants, fared
particularly badly in unhealthy conditions. 'They are very hard worked,'
wrote Gough, 'cutting grass for horses in all weathers . . . poor beggars, a
Liberal government will only grant them half a seer of rice . . . ' To make
things worse there was an earthquake and then the heavens opened.
'Rain, more rain, very heavy rain all night', he commented. The men
were in soaking wet tents going down with fever and then the dreadful
cholera. Their only preventive medicine was twenty grams of quinine and
some beer taken daily. On April 30th Gough had 211 men sick. Six had
died during the month and he wrote of the survivors 'it is a very melancholy
spectacle to see the men dragging themselves up to the hospital worn
down with this abominable jungle fever . . . '

Plans were now drawn up for an invasion of Bhutan proper in which
the left columns were to advance from Buxa to the capital, Punakha, and
the right from Dewangiri to Tongsa. The Government of India, however,
wanted to bring the war to an end and during the rainy season negotiations were begun, much to the disgust of Tytler who resigned.

Even before the recapture of Dewangiri the Paro Pönlop (presumably
the older man whom Eden had met) had been making peace overtures
but was told that the British could only negotiate with him if he had been
accorded full powers to do so by the government of Bhutan and that no
treaty could be concluded until amends had been made on the basis of
the terms already stated: that all the Bengal duars should be surrendered
as well as some land on the left of the Teesta; that the treaty document
extorted from Eden should be handed over to be destroyed together
with apologies for his treatment; that the captured guns should be
returned; that no subsidy payments would be made until then and if
necessary they would be recaptured by force. If these terms were fulfilled
and if all the captives were returned the Government of India would pay
25,000 rupees, to be increased to 50,000.

The Political Agent, Lt-Colonel J.C. Haughton, was convinced that the
Paro Pönlop was not empowered to speak for Bhutan as he had learnt
that the Bhutanese were still trying to enlist the aid of other powers in
order to continue the war. Tibet had been approached but refrained
from action and Nepal had refused to assist. Nevertheless the Dzongpön
of Wangdiphodrung had recently written to the Subhas ordering them to

intensify their fight against the British.

There followed a series of misunderstandings, with the Paro Pönlop appearing to assume that the British had already agreed to suspend hostilities pending negotiations; and agents then arrived to conduct these who were quite obviously not properly accredited.

On June 5th the Government of India wrote to the Deb Raja to say that if he refused to accept the terms troops would be sent further into the country; receiving a reply that made no mention of peace terms and referred only to the restoration of the duars to Bhutan for which two envoys would be despatched.

Exchanges of letters continued for several more months but in September the Viceroy wrote: 'nothing short of your absolute submission and the acceptance of the terms laid down will avert hostilities'. This at last led to some action for in November representatives from the Deb and Dharma Rajas arrived to make peace. However this only led to further difficulties as the Tongsa Pönlop rejected the terms unless the money for the duars was given separately to each of the four chief officers: himself, the Paro Pönlop and the Dzongpön of Wangdiphodrung as well as the Deb Raja. The British response was to state that if the Bhutanese were unable to persuade the Tongsa Pönlop to accept the proposed settlement they would make him do so by force if the other Bhutanese leaders would co-operate with them. It is not recorded whether or not this was passed on to the Tongsa Pönlop but shortly afterwards the envoys agreed to sign the terms and no more was heard of him for the time being. Accordingly, on November 11th 1865 the treaty of Sinchula was signed; and the British agreed to suspend hostilities and not to occupy any more territory, although the road building process would continue.

The main provisions of the treaty were: the annexation of all the Assam and Bengal duars and an area on the left bank of the Teesta to be fixed by a British commissioner: a subsidy of 25,000 rupees to be paid the first year subject to the fulfilment of all the treaty terms and the return of the two guns. This would be raised to 35, 45 and finally 50,000 in successive years. In future all disputes with Cooch Behar and Sikhim were to go to the British for arbitration.

These were stringent terms and have been understandably criticised for their harshness by Indian historians. Nevertheless it is difficult not to accept the conclusion that Bhutanese methods of diplomacy largely contributed. Their practice, adopted also by the Tibetans forty years later, was to prevaricate for so long that ultimately they hoped problems would just solve themselves and unwelcome intruders would go away. If foreigners had to be encountered their patience must always be tried by never being offered what they asked for and for the more awkward issues to be simply ignored. This may have worked to some extent in the intricacies of relationships in the past with the Tibetans and even with the Nepalese and Chinese but was fatal in dealing with an impatient western power. Nevertheless there were two major long term benefits. For the inhabitants of the duars the quality of life was enormously improved as they no longer lived in constant dread of cross-border raids; and British Indian capital became available for investment in tea plantations and other forms of agricultural improvement. Later on when the increased productivity of the duars became apparent the Bhutanese were to use it as an argument in favour of an increased subsidy; but the increase was only made possible by annexation and a peaceful frontier. The Bhutanese themselves disliked living in the lowlands and would not have worked the land themselves. There would also have been an even greater problem over Nepalese immigration. Even so this was increasing rapidly in those foothills remaining in Bhutan and was to present a major problem in years to come.

The other great advantage was that the war and subsequent treaty were to a large extent responsible for creating the circumstances for ultimate national unification under a strong ruler now that the constant drain of resources on frontier warfare was over, petty chieftains more easily called to heel and a ready supply of cash from the subsidies was assured for whoever was to master the country.

The signing of the treaty did not immediately lead to a diminution of problems however, and there was one last attempt at prevarication by the Deb Raja who, in ratifying the treaty, ignored the stipulations for boundary demarcation. Only after the British had objected were these finally ratified. The Tongsa Pönlop also continued to be evasive over the return of the guns and the captives, in the hope of getting more money for the guns. The British refused to negotiate with him separately and the Deb and Dharma Rajas were asked what action they proposed to take. Meanwhile the first subsidy payment had yet to be made and the date of the second payment on January 10th 1866 was approaching. The issue of the guns had now become a matter of prestige for an imperial power unaccustomed to such humiliating losses (and even eighty years later, on the eve of Indian independence, the British refused a Bhutanese request for the return of Dewangari on the grounds that it was the place where the guns had been lost).

The Tongsa Pönlop was told that the British intended to march against him and a copy of the letter was sent to the Deb Raja who was informed that as he had not yet said what action he proposed to take with the Pönlop, the British assumed he had no objection to their taking it. In the previous October a British column had reoccupied Dewangari and when it looked as if the Bhutanese were not going to return the guns and were prepared to fight, the column continued its advance. At last letters arrived to say, with some justification in view of the time of year, that snow had caused the delay and that the guns would be returned.

However, Lt.Colonel W. Richardson, commanding the column, was not prepared to take chances and made a forced march to the Manas Bridge where they were to be handed over. When the column arrived it became apparent that the Bhutanese were still divided amongst themselves and the troops were fired on. Conseqently they rushed the enemy position, overrunning it so swiftly that the guns were surrendered and the war finally concluded.

Internal strife continued within Bhutan for the next twenty years until at last a strong ruler emerged. The struggle for power was first and foremost between the Tongsa and Paro Pönlops and their various allies but there was often opposition to the Deb Raja who was rarely supported by all the nobility. Right at the start of this period the Tongsa Pönlop refused to accept the authority of the current Deb who was supported by the Paro Pönlop. He therefore handed over his post to his brother in order to make himself Deb and a juvenile nominee Dharma Raja. The Paro Pönlop therefore approached the British to solicit their support for the ruling authority but was told by Colonel Haughton, then Commissioner in Cooch Behar, that British policy was not to interfere in the internal affairs of other states unless British interests were threatened.

Meanwhile, because of the lack of firm control from the centre the border continued to give trouble. Money was at the root of it for the Bhutanese could not agree amongst themselves on how the subsidy payments should be divided; and chiefs began to take the law into their own hands, obtaining what they considered to be their share from British Indian subjects across the border. The Dzongpön of Wangdiphodrung demanded subsidy payments from the zemindars of Sidli and Bijni, now in British territory, who were told not to pay by Colonel Haughton, who wrote to the Deb Raja to protest at this violation of the treaty. Another incident occurred at the Chuka bridge where a local Bhutanese officer closed the trade route from India and demanded payment of tolls.

Haughton wanted to withhold the subsidy until redress had been received and although the Government of India approved of this the Bengal government would not support it despite Haughton's argument that the Subha of Buxa who had been sent to receive the subsidy was not of the seniority stipulated in the treaty and that this compounded the other treaty violations. However, the subsidy was eventually paid in October 1868 when an explanation was received for the road closure by a junior official acting off his own bat and when the Bhutanese agreed, after intial protests, to go to Darjeeling instead of Buxa, whose Subha was now suspect, to receive the money.

These triangular disagreements between the British authorities themselves often happened in the history of British relations on this frontier, right up to the time of Indian independence. The Machiavellian continuity of British policy in its intentions towards Tibet which some Indian historians have affected to see, never really existed in a situation where there were not only three-cornered differences between political officers, state and central governments within India, but also conflicts of view between them and the India Office in London which itself did not always see eye to eye with the Foreign Office; and all were subject to the political whims of alternate Liberal and Conservative governments with radically different foreign policies. All that can be said is that at various times over two centuries there were nearly always some British officials somewhere who favoured good relations with Bhutan for the prime purpose of establishing relations with Tibet. In the 18th century the motivation was commercial but in the 19th century it was more concerned with the negative purpose of keeping out the Russians. There was rarely agreement on the degree of desirability or the methods to be used to achieve this result.

At this time Haughton's proposal to open a direct channel of contact with the Tibetan government because of the unsatisfactory state of Bhutan, although supported by the Government of India, was opposed by the authorities in Bengal on the grounds that Tibet had not supported either Sikhim or Bhutan in their conflicts with the British and that it would be unwise to upset the status quo.

Conditions in Bhutan were indeed getting worse. The Dzongpön of Wangdiphodrang who had been the Tongsa Pönlop's chief ally during the Eden Mission, was now leading a coalition against him, and also approached the British for assistance which was denied on the same grounds of refusal to interfere in internal matters when no British interests were at stake. However, it was increasingly realised, at least by some of the officers on the spot, that British interests were indeed affected by the internal situation and that there should be discreet backing for any chief favourably disposed towards Britain who appeared strong enough to settle the country. Haughton also thought that a permanent representative from the Paro Pönlop, who seemed to fit this description, ought to be accepted. This was not agreeable to the government in Calcutta although the Bengal authorities supported his later proposal for an agent from the government of Bhutan, funded by the British, to be stationed at Darjeeling.

The problem was to know who really was the government of Bhutan for by now there had been a shifting of alliances and the Paro and Tongsa Pönlops were for once on the same side, in opposition to the Dzongpön of Wangdiphodrung, and jointly protested at what they thought was British connivance at their enemy's recruitment of Nepalese soldiers. Haughton had, in fact, tried to stop this but had been censured on the legal grounds that as Nepal was an independent country Britain had no right to interfere. The Dharma Raja now complicated matters by writing to Haughton to say that he should not listen to any approaches from his Bhutanese subjects, to which the Government of India replied to the effect that they had no intention of doing so.

Shortly after this a strong man did begin to emerge in Bhutan; but not the one that Haughton favoured. It was Jigme Namgyal, the former Tongsa Pönlop, Britain's old enemy, who defeated the opposition, killed the Dzongpön of Wangdiphodrung and some of his associates, and became powerful enough to place his own nominee as Deb Raja in 1870.

The British accepted the *fait accompli* and decided that it would be politic, at the start of a new relationship, to accede to some of his requests. These included permission for Haughton's own interpreter to become Bhutanese agent at Buxa with the rank of Dzongpön, despite Haughton's objections; and to revise the boundary near Dewangiri which had been so poorly demarcated that people on the British side were still receiving financial demands from the Tongsa Pönlop. The boundary commissioner, whose orders were not to include any of the Bhutanese hill areas as this would cut them off from valuable forest timber and would lead to raids on British territory, duly completed his report in March 1873. He confirmed that although Dewangiri in the Assam duars had been included in the British side of the treaty, the Tongsa Pönlop had been ordering his officials to collect taxes from residents. Consequently this money was to be deducted from the subsidy, troops were to be stationed at Dewangiri and a bridle road was to be constructed. Over in the Bengal duars at the same time the boundary was retraced and marked out again. A few years later it was reported that the Bhutanese had raised a separate and more favourable line of pillars enabling them to collect revenue from the inhabitants of the area into which they had encroached, and once again the British demarcated the old line.

In October 1875 a Bhutanese ruler visited Indian territory for the first time when the Deb Raja, Dorje Namgyal, brother of Jigme Namgyal, met the Lieutenant Governor of Bengal at Buxa. The meeting passed off well and permission was given by him for the British to open a road through Bhutan to Sikhim. Shortly after this there was more internal feuding and Jigme Namgyal assumed power, without being appointed to any particular office, and opposed the road building project which was, almost inevitably, supported by the Paro Pönlop.

Although the Government of India was disturbed by this state of affairs it was decided not to support the Commissioner's proposal to respond to the former Deb Raja's request for help; and once again a letter was sent to say that British policy was not to interfere in internal affairs. Nevertheless when the Paro Pönlop and the Punakha Dzongpön were finally defeated and fled to India they were given asylum and maintained at the expense of the government, who refused to extradite them when asked to do so by the Deb, on the grounds that the treaty referred only to criminals and not political offenders.

In 1880 a Bhutanese raid on a village near Buxa resulted in the capture of several runaway slaves who were only returned to India when the with-holding of subsidy payments was threatened. In other respects relations had so improved that the British agreed quite readily to hand over a hill area near Buxa which included an important Buddhist shrine.

Even after the death of his brother in 1879, the ever-resilient Jigme Namgyal continued to be the de facto ruler until his death the following year when his son Ugyen Wangchuk became Tongsa Pönlop. Despite his treatment of the Eden mission and his hostility towards the British which did not lessen after the end of the war, Jigme Namgyal had nevertheless proved himself to be the outstanding leader that Bhutan needed and laid the foundation for a unity which his descendants were to build on.

Ugyen Wangchuk's position was challenged when in 1883 one of his main supporters was ambushed and killed, but by marching on Bumthang he defeated his enemies and re-established himself as Tongsa Pönlop. In 1884 there was further unrest when the Dzongpöns of Thimphu and Punakha, joined by the current Paro Pönlop, took up arms against him because he had refused to meet the cost of the upkeep of five monas-teries as a reprisal for failing to receive his share of the British subsidies. When a meeting at Thimphu failed to result in agreement, he marched on Simtokha with 4000 men, captured the dzong and then at a battle just below Thimphu, routed his enemies. The Dzongpön of Thimphu, Alu Dorji, who had been their leader, fled to Tibet. Chinese pleas on his behalf were politely ignored, the Deb was dismissed and Ugyen Wangchuk's own nominee, Yangpi Löpen, was appointed in 1886. Two years later, in the Chumbi valley in neutral ground, a conference took place at the request of the Chinese authorities in Lhasa, who had been persuaded to support the exiled Alu Dorji. At this meeting Ugyen Wangchuk refused to hand over areas of Bhutan to be ruled by the exile and ignored later attempts by the Chinese to support him. After suppressing an insurrection by the former Dzongpön of Punakha, the last flicker of a century of strife, he was able to turn his attention to internal organis-ations and the development of a sound foreign policy.

Unlike his father, and living in a different age when British power was undisputed almost everywhere in southern Asia, Ugyen Wangchuk realised the value of strengthening the British connection and was largely responsible for ensuring that the Tibetans received no Bhutanese help in their war against the British over Sikhim in 1889. He was now complete master in his own house and was secure also in the knowledge that the British, who were delighted to have a strong ruler at last in Bhutan, would help him if his authority was challenged. He accepted the reduction of the power and influence of Tibet as inevitable, although taking care to remain on good terms with the Chinese, and saw that Bhutan's future lay in cultivating the friendship of the Government of India – a policy continued by his descendants although the British have long since gone.

Relations between Britain and Bhutan were now so stable that a long report on relations with Tibet written by one of the Secretaries to the Bengal government, who had been sent as a special commissioner to Sikhim and the Tibetan border, contained surprisingly few allusions to Bhutan. The report was based on an account of conditions inside Tibet written by Babu Sarat Chandra Das, the headmaster of a Bhutanese school in Darjeeling, who had travelled in Tibet in the guise of a religious 'guru', and provided information that no European could give. He made the interesting point that the export of Tibetan goods through Bhutan now exceeded imports although there was a great demand for the latter. Even so, European, especially Russian, cotton cloth was replacing Chinese and there was considerable import of other Russian goods, notably woollens and glassware. There were few Bhutanese merchants involved and much of the trade was carried out by Nepalese traders, who operated between Calcutta, Kathmandu and the Tibetan border. The direct trade route from India through Sikhim was increasingly obstructed by the Tibetans and was to become a major cause of controversy with Britain.

There were two key factors. The first was trade and the British post-war policy, harking back to the days of Hastings, of establishing better economic relations with Tibet and considerably increasing the volume of exports, for which these reports indicated that there was a substantial market. The second and more important involved Britain's global re-lationship with Russia. From the North West Frontier of India and the Afghanistan border, from Chitral and the Pamirs, from Hunza and Leh eastwards, from Nepal and Bhutan to the north east frontiers of Assam, Britain and Russia growled at each other across the roof of the world; and occasionally young officers and detachments of Cossacks and the Corps of Guides encountered each other in the inhospitable wastes of Turkestan.

The British feared that the steady Russian momentum of advance south into central Asia to the borders of Afghanistan, northern India, China and Tibet would sooner or later tempt them forward into India itself. Therefore Bhutan, Tibet's southern neighbour, could not be ignored. In order to counteract this supposed threat from Russia it seemed necessary to gain a foothold in Tibet; and for trade from north east India to be able to pass through Bhutan unimpeded. In 1874 the Commissioner of Cooch Behar had written: 'our relations with central Asia, via Phari, are beginning to take shape and must, before long, under the influence of railways and trade, become of great practical value. Bhutan must have a part in these relations although a subordinate one'.

These relations with Central Asia, particularly Tibet and the Chinese Empire, and the implications for Bhutan, figure largely in the next chapter.

CHAPTER SEVEN

1885–1910: Men of Vision:
Ugyen Wangchuk & John Claude White

In the spring of 1885 the Tongsa Pönlop, Ugyen Wangchuk, signed an agreement with a joint Chinese and Tibetan mission which settled a number of border problems. This mission was soon followed by another which disturbed the British as it was supposed to have inquired into the grievance of the Thimphu Dzongpön, who fled to Tibet, and to have supported the claim for Tibetan assistance towards the reinstatement of the former Deb Raja. This looked as if the Chinese and Tibetans were now asserting claims of sovereignty and were not following the British precedent of refraining from interference in Bhutan's internal affairs.

Colonel H.M. Durand, the Secretary to the Foreign Department of the Government of India, wrote: 'We cannot look with complacency upon the establishment of Chinese influence anywhere south of the Himalayas'. Even so, the government had no wish to come into direct conflict with the Chinese and were not inclined to pay the subsidy to the new Deb Raja, to whom the Chinese were opposed; but in the end the views of the Bengal government prevailed, that as he was the *de facto* authority he should be supported, especially as it became apparent that the Chinese were re-asserting what they claimed to be an ancient authority. The Peking government gazette, for instance, referred to a Chinese demand that future nominations to appointments in Bhutan were to be submitted to the Tibetan authorities who would pass them on to the Chinese Amban in Lhasa for his approval. The British Chargé in Peking reported that as a seal of office had been given to and accepted by the Bhutanese rulers in 1736 the Chinese assumed this indicated a state of subservience. In 1891, as if to emphasise the point, as well as their rejection of the Tongsa Pönlop and the ruling Deb, they sent another seal to the Paro Pönlop who told Mr. A.W. Paul, a British officer of the Indian Civil Service who had been seconded to special duty in Tibet since 1886 (and who in 1890 became British Commissioner at the Anglo-Chinese commission).

None of this affected relations between the British and the Bhutanese; and in return for the visit made to Paul by the Paro Pönlop and a repre-sentative of the Tongsa Pönlop, another British mission to Bhutan was proposed, which appeared to have the support of both parties. This was rejected by both the Bengal and Indian governments for whom recollections of Eden were still too strong. However, in the usual compromise way dear to bureaucracy, they did send the Bhutan Vakil, or Agent, who was stationed in Darjeeling, ostensibly on a private visit, with instructions to report back on the political situation. The British were still being cautious about giving all their support to the Tongsa Pönlop and kept their options open with the Paro Pönlop, just as Ugyen Wangchuk was at first equally hesitant as between Britain and Tibet ten years later.

Despite the improved relations between the two governments and the more stable internal situation, frontier problems still continued and in 1892 an Indian official was captured and only released in return for a cash payment. Once again there was consideration of withholding the subsidy until explanations and apologies were received but in the end no action was taken except to set up a military post at the place from where the Bhutanese raiders had debouched and to charge the Bhutanese government for its cost, which was deducted from the subsidy.

From now on the Indo-Bhutanese border was to present few problems whilst the Bhutanese, Sikhim and Tibetan frontier areas were to occupy an increasing amount of attention.

In 1888 the Tibetans had occupied a twenty mile deep strip of Sikhim adjoining the Chumbi valley and were expelled by a small British force. The Tibetans had over two hundred men killed for the loss of one British officer and three men. Ugyen Wangchuk, who was astute enough to realise the strength of the British position, was largely responsible for ensuring that no assistance was given to the Tibetans at this time. Two years later the Sikhim–Tibet convention was signed between Britain and China whose suzerainty over Tibet was recognised by Britain. This was followed in 1893 by Trade Regulations, agreed also by the Chinese and British, but the Tibetans announced that as they had not been party to these agreements they did not regard them as binding. The Chinese were not at that time in a strong position to enforce them because of their war with the Japanese between 1894 and 1895 and were in no mood to support Britain during the Boxer rising of 1900–1901 when Peking was occupied by European and Japanese Troops. Consequently there was a period of frontier bickering when the Tibetans destroyed the boundary pillars that had been erected and were alleged to have stolen Sikhimese grazing land although it was never proved. They certainly placed stone walls across the tracks leading from India so that Yatung and Giagong could not be used as trade marts as agreed in the Trade Regulations.

In 1901 an attempt was made to resolve these issues. It was led by John Claude White, of the Public Works Department until seconded to the Political Service as assistant political officer with the expeditionary force to Sikhim and Tibet in 1888. Like some of the doctors from the Indian Medical Service he was to prove just as competent in this role as his administrative and military colleagues and in some ways more understanding of the nature of the hill people of Sikhim, Tibet and Bhutan. However,

on this occasion his efforts were unsuccessful as the Tibetans refused to
co-operate and it is difficult not to sympathise with their predicament,
being kicked around as a political football between Britain, China and
Russia.

At this time local problems on the northern frontiers of India were
seen in Calcutta (still the seat of government, until it moved to Delhi in
1911) and London within the wider context of Russian expansion between
the Black Sea and the Caucasus and into the lands of the Tekke Turkoman.
In fact the Russians were only doing much the same as Britain had done
in India in the previous century, moving into territories 'to restore order'
on the frontiers, or under 'the Doctrine of Lapse' when the 'forward
policy' was operative as it continued to be in the early years of the 20th
century during the expansionist period when Curzon was Viceroy.
Curzon was also fervently opposed to the Russians and as his views were
only partly shared in London there were to be a great many mistakes and
misunderstandings over relations with Tibet that are beyond the scope of
this book.

In 1903 a Tibetan frontier mission was despatched under Colonel
(later Sir) Francis Younghusband of which White was a member. They
reached Kamba Jong where they remained for five frustrating months
unable to undertake any proper negotiations with the Tibetans. The
following year therefore, with Curzon's enthusiastic support and luke-
warm backing in London, a large scale expedition with a substantial
military force entered Tibet. The British government had been anxious
to sound out Bhutanese attitudes and in October 1903 the Tongsa
Pönlop had been invited to meet Younghusband. At that time however
the Bhutanese were undecided about committing themselves to the British
cause; understandable enough in view of their much longer association
with Tibet and long history of relations with China, of the still fragile
unity in the country and the Paro Pönlop's known support for the Chinese.

Ugyen Wangchuk therefore responded cautiously, sending his cousin,
the Thimphu Dzongpön who turned out to be a great success, getting on
well with the British officers and Younghusband who called him 'The
first sensible man I have met on this frontier'. The Dzongpön agreed to
allow the British to construct a road on the Amo Chu–Di Chu route,
thus considerably shortening their supply line. He also met delegates sent
from Lhasa and tried to negotiate between the parties. His reception and
success decided Ugyen Wangchuk which way to turn and in June he
offered his own services to the British as a mediator. By then, though, it
was too late to do much as the mission was now determined to get on to
Lhasa. He was asked instead if he would impress on the Dalai Lama the
uselessness of resistance. He therefore joined the mission and accompanied
them on the march through Tibet. During all the subsequent negotiations
he proved to be very helpful, especially as the Tibetans on a number of

occasions showed their preference for dealing with him in the first instance. He also got on well with Younghusband and his officers who called him 'Alphonse' because of his rather Gallic appearance: short and well built with a small 'imperial' beard, and usually sporting a grey Homburg hat.

The frontier commission and its military escort made slow progress, neither side being willing to shed blood unnecessarily. Younghusband also knew that an advance to Lhasa was only grudgingly supported by Brigadier J.R.L. Macdonald, the commander of the military escort, who was his senior. He was aware also that not every one in Calcutta shared Curzon's views and that the cabinet in London were strongly opposed to them, partly because they had no wish to antagonise Russia whose support was needed at that time for British policy in Egypt. Only after the eruption of fighting, first at Guru where the Tibetan General was largely to blame, although he had been placed in an impossible position, and then at Karo La, was agreement given for the march on Lhasa, which they reached in August 1904.

The Dalai Lama fled and a new treaty was signed after a great deal of wavering by the Regent and the Tsongdu, the assembly of monks. The fact that it was signed at all was largely due to the assistance, which Younghusband readily acknowledged, of three people: The Chinese Amban, or Agent, whose stock had fallen and saw a chance to enhance his prestige through a mediatory role; the experienced and knowledgeable Nepalese representative and Ugyen Wangchuk. The previous treaty was re-confirmed with the addition of clauses permitting trade marts to be established at Gyantse and Gangtok, new roads were to be made, the access to Lhasa of the British Trade Agent at Gyantse, British occupation of the Chumbi valley and payment of an indemnity. The last two were later amended by the British government for fear of alienating Russia.

In 1903, White, Paul's former assistant, took over the duties of political responsibility for Bhutan as well as Sikhim. He was the architect of Anglo-Bhutanese friendship and an outstanding example of the many lesser known Imperial administrators now largely forgotten, who successfully managed to identify themselves with indigenous people whose causes they espoused, even if necessary against the policies of their own government. He is still remembered in Bhutan. White had known Ugyen Wangchuk on the Tibetan expedition and at his suggestion Wangchuk attended the Indian durbar given by the Prince and Princess of Wales (the year after the great durbar of the Prince's father, King Edward VII) at which assemblies of rulers paid their homage. A party consisting of the rulers of Sikhim and Bhutan, and their entourages toured India. It was the first time that most of them had left their mountainous homelands and, according to White, Ugyen Wangchuk 'took the most intelligent interest in whatever he saw' whether they were cotton and paper mills, ironworks, the mint, or even warships.

Although Ugyen Wangchuk had been impressed by his reception a problem arose that could have upset the cordial relations that had been established. Charles Bell, the settlement officer on the Kalimpong estate, reported that a strip of territory of about 70 to 80 square miles on the western border of Bhutan, adjoining Sikhim and Tibet, had been wrongly held by the Bhutanese ever since the treaty of Sinchula. Article II of the treaty had stated that the hill territory on the left bank of the Teesta should have been ceded to Britain; but this had not been done. The revenue surveyor had reported in 1877 that 'a more difficult country could not be met with . . . even the few Bhutias I had with me knew little or nothing about their own country . . . ' In fact they probably knew more than they let on for he had been deliberately hoodwinked. The landlord was Mimba Kazi, the former translator of the court at Darjeeling, who had been with Eden in Bhutan. He had incited the Bhutanese to join the people of Sikhim in a rising against the British and when he failed he had fled to Bhutan. As Eden had refused to rescind the ban on his return to British territory, despite his helpfulness on several occasions, he had a vested interest in ensuring that his lands were inside Bhutanese borders. He was supported by the Bhutanese villagers, who feared his power, and were also, in this area, strongly opposed to the British. It was not too difficult in that sort of unmapped country to point out the wrong river to a surveyor who had no means of checking and no local support to rely on.

Bell recommended that the land should revert to Britain on the grounds that most of the inhabitants were now Nepali immigrants who were ill-treated by the Bhutanese and wanted British rule; and that the area was within the jurisdiction of the Paro Pönlop who was not well disposed towards the British. The Lieutenant Governor of Bengal thought that it would, however, be a political mistake to put forward a claim that had been dormant for forty years as 'the Bhutanese government is just now more disposed to be friendly and to come in closer touch with the British government than at any previous period since the time of Messrs Bogle and Turner . . . ' He also considered that the very product-iveness of the land on which Bell had laid such stress, was in fact a strong argument for not taking it over. 'Bhutan', he wrote, 'is far from being a rich country and can ill afford to part with productive lands'.

Fortunately he was supported by the Government of India and by the Secretary of State in London; and Ugyen Wangchuk's goodwill and diplomatic skill were suitably recognised. Ugyen Wangchuk's tour of India was returned by White's first visit to Bhutan in 1905. His mission included Major F.W. Rennick of the Intelligence Department, Mr. A.W. Paul who went at White's special request, a confidential clerk, an escort of 24 Indian soldiers, two Sikhim Pioneers, two Sikhim policemen, and the pipes and drums of the 40th Pathans. The warmth of the Bhutanese reception and the success of the mission were in striking contrast to the experiences of Eden's mission forty years before.

They left Gangtok in Sikhim on March 29th winding their way upwards through forest clad hills bright with white magnolias and scarlet rhododendrons in full bloom, the sides of the road carpeted in mauve and purple primulas. Out of the forests they emerged into clearings from whence they gazed across a sea of hills and an 'uninterrupted panorama to the plains of India'. Higher still, they ran into snow which turned into a raging blizzard and even penetrated the chinks of the wooden huts where they slept at a transport station on the Sikhim to Chumbi road, built for the Tibetan mission. They struggled on to the Natula pass at 14,780 feet where the snow was so thick that White was unable to ride and had to plod along on foot. They descended to Pema in the Chumbi valley where Major Rennick and a third of the coolies were found to be suffering from snow blindness. The next day the party was met by Kazi Ugyen Dorji, the Bhutanese Agent who arrived via Jenglap after a difficult crossing. At that time he was Agent of the Bhutanese government in India and was there given the Sikhimese title of Kazi, when he also became the Assistant to successive British Political Officers. An old friend and near relative of Ugyen Wangchuk, he was appointed Gonzim (Chief Chamberlain) of Bhutan in 1908 and became the most influential official in the Kingdom, a tradition perpetuated by his descendents. His grandson, Jigme Dorji, was to become Lonchen (Prime Minister) of Bhutan.

Shortly afterwards a rock fall led to the injury of a pony which had to be shot and two mules died from eating poisonous leaves of a small rhododendron. They were not helped at this stage of their march by completely erroneous maps which failed to show the Kyanka stream which they were following uphill and near which they pitched camp.

They passed 'robber caves', crossed delightful glades and upland swards 'forming rich grazing grounds' and noted the proliferation of trees: spruce, larch, silver fir, holly, oak and pines as wells as rhododendrons, before crossing the Lungri Sampa to a camp where their chief protection from the wind was 'in the walls of lateral moraines of which the valley presented some excellent examples'.

Despite afternoon and evening snowfalls they managed to shoot six pheasants which made a welcome addition to the pot. Then, climbing once again, they experienced 18 degrees of frost on their way up to cross the passes of the Massong – Chung Dong range which had never before been crossed by Europeans. They marched on frozen snow hard enough to ride on, as far as the final ascent, and White's cook (a Mugh, from Chittagong in the Arakan where all the best cooks came from) even managed to ride up to the top. The pass at Kyula was at 13,900 feet and looking back they could see the whole of the Jaylap range. In front of them was a steep dip between themselves and Ha La pass known as the 'bridge of death', offering no shelter from storms and no source of firewood, with precipitous cliffs to the north and a deep snowdrift in the south. However, they were fortunate enough to traverse it in calm conditions without trouble and reached the Ha La where they joined their offerings with the many others left there by grateful travellers for the spirits of the pass. They could now see the towering mass of Chomolhari rising up in the distance and nearer still snowy peaks of the Massong Chung Dong.

On descending from the heights they were met by the Tongsa Drönyer who had been detailed to accompany the party during their stay in Bhutan. At Tsangpa-Pilau they found three small riding rules awaiting them, sent by the Paro Pönlop, which they found to be excellent. On these they followed a good road to Damthong at 10,400 feet where they found awaiting them 'a zareba of fresh pine boughs encircling a well laid out camp' in a beautiful setting of gently sloping grassy glades leading to a series of wide valleys with at each side 'a deep fringe of fine trees of every age'. White noted that 'the Bhutanese seem to have acquired the secret of combining in forests self-reproduction with unlimited grazing'.

When they were comfortably settled into their tents in this delectable camp the Tongsa and Paro officials and the Ha Zimpön and Nyerpa brought further salutations from the Pönlops in the form of a piece of silk for White and rations for everyone.

The next day they passed through an open valley noting the small shrines perched on every commanding promontory. They crossed the beautiful plain known as Gyang Karthang where an annual dance and fair were held and at every village the inhabitants turned out to greet them with wayside tea.

The mission was now in the hands of the Bhutanese government which treated them as honoured guests and took over the administration, transport and arrangement of camp sites, leaving the party free to visit forts and monasteries untroubled by the problems of housekeeping or logistics.

On the way to the top of the Chiuti La they caught glimpses of the Ha valley where Eden had camped. At the top of the pass they were met by a servant sent from Paro with murwa in order to keep out the cold. His experiences were in such sharp contrst with Eden's that White suspected that his predecessors had been deliberately guided away from the proper route to a cattle track.

They saw the Drugyel dzong in the distance and reached the monastery at Gorina where White compared the brass openwork overlaying the altar hangings favourably with anything he had seen in Lhasa. On the ridge below they were greeted with salvos of artillery, fired from iron. tubes bound with leather and were met by the Paro Pönlop's band and three 'richly caparisoned' mules. Slowly they descended a clayey slope which would have been impassable in wet weather. Down on the plain they passed by the Paro dzong and its bridge through a quadruple avenue of willows towards Paro itself where on a level plain their camp had been pitched, at the entrance to which 'a new Swiss cottage tent' had been erected. This was a very different reception to Eden's experience of trying to find a campsite at Paro.

White was now free to take in his surroundings down to the smallest detail. He was intensely interested in practical things: in agriculture and forestry, in flowers and birds, in geological structures and soil changes (he had noticed that rhododendrons did not grow in this part of the country because of the absence of peat) as well as in the details of the Constitution and the offices and functions of all the officials he met. This awareness of everything around him, his knowledge of a wide variety of subjects and keen interest in arts and crafts, together with his unpatronising and friendly attitude to people of other races made him the ideal observer. Even the strange custom of feeding mules with eggs did not escape his notice. Each mule in the camp was given two or three raw eggs broken into a horn and poured down the throat of the animal to strengthen them for the day's march. They all throve on this strange diet.

The following morning the Paro Pönlop, accompanied by his young son, made a formal call on the mission. He was about 56 and, according to White he was 'a fair man with a weak, discontented, though not unhandsome face'. The son was 'a most ill-mannered cub who would have been all the better for a good thrashing.' He must have been a little fiend for the generally tolerant White to have described him thus. The boy's mother was the Pönlop's second wife who ruled her husband with a rod of iron. She had given him her own daughter by a previous husband as his junior wife to prevent his affection from alighting elsewhere. Both women lived together in an attractive house across the valley, as no women were allowed in the dzong after dark.

White was also critical of the Paro Drönyer: 'A low drunken ignorant fellow, the only person with whom I had any trouble. Going about in a state of maudlin intoxication from early morning, it was difficult to keep him in his place, for under the pretext of friendliness and relationship to the Pönlop he used to walk into one's tent at the most inconvenient time, asking for anything from an old solar topee to our mess kit. Finally I had to purchase a temporary respite with a present of a pair of binoculars that he badgered everyone for and at last we parted from him almost sober; but he was the one exception to the other officials and the people throughout the journey were extremely well behaved and very friendly.'

The morning after the call from the Paro Pönlop White rode to the dzong to return the courtesy, crossing the moat by the heavy drawbridge leading straight to the third floor. They turned to the left under a huge gateway into the eastern courtyard in a corner of which was a series of rooms used by the Pönlop. They entered a long low room filled with retainers seated in four rows, two on either side facing each other, reminding White of descriptions of baronial halls in medieval England, heightened by the shields and spears, matchlocks and bows and arrows hanging from the walls.

Presents of a rifle and ammunition were given to the Pönlop and a knife, binoculars and magnifying glass to the son before White took his leave, having first obtained permission to look around the dzong of which even Eden had written 'It far surpassed the expectation we had formed from anything we had heard of Bhootian architecture'; and Turner before him had been greatly impressed. White and his party visited the public Gompa and the great hall which he considered to be even larger than the Potala in Lhasa where the Tibetan treaty had been signed. It had a particularly impressive hanging lattice work of pierced brass. They met the head of the monks, Lama Kunyang Namgyal whom White and Paul had known on the Tibetan mission where he had exercised a good influence over the monks. He took them round the dzong seeing the same fascinating sights that Turner and Eden had described.

The Dzongpön gave them a Bhutanese lunch of scrambled egg and sweet saffron rice washed down with murwa (beer) and chang as well as milk, walnuts and dried fruit. The armoury, said to be the best in the country, was in a fine room with a large bow window facing south and looking down the valley. In the outer courtyard they saw men making gunpowder and silversmiths and wood turners at work and White liked the 'air of bustling activity'.

They continued on their way the next day, camping for the night in grove of walnut trees, and as always White showed himself to be a close observer of men and nature, his comments covering subjects as diverse as the game of quoits played by boys, an unusual succession of prayer walls and the contrasts of the countryside, where thickly wooded slopes covered with masses of flowering pears and peaches gave way to barren hills with sparse and stunted trees. They also saw the well cared-for house of the former Paro Pönlop, whom Ugyen Wangchuk had allowed to return from exile in Kalimpong to die in peace at home.

The next camping ground beside an enormous weeping cypress was spoilt by the howling wind roaring up the valley and they were glad to be on the move again past a cantilever bridge carrying a wooden channel to irrigate the rice fields. White wrote that he had often noticed 'how remarkably skilful the Bhutanese are in laying out canals and irrigation channels and the clever way in which they overcome what to ordinary people would be insurmountable difficulties.'

They passed the knoll where the Punakha Dzongpön had been over-come by Ugyen Wanchuk's forces during the civil war in 1885. It was said to have been done by an act of treachery in the course of a parley but Mr. Paul had a different version. He thought that the peace talks had been genuine enough but that a quarrel had arisen amongst the supporters which had led to the stabbing of the Punakha Dzongpön. He was convinced that Ugyen Wangchuk had had no hand in anything treacherous.

Shortly after this they reached the Tashicho dzong on the outskirts of the capital, Thimphu. It was 'an imposing edifice in the form of a paral-lelogram' the longer sides parallel with the river. Unusually, it had two large gateways, one of which was only opened for the Deb and Dharma Rajas. Inside were the chapel and private apartments of the Dharma Raja and the Thimphu Dzongpön's personal and official quarters. The square tower had only been built a few years before to replace the original damaged in an earthquake. The northern section was occupied by the state lamas and not open to laymen: the inner courtyard led into a fine audience hall decorated with frescoes, silken ceiling cloths, embroidered curtains and banners; and on the western side was a succession of chapels, one of which was said to contain a thousand images of Buddha. The elephant tusks supporting the altar were even larger than usual in Bhutanese shrines.

The next day the mission continued on its way as Thimphu was not then the permanent capital. Today the Tashicho dzong is the Whitehall of Bhutan situated on the edge of an expanding town. (By the middle of this century, because of damage from fire and earthquake, only three of the chapels were undamaged and much of the structure was in such a shaky condition that it was completely rebuilt between 1962 and 1970 following the pattern of the original and reconstructed in the traditional materials of stone and wood.) At Simtokha dzong White thought that one of the statues was an unflattering likeness of the Kaiser. Next day, after going through a wet zone with a completely different climate, they reached the ancient captial of Punakha.

They made a ceremonial entry the next morning in heavy rain along a road of thick clay on which it was difficult to keep a footing. They were preceeded by musicians and dancers who led them across the bridge over the river Mochu to the sound of a fifty gun salute. They found their camp awaiting them, including a two roomed wooden house, a large 'Swiss Cottage' tent for White and a smaller one for Major Rennick. Also awaiting them were the Tongsa Pönlop, the two Punakha Dzongpöns, the Shung Drönyer and the Deb Zimpön, all of whom were known already to White. The Pönlop and the Dzongpöns had been with him in Tibet.

The following day, after finishing off an accumulation of official work

with his confidential clerk, White began a series of courtesy calls which were
in turn returned. The most important of these was on the Deb Raja who
was a recluse occupied with spiritual affairs. This was because a reincarnation
of the Dharma Raja had not yet been found. Until then he was standing in as
the Dharma Raja's 'speech incarnation' and his spiritual duties weighed more
heavily than the temporal.

The next day the whole party proceeded to the ceremonial durbar, White
and Rennick in full dress uniform preceded by an escort of the 40th Pan-
thans commanded by their Subadar, Jehandad Khan. The durbar hall was a
wide-balconied chamber covered in silken hangings and embroideries. In
front of a high altar and its images on a raised daïs sat the Deb Raja clothed
in yellow silk, his lamas ranged behind him. To the right were four scarlet
covered chairs for White, Rennick, Paul and the Subadar, each with its own
table and refreshments. Behind stood orderlies with the gifts that were to be
presented. Opposite on a low daïs sat Ugyen Wangchuk in a robe of dark
blue Chinese silk and below him were ranks of officials. At the lower end of
the hall the men of the escort were seated; behind them were rows of junior
officials and lamas sat in the aisles leaving just enough room for four officers who paced up and down with whips and batons with which to keep order.

After a clerk had read out on his behalf a short address in Tibetan, White
accompanied by Rennick, carrying on a cushion the insignia and warrant of
Knight Companion of the Indian Empire, placed the ribbon around Sir
Ugyen's neck and pinned on the star. The recipient then rose and gave his
thanks for the award after which he was presented with gifts, including a
rifle, a number of framed photographs and the usual scarves.

This was not the end of the proceedings however for there began 'an
almost interminable procession' of lamas bringing scarves to Sir Ugyen who
was almost smothered in them. Then the whole nave filled up with gifts of
various sorts, including heaps of tea and bags of rice and corn, rolls of
fabric, little bags of gold dust and heaps of rupees. Tea and refreshments
were served and betal and pan passed around. Finally a large cauldron of
chang was ceremoniously blessed and a small portion poured into Ugyen's
hands. A wooden spear with a red cloth and a white scarf were also blessed
and waved around his head. Finally there were .prayers led by the Deb Raja
and intoned by the lamas.

Describing the ceremony White wrote: 'It says a great deal for the change
in conduct of affairs in Bhutan and the anxiety to show respect to the British
government that they should have made the presentation of the decoration
. . . the first occasion of so public and elaborate a ceremony.'

After the ceremony they visited the dzong. Access was by two cantilever
bridges whose gateways of heavy timber were studded with iron. There were
defensive towers at each end and the only entrance was up a flight of re-
movable steps twenty feet high. On one side was a massive masonry wall built
from river to river commanding the open plain. Inside, the buildings

"Crossing a Torrent in Bhutan", engraving by William Daniell after Samuel Davis (1837?).

Taktsang (Tiger's Lair) Monastery (White, 1906).

Chöten at Gorina Monastery, Paro (White, 1906).

Ugyen Wangchuk with the Raven Crown and the K.C.I.E. insignia (White, 1905).

The last Deb Raja, Druk Desi Choley Tulku Yeshey Ngudup (White, 1905).

Presenting the subsidy of 50,000 rupees, 19th December 1907 (Hyslop, 1907).

Ugyen Wangchuk with John Claude White (standing), Major F. W. Rennick and A. W. Paul (right), 1905.

King Ugyen Wangchuk with soldiers and chief retainers at Punakha, 19th December 1907.

Group at Punakha, 19th December 1907. Standing from left: Capt. Harold Hyslop, Ugyen Dorji, Punakha Dzongpön Palden Wangchuk, Major F. W. Rennick, Thimphu Dzongpön Kunzang Thinley, Deb Zimpön Kunzang Tsering; seated from left: Capt. Campbell, John Claude White, King Ugyen Wangchuk, Paro Pönlop Dawa Penjore.

The installation ceremony of the new king, 17th December 1907. From left: John Claude White, Ugyen Dorji (standing), King Ugyen Wangchuk, Dratsang Khembo.

Sealing the Oath of Allegiance.

Ugyen Wangchuk with Royal Bodyguard, Tongsa, 1905.

Ugyen Wangchuk with senior ministers and officials, Tongsa, 1905.

Ugyen Wangchuk with his family and personal servants at Wangdi Chöling, Bumthang, 1905.

Ugyen Wangchuk with his sister, daughters and niece at Wangdi Chöling, Bumthang, 1905.

"The Lhasa Doctor", Ugyen Wangchuk's personal physician.

formed the customary rough pallelogram, divided into courts.

The first court housed the main citadel eighty feet high and a number of two storeyed blocks for lay officials. The second court was similarly divided by the main durbar hall occupying the whole width and a smaller hall to the east of it. The next court housed 3,000 lamas whose cells were on two sides. There was a large temple in the centre and store rooms beneath.

Their stay in Punakha passed pleasantly. White gave a dinner party attended by Sir Ugyen and the Dzongpöns who so much enjoyed the magic lantern show that by special request Major Rennick gave a second display at the dzong, mostly of slides depicting scenes of Tibet, India and Europe.

The services of the mission's medical assistant were much in demand and on one occasion he had to attend to a convicted murderer who had received the usual punishment of having his right hand cut off. Although the tendons had been severed it had been done in a manner intended to be merciful so that the forearm was not lost.

White and Paul also visited the monasteries of Talo and Norbugang, passing through glades of pear and clematis to reach them. At Talo there were small well-kept two-storeyed houses with carved verandahs and painted façades scattered over the hillside, each with its garden of flowers and trees. There was also a huge temple as well as the residence of the former Dharma Raja. The head lama sent his band to meet the party with attendants bearing oranges for their refreshment. They were led to an embroidered tent where they were given tea and liquor before being shown around. They saw the caskets of the first Shabdung Rimpoche and his most recent successor as well as some beautifully carved pillars and canopies. In describing these White referred to Bhutanese art and workmanship as 'both bold and intricate'. He regretted the present impoverishment of the country and the apparent lack of encouragement for the continuance of these skills.

At the temple of Norbugang the chapel was full of excellent specimens of metal and embroidered and applique work; and three kinds of incense were being manufactured by mixing into a paste finely powdered charcoal, aromatic herbs and rice water.

Back at Punakha the ladies and other relatives of the late Dharma Raja who had entertained the party to lunch, returned the visit and the lamas stayed to dinner. White noted that the Bhutanese were very appreciative of European food and being Buddhists, without any caste problems, regarded it as an honour to be invited to meals and anxious always to return the hospitality. Although the officials were usually abstemious they all took wine. Afterwards gifts were usually given and those most appreciated were models of animals, especially animated ones like the elephant, given to the Tongsa Lama, which waved its tusks and grunted. The Pathan escort put on a display of Khattak dancing and an archery meeting was held for the soldiers.

The day before their departure White and Paul took formal leave of the Deb Raja who showed them special favour by rising to greet them. He sent his thanks to the Viceroy for sending the party and expressed 'the hope that he would continue to favour his little state whose sincere endeavour was to carry out the wishes of the British government'. Leading officials visited the mission's quarters bringing letters for the Viceroy and for senior British officials; and the Thimphu Dzongpön, acting as their spokesman, made a speech. He said that as according to Bhutanese custom letters were always wrapped in a scarf they had therefore selected the whitest of scarves without blemish 'in which to envelop their letter to His Excellency and hoped that its purity would be considered an emblem of their own perfect purity of mind and intention.'

The first camp on their return journey was at Wangdiphodrung where the dzong was built in two sections connected by an enclosed and loopholed bridge and had a more interesting interior than any except Drugyel dzong. White noted that there had been no alteration in the stream since Turner's time 120 years before.

The next day, on a beautiful morning, they followed a bridle path up the right bank of the Tangchu for six miles, passing the summer residence of the Punakha Dzongpön high up above the path and shortly after pitched camp in the middle of a grove of pines and near a lake. White's little Tibetan spaniel, his friend of many journeys in Sikhim, died of a heart attack on the next day's march but their spirits were lifted up again the next day by the sight of snow-capped mountain ranges and lush valleys filled with rhododendrons, oak trees, chestnuts and walnuts, all in their new foliage. Despite the heavy rain that night they remained comfortable on a camp site which had been levelled for their tents and where mats had been laid. Here also a herd of cows had been brought to give them fresh milk.

The next day they had to trudge through thick clay as the rain had ruined the road surface. They met with more rain as well as heavy fog as they crossed the top of the Pele-la at 11,000 feet descending to 9,400 to camp at Rukubji. On the march once more they again passed through strikingly beautiful country but marred by rain and mist. The mules began to tire so that the following day their progress became slower down steep zig zag paths through rocky country leading right to the walls of the dzong at Tongsa. Here they crossed a stone-flagged courtyard through a gateway and on to their camp a few hundred yards away where they were met by retainers with 'gaily caparisoned' ponies and mules although they were hardly necessary as the Punakha Dzongpön had already placed excellent mules at their service. Amidst a salute of guns reverberating through the rocky gorge they emerged from the bridge to be met by minstrels, singers and dancers who ceremoniously ushered them into the camp where Sir Ugyen was waiting to greet them with tea and milk. He sent four picked men to carry Mr. Paul who had suffered from a bad back, although he declined the offer. White, however, was obliged, much against his inclination, to ride up the ladder-like steps to the dzong with specially selected men on either side of him to hold him in the saddle so that he could not fall off, exactly as Pemberton had described.

The Tongsa dzong had suffered in the 1897 earthquake and the upper storeys of the Pönlop's residence had had to be rebuilt. Behind it was the main tower surmounted by a gilded canopy and the usual courts and buildings, including some very fine temples. In the last courtyard was a lofty chapel in which Sir Ugyen was in the process of organising the erection of a gigantic sitting image of the 'coming Buddha. Below the east wall was another building situated in a ravine containing prayer wheels worked by water. There were two sets of these, each axle containing three 'Manis', or cylinders, of prayers, one above the other. As they had not been used for some time White and his companions, 'having nothing better to do, assisted in putting them in order, by clearing out the waterways which had been blocked with stones and rubbish, and hoped 'that it may be placed to our credit as a work of merit'.

Early one morning during their stay at this hospitable place the members of the mission watched the spring ceremony of blessing the rice fields in which the women defending an irrigated upper field were attacked by the men from an unwatered lower one. When, as on this occasion, the women managed to drive the men off, a good season is forecast with increased fertility and enlarged flocks. They also watched some dancing by the lamas whose robes had been presented by Ugyen Wangchuk.

From Tongsa dzong they began the last leg of their journey home, passing through country that changed from narrow gorges to broad valleys with hundreds of yaks in the upper ones and barley, buckwheat and mustard fields in the lower. The substantial nature of the buildings showed that they were entering a prosperous and well governed area and at Gyetsa there was a good solid rest house for travellers. The next day they had a plethora of mules to choose from as the Tongsa Pönlop's nephew and sister had both sent some to augment those already provided by Ugyen Wangchuk himself. They saw his sister's house as well as his own delightful summer house and echoed Dr. Griffith's eulogies on the beauty of the countryside with masses of violet primulas and scarlet rhododendrons. There was a great deal more cultivation than in his time, much of which had begun after the intercine quarrels had ended eighteen years earlier.

Sir Ugyen visited them in camp bringing his sister and two of his daughters as well as the daughter of the Thimphu Dzongpön. They all wore the attractive and distinctive Bhutanese costume of a long piece of cloth woven into coloured stips, draped round the figure and fastened at the shoulder by a silver brooch and confined at the waist by a band of cloth.

White particularly enjoyed the next few days as they were the private guests of Sir Ugyen in his home district and it gave him 'a much deeper insight into the customs of the Bhutanese'. They were shown round his home, built in the customary courtyard style, including a silk factory where girls were weaving silk and cotton fabrics. They also watched an archery contest and their host gave White some books on early Bhutanese history, survivors of a large collection destroyed by fire. His life had been difficult as his wife had died shortly after the birth of their second daughter and he had found solace in the reading of history. He impressed his guest by his unusual interest in general subjects 'both foreign and domestic' and by his great sense of responsibility towards his country. The two men discussed many schemes for improvement and White bitterly regretted that the process of Anglo-Bhutanese co-operation had not begun twenty years earlier, when Paul had first suggested to the government that White should hold the office of Political Officer to Bhutan as well as to Sikhim. During those years there had been wholesale cutting of valuable Bhutanese forests along the disputed boundaries of the duars, presumably by British Indian subjects.

The members of the mission enjoyed themselves for several days being entertained by Ugyen Wangchuk and his family. They visited the ancient temple of Jampai Lhakang and at Kujé Lhakang they saw what was said to be an impression of Padma Sambhava's back which had formed as he reclined against the rock: also his holy water bottle and a weeping cypress that had taken root from his staff. They were entertained by Sir Ugyen's sister at a house-warming to which White responded by holding a magic lantern show and the escort gave a military display. As always White was intensely interested in practical things and returned to the monastery in order to see the carpenters and carvers at work, the latter using tools without handles and the former only dowels and no nails.

When they left after giving the usual presents, although by now the stock was getting low, the family accompanied them to the main bridge where they presented scarves before departing with obvious reluctance. The mission returned to its old campsite at Gyetsa where they were met by 'bevies of songstresses' a custom that appears to have been more prevalent in Pemberton's time. Sir Ugyen who preceeded them, met the party and took them to the dzong where the lamas danced for them 'in gorgeous dresses of every imaginable colour, to the accompaniment of weird tom toms and huge trumpets, flutes and cymbals, which produce a strange and unusual but rather fascinating music of their own'. Continuing their march in pouring rain Sir Ugyen once again rode ahead of them to the next camp in order to greet them on arrival with refreshment. He and White not only held long talks on Bhutanese affairs and new methods of government but also discussed such mundane matters as methods of preserving provisions and the making of the chutneys included in the mission's stores.

At the top of the Pele La pass they took their leave of this remarkable man. The escort, who had acquired a great respect for him, presented arms and gave three cheers. White wrote: 'I think he felt our departure as much as I can honestly say I did and I cannot help repeating myself and saying again that no host could be more courteous, more hospitable and more thoughtful of his guests . . . '

They continued a slippery wet march to their next camp and then had a long haul to Samtengang, seeing new flowers each day including a large white rose, white and mauve irises and a giant lily (*lilium giganticum*). To start with they followed a different route from their outward journey on the right bank of the river until once again having to ascend the Dokyong-la Pass which they found easier this time. Simtokha the Thimphu band and dancers met them and played the three miles to their camp on the wide plain a mile from the dzong making what White called 'a goodly procession with their led and ridden mules and gay trappings, monks on ponies, orderlies in bright uniforms, bands of musicians and dancers and all the rest of our motley following . . . '

At their camp a new wooden house had been erected which had a large room and windows facing away from the prevailing winds. They were welcomed by the Thimphu Dzongpön and other officers at a table decorated with the finest peonies White had ever seen. A cauldron of chang was blessed, a ladle poured over the hands, the sacred flame touched and a series of teapots brought in, each with a different type of tea donated by different officials.

The next day they paid their farewell call on the Deb Raja 'who expressed his gratitude to the Viceroy for 'sending such friends to see him' and trusted that relations between the two countries would be 'as pure as a white scarf with no blot to mar its whiteness and as dissoluble as water and milk when mixed'. They then adjourned to the Thimphu Dzongpön's room for a Bhutanese breakfast of bowls of rice, omelettes, sausages and pork before going on to the courts of the lamas where the Abbot showed them dancing classes in progress where the monks were mastering the intricate steps of religious dances. 'It was very pleasant', wrote White, 'to find the same cordial wishes and expressions of good will repeated by everyone in turn and to be made to feel so thoroughly that our visit was looked on in the light of a compliment to their country, and that everything was thrown open to us, instead of finding obstacles and difficulties in our way'.

On the return march a combination of incessant rain and a damp unhealthy campsite on a flat meadow beside a river resulted in most of the party contracting fever, including White himself. However they continued on their way, entering a narrow gorge which led upwards towards the plains of Tibet bordered by stupendous cliffs formed by horizontal strata of sedimentary rocks, consisting of layers of limestone, sandstone, slate or shale and quartzites. They crossed the Chinchu six times altogether before arriving at the camp. Ascending the Yakle-La (16,800 feet) they found the maps to be hopelessly wrong. After a steep descent they followed the valley for six miles and set up camp at a good spot on a spur with fine views of the Chomolhari glaciers. They stayed there for a couple of days, visiting the ruined dzong where the Bhutanese had had to keep a strong garrison to defend themselves against the Tibetans who had built a fort inside the Bhutanese frontier. The Dzongpön said that now, however, they relied on the British to defend them against the Tibetans. They did a little more exploring and went to a valley enclosed with glaciers where they saw two avalanches and were taken to a flat slab of rock where human corpses were exposed to be eaten by lammegiers and beasts of prey.

The last leg of the unknown part of their return journey lay over the Lingshi La pass: first through a fertile valley and then along a series of fairly easy gradients, each of which brought them to the top of a cliff until they reached an almost precipitous slope up which they zig-zagged with the laden mules and ponies to the Tibetan fort at the summit, of which the Dzongpön had told them. From there a short incline brought them to the top of the pass at 17,000 feet where they had magnificent views over the plains and hills of southern Tibet. Much of the earlier part of their descent was very steep and snow-covered in places. That evening they dined for the last time with the Thimphu Dzongpön from whom the next morning they received scarves before bidding him and the Tongsa Drönyer, who had been with them all the time, a fond farewell. The latter had proved to be 'a most jovial officer, never under any circumstances put out and ever obliging, an adept at archery and all manly games, fond of a glass but never the worse, a real Bhutanese Friar Tuck with a great fund of information'.

From this point onwards they followed their well remembered route to the Chukya military encampment and from thence to Phari and home.

White's next recorded visit to Bhutan, in May 1906, was part of an exploration he had long wanted to make of Eastern Bhutan and part of Tibet. On this occasion he found that the best point of entry was via Gauhati in Assam from whence he trekked up into the hills. In the low-lands on the approach march the mosquitoes were very trying, especially at night, and the plague of horse flies that attacked the mules, oxen and in particular the elephants, of which he had five on this journey, were even worse. With Mr. F.C.W. Dover, the Sikhim Engineer, he reached Dorunga at the foot of the hills, which was almost deserted in summer, in contrast to a winter visit with Sir Ugyen a few months earlier when it was being used as a cold weather mart. On that occasion they had entered the hills a little further to the west and had seen masses of *Cypredium Fairianum* covering the magnesium limestone hills, an orchid of which Sir Joseph Hooker, the great botanist, had sent a specimen to Kew from Sikhim in 1860.

They had a wet and difficult struggle to get to Dewangiri, much of it along the bed of a stream which they only just managed to cross before it became too swollen although the coolies were cut off. One of the elephants bolted and a baggage mule was carried off by a tiger during the night. The party was met by the Tongsa Dzongpön who accompanied them to his residence at Chungkar where they had a good camping ground with views of distant snows. Here White's 'vaccinator', who had accompanied him for this purpose, vaccinated over a hundred people against a small-pox epidemic. Amongst these people he noticed a number of small boys smoking cigarettes, 'which shows that the latest vice has penetrated even into these wilds'.

Their route led them to Denchung where they camped; then over the Yuto La pass at 8,300 feet and on through woods of oak and rhodo-dendron to Tashigang where the dzong was sited between two rivers and contained the usual courtyards and citadels. White was given the Dzongpön's own room but had to ask for the stores of dried mutton and rancid butter to be removed from under the floor. The room was furnished with the skins of several tigers which had been shot the previous year, having wrought much destruction amongst the cattle.

They left Tashigang, where the vaccinator dealt with two hundred people, and took the road towards the small Tibetan state of Tawang from whence trade flowed through Tashigang to the plains. As entry was prohibited into many areas of Tibet they had to follow a long and roundabout route but, as always, White wrote with great interest on everything he saw, whether it was the method of growing stick lac or the construction of suspension bridges made of bamboo and wrought iron chains, water driven prayer wheels or unusual prayer walls. Wherever they halted Mr. Dover dispensed medicines but they wished they had a qualified doctor with them.

Past Tashiyangtse, beside a river full of fish, they journeyed on into the valley from Lhuntsi dzong to Singhi where they were met by the Dzongpön and stayed in a house surrounded by walnut trees. From here onwards their transport problems increased as they encountered swollen rivers whose bridges had been carried away and tracks impassable for animals. They sent the mules and ponies on by a roundabout route and, without much hope of success, set forth on foot. Leaving the Kumchu they branched off from Pemberton's route, going north instead of to Sekang and on to Lhakang dzong, at first through dense jungle and then in more open country from which, when the mist cleared, they were afforded brief glimpses of snow clad hills and glaciers. They managed to cross the Kang-La pass at 16,290 before nightfall, then had a descent of 1,500 feet through snow before crossing a small glacier. Once over the Bod La, 16,290, they were well on their way to the Tibetan border where they found riding mules and ponies sent by Sir Ugyen as well as by the Tibetans. There were also some yaks which had been sent by the Tongsa Dzongpön whose orderlies held on to White each side on the bad patches. At the dzong at Lhakang Sir Ugyen was awaiting them with the Dzongpön and the headman and refreshments of eggs, milk and chang. Their camp had already been pitched for them in a grove of poplars and willows.

They were now across the border and White wrote 'I had hardly expected to receive such a hearty reception in Tibet but everyone vied with one another in trying to make me comfortable and in doing everything they could for me. It was most gratifying and proved beyond dispute that the Tibetans bore no ill will on account of the Lhasa expedition and also that they were genuinely pleased to see me personally'. He thought the only opposition came from the priestly hierarchy and that the common people would welcome British jurisdiction but he deplored the action of the government in London, who instead of sending out hand-picked people had for some unaccountable reason raised insuperable barriers against any Briton who wished to enter the country whilst apparently assisting foreigners to do so. Thus, he wrote, the Tibetans were handed over 'bound hand and foot to the Chinese and all Tibetan officials are now obliged by their virtual masters, the Chinese, to enforce the Chinese traditional policy of exclusion of all Europeans'.

After visiting a number of monasteries and some gold diggings and calling on a Dzongpön who was an old acquaintance from the Lhasa mission White went to the monastery at Lhalung via Tuwa dzong where he was met by Sir Ugyen again, as well as his nephew the abbot, the monks and headmen. During the two days they stayed there White and Ugyen Wangchuk discussed ideas for developing Bhutan. Some years later White wrote 'I often wonder now how he is carrying out all his schemes and wish I had been able to set him a little further on the road towards their accomplishment before my retirement'.

White continued on his way leaving his vaccinator behind as well as his plant collector who was to forward a number of specimens to the botanical gardens in Calcutta. Once over the last pass at nearly 18,000 feet he dropped down towards the plains at Sekang. On the way he had a splendid view of snow-covered hills and the boundary line between Tibet and Bhutan. He noted that all the valleys had once been more densely populated and that there were ruins of old habitations and irrigation channels. The last leg of the journey took him, by way of Nelung to the Phari-Gyantse road to Chumbi and from thence to his Headquarters at Gangtok.

Reporting on political relations, White referred to the comments made by previous British missions, particularly those led by Pemberton and Eden, and disagreed, amongst other things, with their description of the

Bhutanese as filthy in their habits and drunkards. He had found them to be courteous, sober and clean. He also made the interesting and probably valid point that the real reason for the long history of Anglo-Bhutanese discord over the frontier was probably because of Bhutanese dread of fever in the lower hills where only lesser officials were normally sent. Consequently all sorts of people of doubtful character were allowed to settle there, where they could indulge in cattle rustling and do pretty much as they pleased. Sir Ugyen had agreed to send more officials to these areas because of the big influx of 'Paharias': (a general term for hill dwellers), including a good many undesirables fleeing from British justice. 'In a very few years' he wrote, 'the whole of the outer hills will be settled with Nepalese and it will require a good deal of tact and firmness on the part of the Bhutan authorities to keep them under proper control.'

A major problem on the border was provided by shops where vile liquor was sold and the British Commissioner at Rajshahi in Bengal (now in Bangladesh) had suggested a three mile prohibited zone on either side of the border. The Tongsa Pönlop and the council had immediately ordered the removal of eight shops within a mile of the border. White inspected the area and noted that a number of shops were closed, others moved and some allowed to continue, according to local circumstances.

White regretted that he had only been concerned with Bhutanese affairs for a comparatively short time as he could have saved an unnecessary loss of revenue from the seven new British-Indian tea gardens along the border which were not required to pay anything to the Bhutanese government who also received nothing from the sale of timber and hardwood. In connection with these and other issues of the economy White commented that Ugyen's visit to India had 'opened his eyes. He no longer looks upon the plains as absolutely deadly and to be avoided at all costs.' It was White's view, now shared by Ugyen Wangchuk, that cultivation almost everywhere in Bhutan could be much increased, especially as the roads were well aligned and could be developed in order to increase trade with Bengal which at that time was insignificant. Most of the rice was being sent to Tibet.

In December 1907 White proposed an amendment to clause 8 of the treaty by which disputes with Sikhim and Cooch Behar had to be referred to the British, to include 'any other neighbouring states', so that disputes with Tibet could also be settled by Britain. This he thought to be necessary in view of the proposed British withdrawal from the Chumbi valley in 1908 as the British government had disavowed Younghusband's treaty clause demanding a much longer occupation. Unless Britain took some action the Chinese would claim to settle the inevitable disputes that would then arise between the Bhutanese and Tibetans.

He also suggested that in any consideration of a possible new treaty there should be articles concerning the opening and maintaining of roads, the denial of access to hostile powers wishing to traverse the country or the cession of land to any other power; and military forces to be placed at British disposal on the grounds that it was 'a matter of the utmost importance to exclude Chinese influence on this side of the Himalayas'. White was always being fed with rumours about Chinese intruders into Bhutan and a few months later he heard that a Chinese representative had gone there with twenty soldiers and a Tibetan doctor. The following year Captain W.L. Campbell, the British Trade Agent to Yatung, reported rumours of a Chinese mission being prepared.

The Amban at Lhasa had been reported as having said that Bhutan was the southern gateway of the Chinese empire and that he would send an officer there to report on the situation; and the Popon, the Chinese official at Pipi Tang in the Chumbi valley, had ordered the Bhutanese Pönlops to await his arrival at the borders of their districts to conduct him through them. He had apparently addressed them rudely in a letter 'devoid of honorific terms' and 'couched in language we would employ to village headmen'. Ugyen Kazi, the Bhutanese representative had told Campbell that Chinese claims were a fiction, that they had given no assistance to Bhutan in the war with Britain and that Bhutan had never paid any tribute. He assured Campbell that there was absolutely no Bhutanese commitment to the Chinese. All they had ever been given was a seal which had been put in a box and never used, a hat with an imitation coral button (the insignia of an official in the second rank) and a peacock's feather, now half eaten by insects. Campbell might have pointed out that the very acceptance of these things must surely have represented, at least, a sort of insurance policy; and Ugyen Kazi conveniently forgot to mention the annual gifts that had for centuries been received from the Emperor and the returning caravan bearing tribute that had in fact been customary until quite recently.

Bhutanese and British were not alone in playing the game of selective omission when it suited them and playing on the fears of others; or presenting arguments likely to appeal to current prejudices. The Chinese were past-masters at it. When the British arrived in Lhasa in 1904 Chinese stock was at its lowest but first by supporting the British and then by posing as champions of the Tibetans, responsible for the British withdrawal from the Chumbi valley, they had regained a powerful position by this time. The Russians too were dab hands at it, playing on British sensitivities about the security of India and the Suez Canal so that the Foreign Office, the India Office and the Viceroy's Council rarely spoke with one voice.

As late as 1910, the year when the Imperial Chinese empire was replaced by the republic of Dr. Sun Yat Sen, the Viceroy was cabling anxiously about the reported instances of Chinese attempts to interfere in Bhutan because of their annoyance at the Dalai Lama's supposed intentions to travel through Bhutan to India after Chinese troops had entered Tibet. In fact, the Dalai Lama travelled through Chumbi to Kalimpong and stayed with Ugyen Kazi for a week. Apparently the Chinese had told people in Yatung that Bhutan was to be entered by Chinese soldiers and the Amban had proclaimed that Chinese currency must circulate. The Viceroy had made it clear that Britain was in charge of Bhutan's external affairs and would not permit this.

However Bhutan was never really threatened externally, possibly because of the increasing stability of the country under Ugyen Wangchuk who was now to be installed as 'hereditary Maharaja and chief ruler of Bhutan'. Reporting this to be the first such occasion in Bhutanese history, White considered this to be 'a good omen for the future of Bhutan . . . I need hardly point out the advantages to us that such a change means'. He enclosed a letter from Sir Ugyen saying that he had accepted his people's offer in the reliance on the government of India's support. In other words he had had the wisdom to foresee, before others did, that the future lay with Britain, just as his descendants were to see, at the time of Indian independence, that the best prospects for Bhutan's modernisation and security lay, for the foreseeable future, with the new India.

White recommended that the 'Maharaja' should be accorded a salute of fifteen guns, as accorded to the Maharaja of Sikhim. This was no arcane triviality but a very real issue at the time. A delicate relationship had been built up between Britain, known as 'the Paramount Power', and the Indian Princes who still ruled over half the sub-continent. Their states came in all shapes and sizes and numbered 565 in all, varying from Hyderabad with over 80,000 square miles to tiny ones with less than a square mile. Consequently they were divided by the British, who had treaty arrangements with all of them and permanent Residents in the larger ones, into three divisions. The first division included all the 'salute states' of which two were accorded twenty one guns, six had nineteen, thirteen had seventeen and seventeen were given salutes of fifteen guns. Thirty states were saluted with thirteen guns and eleven had nine. The rulers of these states were referred to as Maharajas except for those with only eleven or nine guns who were Rajas. This pecking order was zealously guarded and taken with the utmost seriousness both by the British and the states themselves. White's recommendation, the use of the title 'Maharaja' and the number of guns, are all indications that at any rate some of the British at that time regarded Bhutan in much the same category as the other princely states of the sub-continent.

Agreement was given for White to attend the installation ceremony but not to his suggestion that the opportunity should be taken to enter into a new treaty. The faith of Bhutan's ruler in the British and the Government of India was not yet fully reciprocated and White was told that there was no need to change the treaty until the new government had proved its worth.

On November 27th 1907 White therefore set out from Gangtok on his second official visit to Bhutan, again accompanied by Major Rennick, as well as by Mr. Wilton of the consular service. Captain W.L. Campbell, the assistant political officer, went on ahead to Chumbi to make the arrangements and the party was joined by Captain H.H.G. Hyslop, by special request of Sir Ugyen who had already met him, and an escort of twenty five men of the 62nd Punjabis under the command of a V.C.O. (Viceroy's Commissioned Officer). There were also three pipers, two drummers and a hospital assistant.

On Thursday 5th December, they set forth from Phari on a fine sunny morning and climbed up to the pass at Tremo La where the Bhutanese frontier was crossed. They sheltered in a valley where they received messages of welcome from Sir Ugyen and were met by the Dzongpön's band of drums, gongs and cymbals. The next stretch was through a rocky gorge where the fifteen stone Rennick was carried on the back of a Bhutanese orderly helped by two or three others on either side. On the far side they were met by attendants with mules and ponies which White again described as 'gaily caparisoned'. They discovered that the reins were only meant for ornament and that the animals were led by their grooms who had to drag them over a very difficult road on which it was amazing how they managed to retain their footing. At last after this uncomfortable progression they reached a beautiful spot where they camped in a grove of larch and spruce, with magnificent views.

With their new Bhutanese transport, they left camp to the strains of the escort's pipes, of whose playing Hyslop, a Scot, was very critical. After an attractive march through pine forests to Drugyel dzong on the right bank of the Pa Chu they reached the finest camp site of all where the walls of the guest room were hung with arrows, shields, old guns, saddle cloths and curious bridles. After a meal of omelettes, spring onions, walnuts, milk and warm chang they walked over to their tents which had already been pitched for them. Although it had been a warm day they were glad to sit round a fire in the evening. They passed two days in this sylvan place, taking photographs, pheasant shooting and going to Taktsang monastery, one of the holiest in the country. It was located on an almost perpendicular hillside entailing a very steep climb before they could reach the temple, built in a crevice in a perpendicular rock face. Its gilded canopies surmounted shingle roofs above a top storey of madder red and a lower storey of grey stone. Every natural feature had been made the most of including a narrow path where a missed footing would result in a fall of a thousand feet. A rope of coloured prayer flags spanned a gorge and in a cave where Guru Rimpoche was said to have lived was the most holy of all the shrines filled with small images of Buddha in copper gilt, each one seated on a lotus. There were other temples, each with Buddhas, holy springs, and altars where incense burned and butter lamps shone. In the centre of the gorge was a tiny shrine on a ledge reached by climbing a vertical notched pole eighty foot high. White and his companions refrained from doing this but instead went on to another monastery perched on a spur from where they could see similar projecting rocks, each with its shrine or temple.

Captain Campbell, who had not visited Bhutan before, was fascinated to note how different the people were from the Tibetans in the Chumbi valley where he was stationed. They were shorter but sturdier, with cropped hair and round faces. He also observed that the climate was milder than in the Chumbi valley.

The following day they went on down the valley where they were met by Ugyen Kazi, or go give him his full title, Rai Ugyen Kazi Bahadur, still the Bhutanese Agent in India, and later when they reached Paro, by the Pönlop. They were surprised to find that the dzong had been burnt down since their last visit and although the ruins were still smouldering rebuilding had already begun. They were told that the whole kingdom was contributing either in cash or with labour.

In the afternoon Campbell explored the ruins of the dzong. He thought that the bridge was the finest in Bhutan, of the usual cantilever type but more substantial and elaborate than the others and constructed of enormous beams which 'must have exercised all the ingenuity of the Bhutanese to get into position'. The approaches were guarded by double-storeyed gatehouses through which the roadway passes which served to balance the cantilever. Campbell thought that 'the roadway of the actual bridge resembles in a remarkable degree the covered bridge at Lucerne'. He looked up instinctively for the pictures that were a feature of that bridge and saw instead 'the ever-repeated 'om mani padme hum' painted on both sides of the cross beams of the roof.

The next day, 10th December, Campbell called on the Pönlop at his private house, for like all Dzongpöns, who were obliged to live in the dzongs where women were forbidden entry, he had a house near the dzong where in fact, he spent most of his time. He passed through an anteroom crowded with armed retainers and was received in an inner room by the Pönlop, 'an old man with tired eyes', only about five foot tall and with 'a small and curious shaped head'. He also met the Pönlop's sixteen year old son and his bride of two days.

From then on they were able to make fairly swift progress as they were mounted on the Pönlop's fresh animals and once again camped in the grove of weeping cypresses they had known on the earlier visit. White went down with fever and it was another two days before they could go on their way, riding up the valley towards Punakha. From the pass of Dokyong La they were able to see range after range of snow capped peaks with Chomolhari on the left. They camped at Chalimaphe at the foot of a giant cedar, 250 feet high and 52 feet round the trunk at the base. They spent a whole day there and Campbell took the opportunity to visit Tashichodzong, the summer capital, up the valley of the Wang Chu. He was as impressed as Turner and his companions had been and thought it looked more like a palace than a fort. The building had been burnt down more than once and traces of successive rebuilding were visible on the exterior walls. Otherwise the only new feature, not seen by earlier visitors, was a new tower put up the previous year.

On 14th December they left Chalimaphe on a steep and narrow path repeatedly crossing and recrossing the river and from the top of a pass obtained superb views of the snowy mountains which divide Bhutan from Tibet to the north, including the snow covered mass of Kulukangri and further west a line of glittering peaks leading to the Chomolhari range. Campbell was unable to obtain satisfactory photographs of the snow because of the thick growth of rhododendrons and oaks on the Punakha side of the pass.

Four miles out of Punakha, they were met by a deputation from the Tongsa Pönlop, dressed in coats of Chinese brocade in every hue and bearing scarves of welcome, baskets of fruit, and wicker-covered bamboo containers of murwa and chang. There were also five or six mules with decorated trappings, a band dressed in green and two trumpeters in red. As the dzong came into view they were joined by more people and guns were fired in salute. The procession was an impressive sight with the pipes and drums leading the Punjabis, followed by twenty led mules with brightly coloured saddle cloths, then the Tongsa Pönlop's bodyguard of twenty men in silks and brocades, each with a yellow scarf, who preceded the band, and dancers, all twisting and turning. Then came White and his party, followed by orderlies and servants, mounted and in scarlet uniforms. As they closed into single file across the bridge through the corner of the dzong to the ground they had occupied in 1905, minute guns were fired and everywhere large crowds watched the procession.

The Tongsa Pönlop, (still Ugyen Wangchuk's official designation until after the installation) and his council received them at the entrance to the camp and conducted them up a path covered with red cloth between banks of flowers and shrubs in pots to the mess house that had been built for them. The Paro Pönlop, the Thimphu Dzongpön and other officials were waiting there in order to present scarves to each member of the mission and after offering them refreshment Sir Ugyen welcomed each one individually to Bhutan.

The comfortable camp bore 'evident traces of the impressions they (i.e. the Bhutanese) had brought back from their Calcutta visit for the paths were edged with pot plants and red cloth was laid down . . . ' Each of the senior members of the mission had a little low roofed wooden house with one room and a bathroom and on top of each flapped a line of coloured prayer flags. The walls had windows shaped like port holes for which shutters took the place of glass. They contained no furniture beyond the officer's own camp kit but the mess house had a table and wooden chairs all made without nails in the traditional way. The whole camp was enclosed in a neat rectangle.

The following morning, December 17th – a day when, according to Campbell, 'The Magna Carta of Bhutan would be signed' – at 10 o'clock precisely the procession set forth for the dzong; dressed in their best uniforms preceded by the pipers playing 'Highland Laddie' followed by White's orderlies in Sikhimese dress and the escort of 62nd Punjabis in their ceremonial uniforms. They were received by the Tongsa Pönlop and Council at the entrance to the main gateway and conducted to the hall which was decorated with banners and religious picture scrolls embroidered in silk. The Tongsa Pönlop sat on a central throne with White on his right and the Lama Khembo on the left. The other members of the mission sat on the right of the aisle with members of the council just below them. On the left was the Tango Lama, brother of the late Dharma Raja and himself an incarnation, and other lamas wearing robes of office and brocade hats; and in the gallery was a band of lama musicians. White's orderlies and the escort lined up behind his seat and those of the other officers. At the far end of the room was an altar covered with lighted silver butter lamps facing Sir Ugyen who wore a robe of blue brocade with the star and ribbon of the K.C.I.E. and a scarlet shawl.

The proceedings opened with the formal presentation of durbar gifts from the Government of India beginning with a ceremonial scarf, followed by similar presentations from the head Abbot and then by the lamas taking off their mitres and silken copes, advancing and twice prostrating themselves. This was done also by the Councillors, the Dzongpöns in a body and all the others, most of them presenting rolls of cloth surmounted by scarves although the presents also included a bag of gold dust and five bags of silver coins. The mission was then given scarves, first by the Tongsa Pönlop and then by the council.

After this fairly lengthy business a procession of lamas entered the hall bearing tea pots and vessels of copper and gold and silver for the tea drinking ceremony. Three kinds of tea, an infusion of wild yams, butter soup coloured with saffron, and ordinary Tibetan tea, as well as rice and pan were each offered in turn followed by a long grace intoned by one of the lamas. The head clerk to the council then read out from a parchment scroll the oath of allegiance to the new 'Maharaja' and the great seal of the Dharma Raja was fixed to the document. This was a slow process watched intently by everyone as the paper was first dampened and then the huge five inch square seal was painted over with vermilion before an impression was taken.

Then in turn the members of the council, the Lamas, Dzongpöns and high officials each affixed their seals and impressions in black. The main part of the document read: 'We, the undersigned abbots, lopons and the whole body of the lamas, the state councillors, the chiolahs of the different districts, with all the subjects, having discussed, and unanimously agreed to elect Sir Ugyen Wangchuk, Tongsa Pönlop, prime minister of Bhutan, as hereditary Maharaja of this state, having installed him in open durbar on the golden throne on this thirteenth day of the eleventh month of Sa-Tel year, corresponding to the 17th December 1907, at Paunakha-phodey, we now declare our allegiance to him and his heirs and with the unchanging mind undertake to serve him and his heirs loyally and faithfully to the best of our ability. Should anyone not abide by this contract by saying this and that, he shall altogether be turned out of our company. In witness thereto we affix our seals . . . '

Two copies of the document were prepared, signed and sealed. White then rose and handed Sir Ugyen the Viceroy's 'Kharita', the recognition of status which confirmed Indian princes as officially accepted rulers of their kingdoms in the eyes of the 'Paramount Power', followed by a short speech of congratulation in which he said: 'I have known Bhutan for many years; and with an intimate knowledge of the political questions relating thereto, I am convinced you have taken a wise step in thus consolidating the administration of the state. Sir Ugyen has been my friend for many years and you could not have made a better choice. His integrity, uprightness and firmness of character commend him to everyone and his accession to the Maharajaship is not only a gain to Bhutan but is of great advantage to the British government who will henceforth have a settled government with a man of strong character to negotiate with'.

The other members of the British mission then congratulated Sir Ugyen on becoming King of Bhutan ('King is a more appropriate translation of the Tibetan 'Gyelpo' than 'Maharaja') and presented him with white scarves, before they all moved on to the King's apartments for refreshments.

The next morning The King visited White and was given presents for his family, including broadcloth, silk and cotton piece goods, tools cutlery, sewing machines and mechanical toys. The Councillors, who visited in the afternoon also received presents, the Thimphu Dzongpön obtaining a galvanic battery that had given as much pleasure as a similar gift during Turner's mission in 1783.

They spent a few more days in Punakha, during which time White handed over the subsidy of 50,000 rupees, which by the treaty of 1866 the Government of India paid annually in return for the duars. He also attended a private Council meeting, at the King's request and as a personal friend.

During these days, White, Campbell and Hyslop visited the Punakha dzong and called on the head Abbot who was then the supreme head of the church in the absence of a Dharma Raja, for whom no incarnation had yet been discovered; and Hyslop and Campbell visited other dzongs in the neighbourhood. On the 22nd December the Thimphu Dzongpön sent the mission a complimentary lunch. Campbell didn't think much of the 'huge dish of rice flanked by two bowls, one of eggs cooked in butter and flavoured with chillies and onions and the other containing a kind of fish stew' and wrote rather disdainfully, 'The Bhutanese have practically no idea of cooking; and Chinese notions which have spread in Tibet to a considerable extent do not appear to have reached them.' He thought a little better of the next course of pork, liver and black sausages several feet long which were excellent eating once their unprepossing appearance was forgotten, and enjoyed the chang and rakshi, a yellow spirit which he found to resemble Chinese rice wine.

The next day they visited the Talo monastery, the residence of the Dharma Rajas, incarnations of Shabdrung Rimpoche: they were met by the Tango Lama who lived there, and was, according to Campbell, the friendliest person he had met in Bhutan. The principal temple was at the top of the building and was reached by the usual breakneck ladders. Inside, the whole of one wall was occupied by an altar placed in front of a row of gods and goddesses in brass and silver. The usual carved woodwork was here replaced by beaten brasswork, even the pillars being covered in metal. The walls were hung with sacred scrolls of appliquéd and embroidered brocade and Campbell thought it the best temple he had seen in Bhutan. They were even permitted to view the empty private apartments awaiting the next Dharma Raja. The last incarnation had been dead for three years and the sitting room bore no trace of his personality although in one corner a faded cushion and a small table marked the spot where the holy man used to sit.

On Christmas day White took photographs of the King and his council as well as distributing 'doles' to the poor of the neighbourhood and that evening he gave a dinner party for the King and council followed by a magic lantern show. As a highly accomplished amateur photographer, White took every opportunity to record Bhutan, its landscapes, architecture and people, as well as the formal state occasions with the King and his ministers. The finest of his and Captain Hyslop's photographs from their private albums have been selected to illustrate this book.

The next day the mission broke up, Campbell going back to Chumbi with the escort and Rennick and Hyslop to India via Buxa. White stayed on for a few days to discuss schemes for development with the King, including projects for education, population, trade, roads, minerals and the possible cultivation of tea, for all of which the greatest restraint was the lack of funds.

White was deeply moved when he took a final farewell of the country he had grown to love and of its ruler who had become such a good personal friend. The King walked with him for four miles until they halted and talked for a couple of hours under the shade of a large pine tree, once again planning beneficial developments, until they had to bid each other goodbye.

White returned by way of Paro and then followed a hitherto unknown route southwards passing Bité dzong to Jaigaon (near the modern border town of Phuntsholing) and then westwards along the boundary looking for land which might be suitable for tea growing on the Bhutanese side as well as for copper deposits. He then turned eastwards to look at a coal mine on the northern slopes of the Himalayas which were also the haunt of every kind of wild animal, including elephant, rhino, tigers, leopard, bison, python, sambur and cheetah.

White retired shortly afterwards. When he and his wife left the home they had built in Sikhim with its English rose garden, they were accompanied by the Maharaja and Maharani; and almost the entire population turned out to bid them farewell. At Gangtok two coolie loads of letters were received from Ugyen Wangchuk, his family and senior Bhutanese officials. Of all the Britons who went to Bhutan he was the most perceptive and the most important. The part he played in identifying Sir Ugyen Wangchuk as a future leader of a united country after years of civil strife, and of ensuring the support of the British government, will never fully be known although it must have been considerable. The Government of India, ever suspicious of the intentions of Russia to the north west and wary of the Chinese in and beyond Tibet, wanted nothing better than a stable and well ordered state in Bhutan and welcomed the opportunity to encourage the development of a strong hereditary kingdom similar to those of the Princes and Maharajas with whom it was accustomed to deal. Certainly Ugyen Wangchuk had impressed all the British officers with whom he had come in contact on the Tibetan expedition and during the tour of India by Bhutanese and Sikhimese notables; but it was the rapport established with White which led to the development of firm friendship between Britain and Bhutan, replacing a century of abrasive relations.

Even without the knowledge of British support Ugyen Wangchuk's character and authority were such that sooner or later Bhutan would have become a united kingdom. Nevertheless, the support was welcomed not only by the king but by most leading Bhutanese as a bastion against any further Tibetan or Chinese incursions and as a source of financial and technical aid. This, alas, was never forthcoming on anything like the scale that Ugyen Wangchuk and White had planned and it was not for another forty years when the newly independent Government of India took over the British role that the sort of assistance they had envisaged was unstintingly given.

CHAPTER EIGHT
Political Officers and Bhutan 1910–1947

According to Charles Allen and Sharada Dwivedi in their fascinating book *Lives of the Indian Princes*, the tiny Indian Political service of less than 130, drawn from military officers and civilian administrators, had the responsibility for maintaining relations between the Viceroy from whose political department they took their orders, and the states. Some of these such as Hyderabad had First Class Residents. Others, grouped together, had Second Class Residents with subordinate Political Agents as well as junior Political Officers working as Secretaries, Under Secretaries and Assistant Political Agents. In their *Manual of Instructions to Officers at the Foreign and Political Department*, (1924) from the experience of historical precedent, they were told that their first duty was to cultivate direct, friendly, personal relations with the Ruling Kings and chiefs and thereafter to 'leave well alone; the best work of a Political Officer is very often what has been left undone'. His task was not to interfere except when there were real instances of misrule to the detriment of the people. Although there were exceptions most of them were remarkable men whose legacy lingers on.

Bhutan had no Resident and contact was maintained from the time of Paul and White onwards by the Political Officers in Sikhim who followed the admirable precepts of their service about not interfering although all of them wanted Britain to do more to assist Bhutan's development. This chapter is largely devoted to the pressures they exerted and the limited successes they achieved. Most of them managed to make at least one visit to Bhutan but all wrote annual reports on the country and its relations with Britain, from 1912 until 1947.

In February 1908, just before going home to retire, White had once again taken up the issue of a new treaty, urging an increased subsidy and assistance towards the development of natural resources. If these were not forthcoming 'the inevitable result will be to drive her (Bhutan) into the arms of the Chinese . . . already Mr. Chang (the Chinese Agent in Sikhim) is attempting to make a coalition of Eastern hill states against us'. It is difficult to judge how far White's use of the current bogey was based on reality and to what extent he himself believed it.

He was not alone in this for practically all the British Political Officers and Trade Agents on the Sikhim, Tibet and Bhutan frontiers used the fear of either Chinese or Russian expansion to support their claims for aid to Bhutan in the knowledge that issues were judged in Calcutta in the international Asian context. In most cases, certainly in White's, they themselves supported Bhutan for more intrinsic and praiseworthy reasons but knew that the purely national needs of a poor country would cut little ice in Calcutta and even less in London.

The new King himself wrote to the Viceroy to seek British help for the development of natural resources, requesting the help of 'European gentlemen to open tea gardens, to work gold, silver, copper, iron and coal mines if any be found, and to open rubber plantations . . . ' He also asked for assistance in constructing a trade route to the frontier. Almost certainly he and White, with whom he had often discussed these matters, had colluded in this.

Later that year, the new Political Officer, C.A. Bell, who had been the Kalimpong settlement officer (p.140) in a résumé of British relations with China, Tibet and Bhutan, wrote: 'our policy with regard to Bhutan should be to show her all the friendliness we can and if opportunity offers, to make a brief treaty with her so as to enable us to control her foreign relations while leaving her absolute freedom in her internal affairs. This will enable us to keep Chinese agents, Chinese troops and Chinese influence generally out of the country . . .'

He considered that there was no need to consult with China or send a copy of any treaty as Britain had never recognised Chinese claims to sovereignty. These had only been based on the fact that Bhutan still sent annual tribute to Tibet which was subordinate to the Chinese government. The Bhutanese claimed that these gifts were merely spiritual offerings to the Dalai Lama. Both the Bhutanese and the British conveniently forgot the annual tribute that used to be sent to China direct or the references to Chinese protection made to the early British missions.

Bell also reported that there was a great change of attitude towards Britain since the Tibet mission and the cordial personal relations established then and on White's subsequent journeys. His continuance of the pressure begun by White began to pay off. A letter to Lord Morley, the Secretary of State, signed by Kitchener and six members of the Council, as well as by Lord Minto the Viceroy, referred to their anxieties about the Chinese activities in Tibet where their troops had been reinforced, the Lhasa garrison increased and the Tibetan army re-trained with instructors from China and Japan who had supplied consignments of rifles and ammunition. 'It is clear that the status quo in this part of the frontier has been materially altered,' they wrote, referring to a recent speech by a Chinese official who had rather colourfully described China, Tibet, Nepal, Sikhim and Bhutan as the molar teeth side by side in a man's head. 'The time has come', the letter continued, 'to frustrate the evident designs of China on Bhutan and local conditions are favourable for a blocking policy'. They concluded that 'the increase of the subsidy is desirable and we should not resist the declared wishes of the Maharaja to open up his country for development by roads and the investment of outside capital provided that the capital is of British or British-Indian origin and that the process of development is gradual . . . ' It was acknowledged that there were risks in the development of a backward state on India's borders and the provincial governments of East Bengal and Assam were not keen on an extension of tea gardens on the grounds that clearance of forests and denuding the banks of streams would lead to flooding within their states. They were also apprehensive about the inevitable influx of Nepalese immigrants. Nevertheless the Government of India considered that any risks were justified if Bhutan's external relations could be secured by treaty. It was recommended therefore that Bell should be empowered to enter into secret negotiations with the King . . . 'these measures will adequately secure our position on the north east frontier at a comparatively small cost . . . '

After a long distance consultation between Culcutta, the India Office, the Foreign Office and the British representatives in Peking, it was agreed that a new treaty should be proposed by which in return for control over foreign affairs Britain would increase the subsidy and help to develop natural resources.

Towards the end of 1909 Bell began making his preparations to go to Punakha and asked if he could take 100,000 rupees with him to hand over on the spot as an impressive gesture of good will if the proposed treaty alterations were accepted by the Bhutanese. The money was to be packed securely in boxes each holding 2,000. 'The actual presence of the money will stimulate them to agree to our terms', he wrote. In the unchanging tradition of bureaucracy he was permitted only to take half this sum, the rest to be paid only if the treaty was signed. Bell protested strongly, 'Bhutan is in urgent need of money and it is largely this consideration which will influence them to accept the sacrifice of their independence,' he wrote, and once again raised the Chinese bogey to frighten his masters. Speed was essential for as soon as the Chinese heard of what was in the wind 'they will do their utmost to frustrate the negotiations'. As so often happens in bureaucracies, where the initial stonewalling is done by uncommitted middle ranking officials interested only in safe-guarding their own positions, pressure from the field in the end won the day. The acid little minutes in the Secretariat files commenting on the tendency of officers in the field, especially in Sikhim and Bhutan to identify themselves too enthusiastically with the needs of the people of those countries and to produce specious arguments designed to appeal to the Secretariat's current preoccupations in support of their favourite projects, are all too familiar.

Bell submitted a draft treaty which was approved although the usual central government wariness asserted itself when the proposed clauses subjecting it to ratifications by the Viceroy and Council and the Maharaja's Council were deleted. The treaty was to be solely between Bell and Ugyen Wangchuk leaving the Government of India and the British cabinet free to disavow it as they had with sections of Younghusband's treaty. Bell again protested and in the end was permitted to use his discretion if he thought that additional signatures would increase the treaty's validity.

Accompanied by Captain Robert Kennedy, he at last set forth in January 1910 and wrote from his first camp just across the border to say that he had prepared the ground by having a preliminary meeting in Darjeeling with Ugyen Dorji who had taken a draft in English and Tibetan to the King.

Describing his journey, Bell wrote: 'We marched rapidly to avoid Chinese interference . . . and interference which was dreaded by Pemberton in 1835 . . . If the Chinese had succeeded in intervening and in preventing the Bhutanese from signing the treaty . . . it would have ensured Chinese control over this country. We were in fact playing for high stakes and it was therefore essential that I should make as sure as possible of my ground before starting into Bhutan . . . '

Three marches from the capital he learnt that a party of Chinese traders from the Chumbi valley had arrived and he thought that there was 'very little doubt that they were secret service men employed by Mr. Cheung, the commissioner of Chinese customs at Yatung . . . '

There is as little real evidence of a serious Chinese threat as there had been of a Russian one towards Tibet before the Younghusband expedition which, on reaching Lhasa, found that the stories of Russian arms and troops were quite without foundation. How far Bell and the other Political Officers believed in the threat themselves or how far it just suited their purposes to appear to do so it is difficult to tell. In all probability they did believe it up to a point for the British on the frontier as well as in the Secretariat were by then obsessed with the intricacies of the 'Great Game'.

On arrival at Punakha Bell found that the King 'had done his work very well'. The whole council, including the Paro Pönlop had assembled and the intitial scruples of some council members opposed to the surrender of foreign policy control, had been overcome. On the 8th January 1910 the treaty was signed in the marquee in the compound of Bell's camp, with Bell and his assistant, Kennedy, in full uniform. It was 'first explained to the Maharaja in the presence of the Council that he must not enter into any agreement with the authorities of foreign states without the assent of the British government and that he must not, without the consent of the British government, permit agents or representatives of foreign powers to reside in Bhutan, or part with land to the authorities, representatives or officials of any foreign state. These conditions he accepted in their entirety'. The treaty was signed with the Dharma Raja's large red square seal, placed on all documents of major importance, as well as the King's own seal and those of council members entitled to have their own seals and, at Bell's insistence, the seal of the monk body. 'Even if anything untoward happens to the Maharaja and his family', he wrote, 'there will be no getting round so completely sealed a document'. He had insisted on this as all his experience in frontier districts had taught him that 'chiefs are always ready to back out of agreements to which they are not finally committed'.

By one o'clock the signing and sealing were finished and, according to Bell, Bhutan was then 'incorporated in the British empire'. Had this view been fully accepted in Calcutta, Delhi and London, Bhutan might have fared better than she did and might have benefited from the practical assistance offered to some of the Princely states. On the other hand she might then have gone the same way as Sikhim when the state was taken over by the Republic of India. The muddled thinking over her status, apparent in many of the Government of India's files right up to the time of Indian independence, may in the end have been for the best.

Ugyen Wangchuk told Bell that he would also at all times provide whatever assistance the Government of India might ask of him and offered to make land available for the residence of any British official to be stationed in Bhutan, thanking him for the grant of land at Kalimpong made available for a Bhutanese Agent and for the British agreement to Bhutanese use of the Calcutta mint for making a new die for copper coins.

In forwarding these comments Bell recapitulated the advantages that had been gained by the treaty at a time when British prestige had fallen because of their withdrawal from the Chumbi valley which the Chinese were claiming as a victory and there had been a danger of Bhutanese rejection of the treaty's terms for fear of China. 'By obtaining this control', he wrote, 'over the external relations of Bhutan we have removed the Chinese menace for 220 miles of a very vulnerable frontier'. If Chinese troops had been sent to Bhutan 'the tea gardens and villages on 300 miles of border country would have been untenable . . . ' He thought there had been a real danger of Chinese colonisation as was happening in the south east corner of Tibet. There could now be a great increase in trade and Britain could safely accept Bhutan's invitation to exploit the forests and mines of the lower hills. Reference of disputes with Cooch Behar and Sikhim to the British goverment was now obligatory.

Back at Gangtok a month later Bell wrote to say that the Chinese must by then have heard about the treaty for despite the attempts at secrecy Bhutanese officials had been consulted about the auspiciousness of dates for the signing, some of whom may have responded to the advances of Chinese spies. The size of the meeting, the large number of boxes containing money and the supplies of arms and ammunition (taken to the King at his request) must all have given the game away even if the

Chinese hadn't already been told by the Paro Pönlop who was in frequent correspondence with them. Bell thought that the treaty should therefore be made public, otherwise the Tibetans and Bhutanese as well as the Chinese would think that the British were afraid to announce it because they were unable to enforce it. There were rumours of a proposed visit by a Chinese official and the King had asked what he should do. Bell had told him that any letter from the Chinese should be sent to him by Ugyen Dorji for his advice on how to respond. The Foreign and India Offices agreed and the treaty was officially proclaimed; although after subsequent statements by the Chinese in the next two years some officials wondered if, in fact, they had ever been directly informed.

In common with most of his predecessors Bell kept a diary and although this added nothing to what was already known geographically about Bhutan there are some interesting observations. He noted that as soon as he had crossed the border all cultivation virtually ceased as the area was sparsely populated. (White had already remarked how the Bhutanese disliked living at low altitudes and dreaded the dense and dripping forests). 'By comparison with Kalimpong and Sikhim this part of the country could support 150 persons to the square mile. At present it can be only 20 or 30'. The road from Bahsa to Chuka had been examined by Mr. Dover, the former State Engineer from Sikhim, who had estimated a cost of 55,000 rupees to make it mule-worthy.

Bell wrote glowingly of the hospitality he had received, being met by officials and bands wherever he went and by the King and Council at the entrance to the mission's camp where they walked along a red carpet bordered by pot plants to the same little bungalows used by White's party. He reported that the King had struck him as being a capable ruler and very friendly towards Britain. He was trying to secure the safety of the state by appointing to all the principal posts the members of his family and their supporters. Even in the eastern region all the main posts seemed to be held by people from the King's family who came from the centre. Nevertheless, and perhaps in the circumstances hardly surprisingly, the Paro Pönlop was as hostile to Britain as when Bell had first encountered him in 1904 when making the Amo Chu road survey. 'He is the leading chief in Bhutan and his revenue is greater than that of any of the others . . . by assistance rendered in an internecine quarrel some twenty years ago he has established a claim to the Maharaja's gratitude. The Paro Pönlop requires watching'.

The King presented Bell with three scarves of different colours instead of the usual single white scarf as well as one of five gold medals struck to commemorate his ascending the throne, the others being for Paul, White, Younghusband and Macdonald, the leader of the military escort on the Tibetan mission. It is interesting to note that he also referred to Bhutan as being part of the British Empire.

On his way back Bell met the former Deb Raja returning home to see if he could be re-appointed, although by then, as Bell knew, the work was being done by the King himself who had no intention of letting any power slip from his hands. He learnt also that the Paro Pönlop had tendered his resignation which had been refused until such time as he had rebuilt the dzong, a very expensive undertaking. However, when they reached Paro they saw that the work was nearly completed and found the Pönlop to be perfectly affable. He had a long discussion about religion with Bell, who had become a well known Tibetologist and was later (as Sir Charles) to become the Government of India's representative with the Dalai Lama during his period of exile in India.

In the summer of 1910 Bell had forwarded a letter from the King confirming that Bhutan would not enter into an agreement with any foreign power without the consent of the British government or permit the entry of agents of foreign states. Relations with the Chinese continued to vex political officers in Sikhim and Bell was sent a copy of a letter from the Amban to the Paro Pönlop who continued to favour the Chinese cause. At least it suited the King to say this and the British, who supported him, to believe it. Possibly the Paro Pönlop was doing little more than continue the tradition of backing his rival's enemies, provided his own security was not affected, and of hedging his bets just in case of a British withdrawal.

Bell was also sent by the King a letter from the Amban addressed to the Deb Raja, to the Paro Pönlop and to himself as Tongsa Pönlop ignoring his new office. This referred to the future posting of Chinese troops to Bhutan and warned them to offer no resistance or attempt to summon help from elsewhere. Bell, who had been warned by the Dalai Lama that the Chinese were fond of proceeding by 'tentative aggression', thought it was just a piece of deliberate kite flying to test British claims to control Bhutan's external affairs. He was told not to reply and that representations would be made in Peking, where H.M. Chargé d'affaires duly took up the matter. He was blandly informed that Bhutan was a vassal state that had paid tribute and had received letters patent in 1891 when the Imperial seal had been bestowed; and that the Amban had acted in accordance with precedence. The British response was a note of protest enclosing copies of the Anglo-Bhutanese treaty of 8th January that year and the firm statement that Britain could not allow any 'administrative changes in Tibet' (a euphemism for the imminent Chinese occupation that year) 'to affect or prejudice the integrity of Nepal or of the two smaller states of Sikhim and Bhutan and that they are prepared to protect the interests and rights of the people of those states'.

Bell argued that the Chinese lack of opposition to British entry into Sikhim in 1888 or of action over the Tongsa Pönlop's refusal then to go to Lhasa to discuss reprisal against the British, the lack of Chinese punishment for the official responsible for the burning of Paro dzong or of assistance towards rebuilding, and the lack of objections to White's mission in 1904 or to the King's enthronement in 1907, were more than adequate grounds for discounting Chinese claims. The British government, however, preferred to rely on the time-honoured argument of the *quid pro quo*, writing to Peking to say: 'H.M.G. have recognised Chinese interests in Thibet (sic) and have been unwilling to embarrass her in any action there so long as she adheres to her own pledges and does not prevent the Thibetan government from fulfilling its treaty obligation. But no attempt of the Chinese government to exercise influence over states so remote from the sphere of direct Chinese interest and in such close relation with the government of India as Nepal and Bhutan can possibly be tolerated'.

The Chinese, however, refused to relinquish their claims and in April 1911 reasserted that Nepal and Bhutan were vassal states. The next month the Trade Agent in Yatung reported that a Chinese official had left for Bhutan in order to cultivate the friendship of the Paro Pönlop, who continued to be very friendly with the Chinese Trade Agent. in Gyantse.

Bell emphasised that it was so essential to ensure that the Chinese did not undermine the position secured by the treaty that there should be no British interference with Bhutan's internal affairs even if British officials, tea planters and others did sometimes become frustrated by Bhutanese administrative methods.

Bhutan's status was defined that year in a Government of India Foreign Department secret memorandum to the Secretary of State referring to Bhutanese subjects in Siam, whose status had been queried by the British Minister in Bangkok, who received the reply 'there is no doubt that Bhutan is a native state of India under the suzerainty of H.M.G.'

In 1911 the King made a nineteen day journey to Delhi 'to pay homage' to the King-Emperor, at the Delhi durbar; and returned full of ideas for Bhutan's development as a result of what he had seen in India.

The following year the Chinese threat to Bhutan was eliminated when in 1912 they were expelled from Tibet after an uprising which had at first seemed so unsuccessful that the Dalai Lama sought British protection. He fled to the British Trade Agency at Yatung where Mr. Macdonald protected him from the pursuing Chinese before smuggling him in disguise to Sikhim and from thence to Calcutta. On his ultimate return to Tibet British influence replaced Chinese to some extent, although western developments such as the telegraph line to India and the arming of Tibetan soldiers with modern weapons was disapproved of by the more conservative monks whose affinities remained with the Chinese. Consequently the position of the Dalai Lama, now a secular as well as spiritual ruler, was to prove an uneasy one.

The Government of India now regarded Tibetan and Bhutanese affairs as so important that it was decided to retain control despite proposals, arising from the great increase of work at the centre, to return to the governments of Bengal and Assam the powers to deal directly with those states bordering their territories.

Bell prefaced his annual report for 1912–13 by commencing that Anglo-Bhutanese relations remained friendly; and this refrain was repeated in every subsequent report for the next thirty five years. Other recurring themes over this period were: the mainly satisfactory, if not very large, trade figures, except during world wars and depressions, with Bhutan having a healthy balance of exports over imports; the regular payment of the subsidy; the continuing problems of the liquor shops and boundary disputes, minor crime and the occasional extradition. This first report also included one of the last mentions of the Chinese whose activities on the frontier had now ceased. It also referred to a change of attitude by Bhutanese officials, particularly the Paro Pönlop, who had hitherto supported the Chinese and were now 'being drawn to our side more and more' . . . There was also mention of the beginning of trade with Bengal and Assam tea gardens.

The next year's report was written by B.J. Gould' 'Officiating' Political Officer in Bell's absence on leave. He was to have a very long connection with Bhutan and Sikhim where he returned as Political Officer from 1935–1945. He had seen the King at Dewangiri in order to be present at a meeting when White renewed his old acquaintance. His object was to propose the development of Bhutan with British capital, with himself acting as the King's agent. This had been agreed in principle by the Government of India and was accepted by the King. Land near the frontier was to be leased for ten plantations, the development of mineral resources and the extraction of timber and bamboo. Unfortunately when White put in a claim for his expenses 'in direct communication with the Bhutan durbar' the King cancelled the appointment and decided not to replace him. Whether he was put out at White's direct approach to his government and not to himself personally, whether White's claim was exorbitant or used as a pretext for cancellation because of opposition from Bhutanese notables, or whether the King himself had had second thoughts about European exploitation as the thin end of the wedge, will not be known until the surviving Bhutanese archives are made public. In any event it was an unfortunate sequel to his long association with Bhutan and White would have been better advised to have stayed in his west country retirement.

In 1914 the report of a British Forest Officer who had undertaken a survey was agreed in parts but the Bhutanese had found it 'too wide ranging for adoption in its entirety'; and the following year Mr. R.E. Cooper of the Royal Botanical Gardens in Calcutta spent six months in Bhutan collecting specimens.

Education which now began to be mentioned with increasing frequency in the Political Officers' reports, was slowly developing, but only˙for a few well connected boys. In 1914 there were forty six boys being educated in Ugyen Dorji's schools at Kalimpong and Ha under teachers provided by the Church of Scotland mission. The following year a new school was opened in Bumthang where boys were taught in English and Tibetan. This was also assisted by Ugyen Dorji, who, according to Bell, 'appears to have made himself responsible for imparting English education to Bhutanese boys'. He died at the end of the year – a man to whom his country owes a great deal.

The year 1916–17, the blackest period of the war, was the only one not reported,; but in 1917–18, Major W.L. Campbell, 'Officiating' Political Officer, who had been to Bhutan with White in 1907, wrote of unsuccessful attempts to recruit soldiers for the Indian army from the Nepalese settlers in Bhutan. A more successful visit had been made by Mr. W.W. Horrell, the 'Director of Public Instruction' (i.e. education) for Bengal and Dr. W.S. Sutherland of the Scotch mission in Kalimpong, who had inspected the school at Ha.

The next year's report by Campbell, now Political Officer, referred to a visit to Bhutan by two ladies, Dr. Cousins and Nurse Brodie, to help deal with an outbreak of cholera that claimed fifty lives.

Bell was back for a year in 1919 and wrote of permission being granted to Octavius Steel and Company to conduct a survey in Bhutanese territory to investigate a project for the harnessing of Bhutanese river water to take electric power to the tea gardens.

For 1919–20 M.D. Macdonald reported that the schools were doing well with 21 and 28 pupils respectively at Bumthang and Ha, as well as others at the Kalimpong High School.

In 1921 Major (later Lt.Col.) F.M. Bailey who as a young Lieutenant, had been Trade Agent in Yatung ten years before, became the Political Officer in Sikhim where he remained for the next nine years until becoming successively, Resident in Baroda, Kashmir and Nepal. One of his first acts was to forward the King's request for further education and training for Bhutanese boys in India. He also asked for an increase of the subsidy from one to three hundred thousand rupees. Presumably he was aware of bureaucracy's habit of automatically halving any sum requested, however deserving the cause. In supporting the application Bailey reminded the government that on the outbreak of war the King had placed all his state's resources at the disposal of the British and contributed a hundred thousand rupees to the Indian Relief fund. Bailey urged the government to agree to the increase although aware of the 'present financial stringency' (familiar phrase) but referred in support to Bhutan's 'ever growing desire for closer political and trade relationships with India'.

The King's letter to the Viceroy made it clear that Bhutan's greatest barrier to development was the ignorance of its people. No one outside the monasteries had been able to read until in 1914 the forty five boys had been sent for education at Kalimpong in the winter and at Ha in the summer. Now, seven years later, four of the Kalimpong boys had reached Indian university entrance standard and the others were ready to go on to further training. The issue now, wrote the King, was 'how best to utilise these lads for the development of Bhutan'. He therefore wanted them to be trained as doctors and vets; in science and in teaching methods so that six of them could take charge of a training school for primary school teachers; in agriculture and dairying; weaving, tanning, forestry, minerals, civil engineering; hydro-electric engineering and printing press technology.

To support his plea for subsidy increase the King reminded the Viceroy that the value of the existing sum of 100,00 rupees was worth much less than before the war; that, for example, the cost to him of clothing all his officials and soldiers was three times as much as it used to be in 1914 but the Government of India was getting a greatly increased revenue from the ceded duars, although he realised that Bhutan had no legal claim to a share of this.

Inevitably, when presented with two proposals for increased expenditure, the government, in true civil service tradition, gratefully accepted the let-out provided by the lesser and rejected the request for increased subsidy whilst agreeing to training in India. Enquiries were made at appropriate institutes about their conditions of entry and as it transpired that some of the boys were not up to standard the total was reduced. In the end, at a cost of 50,000 rupees, including tuition, board and fares, training was offered for three prospective teachers, two doctors, two veterinary assistants, four forest rangers; for three boys in agriculture and dairy farming and one each in weaving, tanning, mining, engineering and civil engineering. 'I cannot find words to thank you for what you have obtained for me', the King wrote to Bailey.

In his first report Bailey referred to a visit made by Dr. J.A. Graham of Kalimpong as the personal guest of the King and to an earlier one to Paro by Lord Ronaldshay, Governor of Bengal, whose intention to invest the King with the G.C.I.E. had been thwarted by Sir Ugyen becoming a victim of the great flu epidemic. However Bailey was able to rectify this the next year, 1922, when he went to Bhutan accompanied by Captain H.R.C. Meade, Bansi Ram, a surveyor, and Lieutenant A.W. Dyer of the Indian Medical Service (whose officers served both in Civil and Military capacities) the Civil Surgeon in Sikhim. He also took with him his wife and Lady Cozens Hardy. They followed White's route to Bumthang and at each halt found 'a beautifully laid out camping ground surrounded with a fence'. They went via Ha and Paro before reaching Tashichodzong where they were impressed by the dzong. Their next halt was at Punakha

and from there they went to Wangdiphodrung where they learnt that
two Indians from the plains had been telling people not to repair the
road for the mission: a faint echo of rising political ferment in India. At
Bumthang they found 'a delightful camp' awaiting them, with specially
planted flowers and trees. They were met by Ugyen Wangchuk whose
son Jigme, the future King, had accompanied them for the previous two
marches.

Bailey thought that the old feuding between the Tongsa and Paro
Pönlops must have ceased as Ugyen had made his grandson Paro Pönlop
on the death of the previous incumbent and all power was now in the
hands of his own family.

However the old issue of inadequate revenue was as troublesome as
ever and neither of the Pönlops, despite the family connection, sent any
funds to the central government except for religious purposes. The original
subsidy of 50,000 rupees was still divided between the two Pönlops and
the only sums available for essential services were the additional 50,000
and a hundred thousand rupees compensation paid by the government
of India for loss of liquor revenue in the frontier areas. Any other
revenue was paid largely in kind and went on feeding and clothing the
enormous body of monks.

On the 28th July Bailey and his party attended a durbar held at the
Kujé Lhakang temple three miles out of Bumthang, visited by White in
1905. There were in fact two temples side by side, the upper storey of
one being formed out of the enormous rock, said to bear the imprint of
the body of Padma Sambhava who lived in an adjoining cave. The durbar
was to have been held on this most sacred spot but as the temple was so
ancient it was considered too dangerous for so many people and the
ceremony was held in the newer one adjoining.

They were met at dawn by the King himself, who conducted the mission
to their seats. Bailey sat on the King's right facing the body of lamas with
the rest of the mission facing inwards on his right. He gave a short
speech before placing the insignia of the G.C.I.E. (Grand Cross of the
Indian Empire) round the King's neck. A long procession of officials
then entered in order of seniority. Each one bowed three times before
presenting his gifts of bales of silk and other materials and money heaped
onto tiger skins. The ceremony ended with a dance by masked lamas.

From Bumthang Bailey's party went on to Tibet, crossing over the
dangerous Monla Karchung pass at nearly 17,500 feet, over glaciers and
soft snow, bypassing wicked looking crevasses. After journeying through
Tibet they returned by way of Talung and Gyantse. Bailey's report of this
journey contained a military route report with minutely detailed descriptions of each march. Mr Dyer's report showed that he had treated
433 cases in the months of June, July and August. Interestingly, in view
of previous medical reports emphasising the prevalence of venereal

diseases there were only twelve cases of syphilis, eight of gonnhorrea and four of goitre. The majority of his patients suffered from chronic ulcers, dyspepsia and constipation. He also had to carry out four surgical operations including an amputation.

In his next three reports Bailey was concerned with educational developments. Although the number in the original schools had dropped and fewer boys were going to the Kalimpong High School, a new school for small boys had opened in Ha and the first qualified Bhutanese teacher was at Bumthang. Of the original 46 boys sent to Kalimpong eleven had passed their Indian matriculation exam.

In 1924 Bailey took the same party as before, except for the doctor, to Punakha to see the installation of Sonam Topgay Dorji, Ugyen Dorji's son, as Governor of Ha province. Bhutan was slowly being opened to a very few select and officially sponsored travellers to whom the beauty of the country came as a revelation. John Easton, on a journey just over the Bhutan border from Kalimpong to Phari, gave what is probably the best description by any traveller of the splendour of Chomolhari: 'Behind us was nothing but mist . . . before us as far as eye could see stretched Tibet, cloudless, gleaming in the midday sun . . . range upon range, furrow upon furrow stretched the brown, barren hills, picked out in chocolate and black, clear cut and distinct, each from each . . . the sun gilding the crests . . . Behind them, thrusting a mighty spire ten thousand feet into the cloudless sky, snowclad, ineffable Chomulhari (sic), divine mother of mountains . . . one pure white spire towering above those furrows . . . '

In Bhutan though, people's minds were now occupied by other matters than scenic wonders for in August 1926 a letter was received by the Political Agent in Sikhim from the 'Tongsa Pönlop Jigme Wangchuk, Maharaja Kumar of Bhutan: to the foot of the high throne, uplifted and five faces of the great King-Emperor of England, powerful, high, prospering in this world, of boundless kindness'. It reported the death of his father, the great Sir Ugyen Wangchuk and went on: 'We have from the past up till now relied on and trusted no foreign power except the British government . . . although we may not have an opportunity of serving you, yet we have no-one except Your Majesty the King Emperor in whom we can hope . . . submitted in a silk scarf of green . . . '

A few days after this Bailey wrote that all parties in Bhutan were waitingto see the Government of India's reaction to the new king and that he therefore wished to go to Bumthang as soon as possible as 'a peaceful continuity of the present dynasty would be in our general interest . . . ' Both the new King and Dorji the hereditary chief minister, were very young and were hoping that the next move would come from the British recognising the succession and so pre-empting any resurgence of the old factionalism. Bailey requested permission to attend the King's installation as White had done for his father in 1907. The government pussyfooted about as usual and it was argued that a personal delivery of the Viceroy's kharita 'might result in committing them more deeply than they wish'. However, as usual, the determined persistence of the man in the field won the day and in the end Bailey, now a Lieutenant Colonel, went the following year with his wife.

He left for Bhutan on the 24th February 1927 and as on the previous occasion found that all the camps had been beautifully prepared. Early the following month they began climbing, marching through snow for most of the way. At Ha they were joined by Major R.L. Vance of the Indian Medical Service, Lieutenant D.B. Sangster, a Subadar and fifteen men of the 3/12th Frontier Force Regiment. Before pushing on they saw 'a very creditable boxing display' at Dorji's school at Ha. At Tashichodzong they were joined by the Reverend Dr. Graham, who had been the King's tutor and at whose school, known as 'Dr. Graham's homes' generations of Bhutanese children have since been educated. He was later to become Moderator of the Church of Scotland.

On 10th March the whole party climbed to the pass at Dokyong La, 10,400 ft., in falling snow. At several places they were met by Bhutanese with ponies and mules, tea and food sent by the King and his officers and later by a band of pipers and Bhutanese soldiers who escorted them to Punakha, where they found a comfortable camp prepared, where the King and his family lunched and later had most of their meals with them.

The ceremony was postponed for a day owing to a mistake in the astrological calculations but on the morning of the 14th the whole party, preceeded by Bhutanese soldiers armed with modern rifles and followed by their own escort, rode to the dzong where they dismounted and walked up a steep ladder covered in white cloth at the head of which they met the Dharma Raja on whom they had called the previous day. In the durbar hall the officers were seated in the centre to the left of the two lamas and to the right of the King and Bailey; and the rest of the party were on the right with the escort behind them facing the body of lamas. There were crowds of Bhutanese onlookers on all sides, some of whom had even climbed up the roof and were looking down from the eaves. After the serving of tea the presents from the Government of India were placed in front of the King who was presented by Bailey with a silk scarf before the officials gave their gifts. His assistant read a speech in Tibetan before Bailey placed the insignia of Companion of the Indian Empire round the young King's neck before presenting him with the Viceroy's 'kharita'.

The King had to perform religious ceremonies for eleven days but asked the British to stay on until their conclusion on the 24th which had been selected as a lucky day for their departure. They enjoyed themselves watching the masked dancers as well as playing cricket, football and rounders, holding a sports day and an exhibition of drill given by the soldiers of the escort. Before they left the King gave them gifts of swords, silks, Bhutanese cloth and a pony for Bailey and accompanied them for part of the way, passing a beautiful village with peach and pear blossom and scarlet rhododendrons in full bloom. They arrived back at Gangtok on 12th April.

In a perceptive minute written after his return Bailey noted the important part the Dharma Raja had played in the proceedings, which was interesting as the office had been considered to be in abeyance ever since 1904 and even more so in view of subsequent events.

In the spring the following year, 1928, Bailey wrote to the Foreign Secretary of the Government of India to describe a visit to Dewangiri the previous February and his discussions with the King there. 'The young Maharaja,' he wrote, 'who has been ruling for one and a half years, commenced his rule happily. He is only twenty three years of age . . . ' Apparently the old King had expresssed some anxiety about a peaceful succession for before the birth of the present King his son-in-law the Deb Drönyer and later the Deb Drönyer's son, the existing Paro Pönlop, were considered likely heirs. Ugyen Wangchuk had at one time even contemplated abdication in order to see his own son safely on to the throne. At the time of Bailey's visit to Dewangiri the Paro Pönlop appeared to be acquiescing in the situation, at any rate outwardly, although Bailey thought that 'if an opportunity occurrred he would not be above an attempt to make trouble.' He was 'to a great extent independent' and collected revenue from a large area, of which only a small amount went to the Punakha and Tashichodzong monasteries and nothing to the central administration. The old King had apparently wanted to curtail the power and position of the Paro Pönlop but had died before carrying out these plans.

In May the situation was eased with the birth of an heir to the young King. Another factor preventing any armed risings was the Paro Pönlop's comparative lack of modern weapons whereas the King had by now, after some years of British assistance, an armoury of five hundred and twenty .303 rifles. In the course of the Dewangiri meeting the King was taken across the frontier to Gauhati for a night and, for the first time, saw a motor car, a train, a river steamer and machinery of various kinds in which he took great interest.

Bailey considered that the major problem facing Bhutan was no longer the succession but was the settlement of so many lowland Nepalese in the lower valleys to which the Bhutanese, who still disliked living at any height lower than 5,000 feet, avoided going if they could help it. There were now estimated to be about 50,000 Nepalese in these areas.

He also referred to a dispute over grazing grounds between the Bhutanese and the Tibetans and wanted confirmation that the Bhutanese government was in its rights to conduct direct correspondence with the

Tibetans on such an issue as it was not one of major foreign policy. Apparently the trouble had arisen because the Dharma Raja, a young Tibetan of twenty three, had given his countrymen a document guaranteeing grazing rights. The King had invited the Political Agent to write to the Dharma Raja, but not wishing to interefere without higher authority, the Agent had asked for copies of the correspondence for forwarding to Delhi. Meanwhile the King was advised to accept the Tibetans' claim for mutual cross-frontier grazing despite the illegal means they had adopted. The advice was accepted but the King showed his displeasure towards the Tibetans for approaching the Dharma Raja knowing him to have no administrative powers and knowing also that his Tibetan mother had considerable influence over him.

This was not the only problem involving the Dharma Raja and in August the King wrote to say that he was reported to have decided to leave Bhutan later that month in order to see Mr. Gandhi before going on to seek help from the Chinese. The King wanted the British to send him back to Bhutan if he turned up in India but the Government of India's reaction was to say that he would be treated as an ordinary refugee. He could not be arrested and returned to Bhutan as no criminal offence had been commited, but 'efforts will have to be made to prevent his leaving India' and the governments of Bengal and Assam were told of this decision.

The young King was now in a very awkward situation. The Dharma Raja, as a reincarnation of Shabdrung Rimpoche, was universally revered; and if force was used the people could turn against the monarchy which was still a comparatively new institution. It was said that the Dharma Raja was attempting, under the influence of his mother, to take back the temporal powers lost by his predecessors many years before. He was also influenced by a number of young men who had been to India and by his brother who had visited Mr. Gandhi. The Bhutanese were prepared to use force if necessary to prevent him going on to Tibet, where the Dalai Lama's sympathies could be solicited, and if necessary also prevent his return from India; but the King was very anxious to be assured of British support in this critical situation.

At this time, the officiating Political officer was F. Williamson who had been Trade Agent at Gyantse and Yatung and had accompanied Bailey to Ha in 1925. Williamson's view was that the Dharma Raja was 'unlikely to have much money and it is hoped that this will render his movements more amenable to supervision by the government of India'. Official reaction to this came in the form of a stuffy minute written by an under secretary in the secretariat in Delhi expressing the hope that 'the Foreign Office will squash this sort of interference in the internal and spiritual affairs of what is not an Indian state. Dorji and the Maharaja seemed to have played Mr. Williamson very skilfully with the Congress fly'. (i.e. the fear that the politics of India's Congress Party were going to be exported). This of course missed the point totally, that such a threat to a monarchy which had staked everything on British support, was not really just an internal matter.

The remark is also interesting for several other reasons: first it indicates that there was no real continuity in British policy. Had there been the sort of continuously Machiavellian policy towards Bhutan, Tibet, China and the whole frontier area, implied by a number of Indian historians, this sort of minute would never have been written. Secondly it also shows that the implications of the Anglo-Bhutanese treaty and Britain's rights and obligations were not understood in Delhi where Bhutan was sometimes regarded as just another Princely state and at others as a totally independent country, according to the knowledge and whim of individual officers and the prevailing political situation in India. At that time with the movement for independence gathering momentum, the last thing that was wanted was any Congress criticism of signs of fresh imperial expansion.

In November the Secretary of the Political (Intelligence) Department referred to the despatch of Bhutanese troops by the Paro Pönlop on his own initative to the Tibetan frontier, ostensibly to prevent the departure of the Dharma Raja, as 'unwise'. The order was countermanded by 'Raja' (as he was then known to the British) Sonam Topgay Dorji. Possibly the Pönlop was playing a double game and his troops, with reinforcements from Tibet, might have been meant not only to restore the Dharma Raja but also to enable himself to pose as the spiritual saviour of the country and even usurp the throne. However, none of this speculation was evident in Delhi where concern was expressed for two oddly conflicting reasons: first, that any attempt to constrain the Dharma Raja violated article VIII of the treaty by which Bhutan agreed to be guided by Britain in external relations: and secondly, and quite paradoxically, that Williamson had exceeded his powers in giving advice to the Bhutanese government. 'It would therefore seem', the minute continued, 'that though the Government of India could hardly care to intervene in the full sense, should a first class crisis arise, the giving of advice by the political officer represents a definite stage on the road to Bhutan's becoming an Indian state'. Yet on a number of occasions in the past, as has been shown, that is just how Bhutan had been regarded.

Further minuting revealed differing views within the department itself. Reference was made by a protagonist for 'native state' status to a despatch by the Secretary of State in 1924 which claimed that Bhutan 'had at least reached a position from which the transition to the status of an Indian state can easily, with the mutual concurrence of both parties, be effected, if this should hereafter appear desirable.'

The affair which gave rise to all this excitement was settled in 1931 by the sudden death of the Dharma Raja, allegedly, despite his youth, from heart failure but now generally ascribed to asphyxiation. The circumstances were certainly very curious as one of his servants was also found dead outside the monastery walls and was said to have poisoned himself. He had been one of those who had accompanied the Dharma Raja's brother on the visit to Mr. Gandhi whose help had been requested to restore the Dharma Raja's powers. Gandhi had declined to discuss the matter and had merely sent a letter to the Dharma Raja who, it was also reported, had been placing deadly maledictions upon the King and had sent men to Tibet to find out if the Chinese would send troops to help him. Finally, damning him still further in Bhutanese eyes, he was alleged to have lapsed from celibacy.

This was not entirely the end of the matter and the King's fears of Tibetan reaction proved to be well founded as he received a letter from the Tibetan government referring to rumours that the Shabdrung (Dharma Raja) had been murdered 'in conjunction with the Paro Pönlop', requiring an explanation as he had been 'entitled to rank and position' under the Tibetan government and going on to say 'you have, without considering his holy qualifications, condemned him as a murderer . . . you are aware you ought to have sent us a report . . . ' which he was then ordered, in somewhat preremptory terms to do without delay,

Lt.Col. J.L.R. Weir, the new Political Officer who had also served an earlier spell as Acting Political Officer, told the Government of India how much the King resented the tone of this letter for 'although the Lamaist church of Bhutan is to some extent subordinate to the Dalai Lama who is the head of the Lamaist religion, the country is, and always has been, independent of Tibet'. He couldn't think why the Tibetans had suddenly chosen to interfere in Bhutan's internal affairs but had been given to understand that certain Bhutanese who were personal friends of the Dalai Lama, had engineered the whole thing and that events in India may now have given Lhasa the idea that as the British hold was weakening in India ancient claims elsewhere could be re-asserted.

Weir raised these issues at Gyantse when he met the Tibetan Trade Agent, a confidant of the Dalai Lama's, and followed it with a visit to Lhasa where he saw the Dalai Lama and members of the government. He heard that they had been justifiably angry at the despatch of the Paro Pönlop's troops to Tibet and his openly proclaimed orders for the Dharma Raja to be arrested or even killed, if necessary. The subsequent news of his death not unnaturally led to a suspicion of foul play. Fortunately Weir was able to produce proof that contrary to general belief, the Dharma Raja had been born Bhutanese and not Tibetan. This took some of the heat out of the argument. Weir also took the opportunity to remind the Tibetans that Bhutan's dealings with foreign states were controlled by the British and that Britain was prepared to support

Bhutan in the matter at issue. The Dalai Lama then assured him that for the Tibetans the case was closed.

The four reports written between 1928 and 1931 by Weir and Williamson referred to other matters as well as the Dharma Raja's death. A Bhutanese had returned from three years training as a mining engineer and two had come back as Jemadars, (Viceroy's commissioned officers junior to Subadar) in the Indian Army. Trade figures were good despite a cholera epidemic with 500 deaths; and the world trade depression had not yet hit Bhutan.

In January 1931 Weir went to Bhutan to invest the King with the insignia of K.C.I.E. Such awards to successive Bhutanese rulers, still invariably described as 'Maharajas', supports later Bhutanese and Indian criticism that the British tended to regard Bhutan as little different from any other of the 'Princely states' of India which owed allegiance to the British crown, although, as already remarked, there was no continuous policy. At least the Princes got something out of it in the way of military and other assistance recommended by resident British representatives. Bhutan appeared to get the worst of both worlds. The refusal of British and British Indian governments to respond to repeated requests for increased financial assistance contrasts unfavourably with the massive aid later given by the newly independent and far from wealthy republic of India.

There was a great fund of good will towards Britain in the Bhutan of the thirties, as evidenced by the reception afforded the visiting Political Officers. Weir, whose party included his wife, daughter and sister-in-law, as well as Lieutenant Maurice Sinclair I.M.S., left Chumbi in the beginning of January and spent two winter months in the country, wrote: 'At our first camp we found evidence of the unfailing thoughtfulness for our comfort which we experienced from all officials of Bhutan throughout our tour'. From Sharitang he went on to Ha where he spent three days, watching, amongst other things, an excellent display of schoolboy boxing. The next day they met up with some riding mules and ponies sent by the Paro Pönlop. He was an unmarried grandson of the late King, who was not interested in 'shikar, riding or manly sports', a tolerant and unambitious person whose chief amusement was stage managing dances performed by monks and soldiers, in which he himself clashed the cymbals.

Weir continued to Wangdiphodrung and on to Punakha, where he was unable to meet the Dharma Raja who was said to be in meditation at a hill top monastery. As already mentioned he died that year and has had no recognised successors. Weir did, however have an extraordinary meeting with a 'straggler' from the Lhasa expedition of 1904, a Mahommedan who had taken to eating pork, whom he set on his way back to India.

He took five days to get to Tongsa where he had a very comfortable camp and from thence he set off for Bumthang for his meeting with the King whose younger brother met the party at the top of the Kyikyi La pass with welcoming fires and hot tea.

At Bumthang the investiture ceremony followed much the same procedure as before and was again held at the temple of Kujé. Leaving their camp and preceeded by a guard of twenty Bhutanese soldiers the British went first to a marquee to change into ceremonial dress and from there along, a red carpet to the hall where, 'after the formality of testing for poison and a grace had been intoned, three kinds of tea were served: a sweet infusion of wild yams, melted butter and milk, and what Weir called 'the usual Tibetan tea'. As well as the presentation of gifts by the mission and the investiture itself there was a great deal of present giving by all the leading officials. Each one advanced followed by servants bearing his gifts for the King to whom he bowed three times, his forehead touching the ground. A scarf would then be produced with a great flourish and handed to the master of ceremonies who received it with equal panache before presenting it to the King whilst calling out the name of the donor who would again bow three times. At the same time his servants hurled the bales of cloth and silk onto the floor making as much noise as possible and then rapidly unrolled them to display their contents. When all the proceedings were over the spectators could hardly see over the barriers of cloth.

Whilst they were at Bumthang the King and his family were guests of the mission at lunch and dinner on most days. The King impressed them by his intelligence and anxiety to learn about affairs outide Bhutan. He spoke and wrote Hindi very well and had a good grounding in English.

They returned via Dewangiri on a road not previously travelled in its entirety by any previous European visitors. It was not easy going in thick snow but Weir thought that if funds were made available for improvement it would make a good feeder road for Bhutan's natural products.

In the report on his visit Weir expressed some anxiety about the future for Bhutan as the population could be in decline owing to in-breeding and the reduction of immigrants from Tibet. Although there were still some fine-looking people in the country, a larger percentage suffered from venereal diseases. Lieutenant Sinclair considered that as many as 80 percent had gonorrhoea or pyrorrhoea and that the prevalence of goitre amounted to an epidemic. He wrote that because of these diseases many were of poor physique and 'only the fittest can survive'. He was kept very busy and treated over thirteen hundred separate cases of various types of illness as well as giving nearly four hundred vaccinations.

Weir was also struck by the poverty of the people and the need for more feeder roads for the carriage of goods to and from the markets in Assam. Politically the country seemed stable, thanks to the 'Maharaja'.

Even though he was still, in effect, little more than the overlord of the province of Tongsa, the internal situation was quiet and relations with British frontier districts were good with mutual co-operation over the capture of fugitives from justice. Even then, sixteen years before the event, the 'Maharaja', expressed doubts about a future relationship with an independent India. 'He fails utterly, like the Tibetans', wrote Weir, 'to understand the policy of the British government towards what he looks on as rank rebellion against established authority. The execution of Mr. Gandhi was his solution to the difficulty. A round table conference, as held in London 1931–2, to enable India to break away from England was beyond his comprehension. The future relationship of a changed India towards Bhutan was a subject of much concern and he very definitely stated to me that if an Indian were ever to be made Political Officer of Sikhim he would never be invited to set foot in Bhutan'. It says much for the King's political acumen that eighteen years later he was to welcome Pandit Nehru as the Prime Miinister of independent India.

In his annual report for 1931–2 Weir was able to write; 'Bhutan has again had a year of internal and external quiet. The Dharma Raja's death had 'closed a chapter of Bhutanese history which was fraught with potential danger to the existing rule'. There had continued to be a number of cross-border arrests. The world depression had affected Bhutanese trade and both imports and exports had been reduced. The former included cotton piece goods, metals, and tobacco leaf; amongst the affected exports were ponies, mules, blankets, wax, butter and cattle. However, a concession to a British-Indian tea company had been re-newed and there were hopes for further developments. Finally, education was now firmly established although only for a very small minority, and the two schools, at Ha and Bumthang, had made good progress. One young man had finished his medical training in India.

Weir also referred to the continuing ambiguity of Bhutan's status: 'It is certainly not a foreign state within the meaning of the 'Extradition Act' . . . It is also not an Indian Native State although its late ruler paid homage to the King-Emperor at the Delhi Durbar in 1911 . . . ' He had raised the issue in connection with the status of Nepalese settlers of whose present nationality he wanted a legal ruling as well as guidance on procedure to be followed in cases where the extradition of such people was requested by the Bhutanese and Sikhimese governments. The Government of India only replied to say that 'they were not in a position to define their views regarding the nationality of Nepalese settlers . . . ' However, they were not prepared to agree to the surrender of British subjects or the subjects of states other than Bhutan for trial by Bhutanese courts. Only Bhutanese subjects, or those with dual nationality, except when it was Anglo-Bhutanese, could be surrendered. This violated the spirit, it not the law, of the treaty and was not of much help to Weir.

Weir had recommended increased financial assistance 'if Bhutan is to advance on more modern lines and is not to be allowed to disintegrate' and this was followed, in his absence on leave, by a financial report written by Williamson, his successor, who described what happened to the existing funds. The King received a hundred thousand rupees per year as subsidy and another hundred thousand in compensation for the removal of the liquor shops within ten miles of the frontier. Most of this money was distributed to officials and monasteries without whose continued support he could hardly survive. The Paro Pönlop was still virtually independent: so much so that the King had never visited the Paro area. In common with other senior officials the Pönlop only supported the present regime out of self-interest, for the money, and for his own enhanced status, for as a united Bhutan was of more consequence vis à vis Tibet and India than a fragmented state, so therefore was its more powerful subjects.

In his report for 1932–33 Williamson wrote that Captain C. J. Morris, the same Gurkha recruiting officer who had been so unsuccessful in 1917, had returned to assess the available Nepalese Gurkha manpower for reserve recruitment in time of war. In the event he was to be much more successful this time. Meanwhile Williamson had visited and been impressed by the fourteen Bhutanese boys training in Shillong with the 2/10th Gurkha Rifles.

That year also Captain George Sherriff and Mr. Frank Ludlow had been permitted to make a botanical visit on behalf of the British Museum. This was the first of six joint expeditions made by this remarkable pair, mainly to Eastern Bhutan and Tibet. Frank Ludlow, a member of the Indian Education Service who had read Natural Sciences at Cambridge before joining the Indian army in the First World War, had given up his post as an inspector of schools in India to start up a school for Tibetan boys in Gyantse, and although it did not long survive monkish hostility, the experience of the three years he spent there between 1924 and 1927, led him to passing most of the rest of his life concerned with the Eastern Himalayas and its flora. He made his first visit to Bhutan in 1923 when he went with Bailey to Dewangiri. He first met George Sherriff, a former regular army officer who had distinguished himself on the North West Frontier, in 1929 when staying with Williamson, then Consul General at Kashgar, where Sherriff had been appointed Vice-Consul the previous year, later succeeding Williamson but resigning in order to devote himself to botanical exploration.

Although both men held political appointments, Ludlow becoming British Resident in Lhasa during the Second World War, on secondment from the army to which he had returned; and Sherriff, who had also rejoined the army before returning to political duties in Gangtok, succeeding Ludlow in Lhasa, it is for their botanical achievements that they are best remembered. For thirty years they were leading contributors to the botanical knowledge of the region, based on the individual and joint journeys they made between 1929 and 1949 and subsequent work in Britain. They built on the work of Dr. Griffith in Bhutan and elsewhere, Sir Joseph Hooker in Sikhim, R. E. Cooper, F. Kingdon Ward and others, including some of the political officers, particularly F. M. Bailey. Between 1933 and 1946 they made six joint expeditions; and in this first one alone they collected nearly 750 bird skins and over 500 gatherings of plants including some that were new to science. Some of the rare species they discovered included a number whose commoner forms are well known to the European layman, such as primulas, peonies and rhododendrons; and they had several plants and shrubs named after them, including *Meconopsis Sherriffii* and *Rhododenron Ludlowii*.

Williamson went with his wife to Bhutan in June 1933, taking with him 'Raja' Sonam Topgay Dorji, who had not only had succeeded his father as the King's Agent but also as the Political Officer's assistant. He also took his personal assistant Rai Bahadur Norbhu Dhondup and Captain D. Tennant of the Indian Medical Service and in the course of their journey they crossed the country from West to East.

They went first from Yatung to Ha where they were met by Dorji who was also the Dzongpön of the area, of whom Williamson wrote 'nothing was too much trouble for him to undertake'. They also joined forces with Sherriff and Ludlow who stayed with them for a month before going on to East Bhutan and Tibet. Major C. J. Morris went with them as far as Bumthang before returning separately.

They stayed for a week in Ha, enjoying themselves, learning to use the Bhutanese longbow. They watched an archery tournament in which the Bhutanese danced and yelled, shook their bows and arrows in the most excited way, sang, and exhorted their arrows to go straight. 'It was a great show' wrote Williamson, 'the best of its kind we ever saw. The archers enjoyed it all immensely, and what is more, hit the target quite often at a hundred and fifty yards'.

From Ha they left for Paro where they were escorted for the last few miles before entering the town by a guard of honour in bright silk tunics with swords in silver scabbards, rhinoceros hide shields and iron helmets.

Williamson wrote that the Paro Pönlop, whom he had met in 1925 'seemed really delighted' to see them. They stayed in a guest house that had been rebuilt since Weir's visit and was now a 'pagoda-like' building where the Pönlop was the mission's guest at most meals and thoroughly enjoyed the cinema show given in the evenings, Charlie Chaplin being the favourite with the Bhutanese. He was then thirty four, short, bald, very fat and unmarried and was known to be a benevolent administrator in the Paro region but apparently paid little attention to the southern and tropical parts where 'Gurkha colonists', according to Williamson's informants, were 'disgracefully exploited by certain young Nepalese landlords'.

From Paro they visited the famous tiger's nest monastery with the Paro Pönlop who accompanied them as far as the top of the Pele La pass. They were unable to visit Tashichodzong because of the death of the Dzongpön and therefore went straight on to Wangdiphodrung. At their first camp site Williamson thought he had never seen so many flies, not even in Mesopotamia during the war. From Wangdiphodrung they made a detour in order to see the dzong at Punakha before going on to Tongsa. They were met by the King's brother, a young man of twenty with whom they became very friendly and were saddened by his death from typhoid shortly afterwards. Williamson heard that he was unable to receive proper medical attention because of interference from the lamas.

A day and half before getting to Tongsa they had been met by bearers carrying a dandy (a lightweight conveyance carried on the shoulders of porters. The author travelled in one up to Mussoorie with his mother in the early twenties before a motor road had been made.) This had been sent for the use of Mrs. Williamson, a gesture that had been much appreciated as women were not normally allowed to use them – not even the King's wife. They were also met by a small escort of soldiers dressed as Gurkhas except for bare feet, under one of the Jemadars who had been trained in Shillong. The King himself met them at the entrance to their camp, 'a fine looking young man of twenty nine, beautifully dressed in a striped silk chuba (tunic) with very decorative Tibetan boots of blue and white with pointed toes'. Before leaving with his brother he stayed with them for some time whilst they were served saffron tea, rice and fruit.

After lunch the royal ladies called. The 'Maharani', as Williamson referred to her, was the King's cousin, a very pretty twenty three year old. She accompanied the King's sisters, one of whom, the 'delightful' Ashi Pedon, had 'inherited a great deal of the political acumen and sound sense of her father, the late Majaraja, Sir Ugyen Wangchuk'.

The royal family dined with the mission and they enjoyed themselves playing 'childish games' like 'Up Jenkins' (an English children's party game of the time). Williamson wrote that his wife became 'very intimate with the ladies whom she now regards as close friends. The absence of irksome religious restrictions and of purdah makes social intercourse as easy as with Europeans and there was an entire absence of any feeling that we were dealing with people whose outlook on life was in any way different from our own'.

Time passed all too quickly. They practised archery most days, had their meals with the Royal Family, played games and had cinema shows every evening. Williamson had frequent discussions with the King, especially about Bhutan's financial needs. They set off on their return journey on 24th July accompanied by the King who went shooting with them at their first camp. He was a good shot but, wrote Williamson, 'religious feeling against the taking of life and the influence of the lamas are so strong that he never shoots at all in the ordinary way'. They took their leave of the King and their Bhutanese friends with regret and continued their journey to Talung in Tibet and from thence back to Sikhim.

Captain Tennant wrote that in most places people were not inclined to seek his services, possibly because of the time of year. Nevertheless he saw a total of 564 patients excluding 200 of the mission's coolies. The most prevalent diseases were venereal ailments, alimentary diseases (intestinal parasites) goitre, rheumatic disorders and dental conditions. At Bumthang he had met a Bhutanese doctor who had returned from training in India.

A year after he had been the King's guest in Bhutan and a few months after a second visit, this time only as far as Ha, Williamson reciprocated his hospitality by taking the King and Queen to Calcutta where they stayed with the Governor of Bengal and called on the Viceroy. Williamson accompanied them everywhere: to the zoo, the paper mills, a munitions factory, even a warship – H.M.S. Emerald. The Governor lent his launch and they went on picnics and from Dum Dum airport the King made a flight in an Avro aeroplane. Nevertheless they confessed to enjoying best of all an amateur production of 'The Yeomen of the Guard'. Before returning to Bhutan they also made a pilgrimage to a Buddhist shrine near Benares. Williamson wrote, 'the impression they made on everyone was extraordinarily favourable'.

Williamson emphasised that the Bhutanese would be a dying race unless measures were soon taken to abolish the existing system of taxation whereby only householders were taxed. Consequently when a young man married he remained in his father's house. As a result few new houses were built and the bulk of the people lived in congested and insanitary conditions. The King wanted to change this and to bring in other improvements, all of which cost money: such as improved communication, training for more potential doctors and teachers, as well as the nucleus of a small standing army to ensure internal security. For the latter he suggested that more Bhutanese should receive training in a Gurkha regiment. In supporting the proposed increase in funds, Williamson wrote, 'It is not necessary to stress the danger to India which would be caused by unrest in Bhutan at a time when China is trying, apparently with some success, to increase her influence in Tibet. More money to ensure the content of the people would go a long way to remove this danger'.

The pleas were forwarded by the Government of India to those of Bengal and Assam for comment and resulted only in some caustic minuting by very senior officers. 'Reforming zeal is natural in the few lucky Political Officers who visit Bhutan', wrote one, 'it is, however, dangerous and one has to be on one's guard against infection'. Another wrote: 'I have yet to be persuaded that reform on modern lines in Tibet, Nepal or Bhutan would suit either them or Bhutan . . . I think we should hesitate long before we should encourage such reforms in a state on our borders of which we know precious little and in which the enlargement of our responsibilites would seem inconvenient and unprofitable'. The chief Secretary of Assam considered, however, that although, in his view, the Political Officer in Sikhim had probably 'been kept in the dark to some extent regarding supplementary revenues collected by the Bhutan state' and that some revenue accrued from the timber trade, nevertheless the government of Assam would support the proposal. In due course, however, the Government of India, with the agreement of the home government turned down the request for an increased subsidy.

In 1935 Gould (see p.173) began his long tenure of office, in the first years of which a visit was paid to Paro by Sir John Anderson (later Lord Waverley) the Governor of Bengal who took with him Lt. J. E. J. Davie as his A.D.C. In 1936 the King himself wrote to request more money and repeated the reasons already put forward by the Political Officers. It was, he wrote, 'in order to benefit my subjects by removing barriers and to create a stronger and more vigorous nation'. He repeated the argument that the national budget was limited by the lack of direct monetary taxation and that lack of finance, together with the innate conservatism of the people made reform impossible; and yet there was an urgent need for good internal communications, a system of education, medical aid and a defence force. In addition to being worried about what might happen in Tibet, he was also 'deeply anxious' regarding the future of his country after the passing of the Government of India Act. 'India is now having handed over to it by the British people the full government of the land that formerly belonged to Bhutan in this Himalayan region. That land has been developed chiefly by the industry and effort of British pioneers and is now many hundredfold more valuable . . . Whilst in the strictly legal sense Bhutan cannot claim further compensation I would respectfully urge that two lakhs (i.e. two hundred thousand) of rupees of extra annual subsidy should be granted'. The cogency of this additional argument still did not prevent the Viceroy, Lord Willingdon, from turning down the King's request on the grounds that in order to ensure the autonomy of Tibet 'against inroads by China or other powers, it might prove necessary to increase financial assistance to Tibet, and that the possibility of increasing the subsidy to Bhutan could not be considered until the Tibet issue was settled'.

Accompanied by Captain J. F. Morgan of the Indian Medical Service and by 'Raja' Sonam Topgay Dorji, who had inherited his father's position as the Bhutanese Government Agent in India and later as Deb Zimpön, Gould crossed the border into Bhutan in May 1938, travelling by way of Ha and Paro to Bumthang where the King was staying for the summer.

In his subsequent report Gould wrote: 'I cannot hope to improve on the full accounts which have from time to time been given by my predecessors of the route and of the courtesies which are customarily extended to a Political Officer when he visits Bhutan. I will therefore deal with the matters which struck me most'. He started with the inadequacy of the financial system which was to all intents and purposes that of a feudal state in which powerful barons still had to be appeased. There was virtually no central revenue and therefore no funds for education or medicine and no foreign personnel were employed to provide the skills and services that the country lacked. The only Bhutanese who had trained outside the country were 'Raja' Dorji himself, a sub-assistant surgeon who acted as the state doctor, two veterinary surgeons, two schoolmasters, three forest rangers, one trained in mining and two in tannery.

Gould's impressions of Bhutanese physical capacity were more favourable than those of other visitors since White's time. He thought that there was 'a very great deal to be said in favour of a system that has produced such people as the Bhutanese who were physically 'not inferior to any of the inhabitants of the Indian frontier', that he had known. A man or woman could carry an eighty pound load in any weather, up to a height of 14,000 feet. Also, 'the people show considerable intelligence and independence of mind in adapting their agriculture and other practices to varying local conditions.

He was impressed by the King: 'a man of entire openness and honesty of mind and naturally inclined to seek the good of his people'. His son, then nine years old, was attending the small school in Bumthang, where he was being educated in Tibetan and Hindi. Gould wrote that it was 'impossible to exaggerate the kindness of his reception by the King and his family and those close to him, who included the Paro Pönlop, 'a stout and inactive bachelor', and 'Raja Dorji' with whom he was particularly impressed.

Gould wrote that from the British point of view 'Bhutanese political sentiment is as sound as could be desired', but that although the 'Maharaja's' family was firmly seated there were two factors that could weaken them. The first was lack of money 'to make his authority fully efficient, particularly in the direction of financial reform'. The second was the decline in population largely due, according to Captain Morgan who had been there, to the prevalence of syphillis in the adjoining area of Tibet with which there was now much more contact. The problem of a declining indigenous population was accentuated by the great increase of Nepalese coming into the south. The two issues were interdependent, for lack of money meant that the King could not afford to travel as this would traditionally entail so many calls on his generosity. He could therefore neither see for himself the needs of the kingdom or be seen as a unifying force by his people; nor could he travel abroad to develop his ideas through observing other places. Indeed he had only twice left the country to go to India; once to Gauhati in Assam and on the other occasion to Calcutta where he had met the Viceroy, Lord Willingdon. Nor was there any money available to defray the cost of a medical campaign against syphillis. Gould emphasised that this was of deep concern to the King and that he and 'Raja' Dorji and their wives would give a personal lead to such a campaign. He wondered if, in the event of an increased subsidy not being possible, assistance could be given with the provision of drugs or if some outside medical body could help. This plea was reinforced by Sir John Anderson who, speaking in Edinburgh, hoped that private funds would be made available for medical surveys in Bhutan, and by Dr. Graham who asked the Government of India to help combat diseases which were leading to depopulation. A few years later in 1941 Captain Staunton of the Indian Medical Service made the first independent medical tour. Previous visits by doctors had been in the company of the Political Officers.

In addition to the control of Nepalese population in the south other needs listed by Gould included the conservation of forests, improvement of communications, 'suppression of the more extravagant forms' of feudalism and adoption of a system of taxation that would provide revenue for reforms including a system of education. Gould was quite impressed by the state troops, numbering about a hundred, whose training had been based on that given to the fourteen men who, on Weir's recommendation, had trained with the 2/10th Gurkha Rifles in Shillong. The British government had also helped with the provision of rifles and ammunition.

Although not immediately successful he refused to give up and in 1941 wrote a long justification for the award of two hundred thousand rupees on the grounds already put forward by Weir, Williamson and himself. He also quoted a number of supporting factors. Most striking amongst these were comparative figures of expenditure per head of population: 110 annas in Chaka, 90 in Mandi, 70 in Sikhim as well as British help for road building, 60 in Tehri Garwhal and only 3 in Bhutan. His plea for support on the grounds of increased Chinese power and designs on expansion was less well founded for at that time China was fighting for her life against the Japanese and her internal divisions between the Nationalists and the Communists were only papered over. Gould also wrote that although the 'Maharaja' was loyal to the British connection, he 'was beginning to have some doubts as to the security of his position and his ability to hold Bhutan in the British interest against any considerable opposition'. The ruling house had only been in power since 1907 and could be in danger unless its power and prestige were increased and unless it had the resources for internal defence. This may have been a rather specious argument, for Gould's predecessors had emphasised the strength of the King's position, despite lack of funds, as an argument for further support.

He opposed the idea of a *quid pro quo* which appears to have been floated in some quarters: that in return for additional funds Bhutan should be invited to become a 'native state' of India on the same basis as Sikhim. Instead he advocated the very policy that in a few years time was to be followed to a large extent by an independent India; 'What is needed', he wrote, 'in a strengthening of the links which were established in 1910 between India and Bhutan independent in all except its external relations, rather than the assumption by the Government of India of responsibilities in regard to the internal affairs of Bhutan'.

The next year, in 1942, at a time when Britain's fortunes were at their lowest ebb, with defeats by the Japanese in Malaya and Burma, set-backs in the middle east and the near success of the German submarine onslaught, Gould, now Sir Basil, succeeded where his predecessors had failed; and an additional hundred thousand rupees were added to the subsidy, half the sum he had requested. It was to be for 'the duration of the war', after which it would be reconsidered. It had been finally agreed, not just because the government in Delhi had at last been moved by the financial and medical arguments that had now so often been put forward, but also, and perhaps more cogently, because of fears about the war situation on the Eastern front. Minuting in the Political Department files shows that there was anxiety lest the King (still always referred to as Maharaja) should, just at this juncture, seek help from elsewhere. There was almost certainly never any real danger of this but shrewd protagonists for Bhutan were prepared to use the argument if it would help their cause.

Gould, who had journeyed through Bhutan with Hugh Richardson in 1941 en route between Tibet and Sikhim, visited Bhutan again officially in 1943. He had suggested a meeting with the King somewhere half way between Bumthang and Dewangiri but the King insisted on going much further towards the Indian border despite the snow and the imminent birth of a child. They met at Dewachu where the Bhutanese team included 'Raja' Dorji and his son Jigme, now Dzongpön of Ha; and on the British side Gould had his assistant political officer, a wireless operator, Captain St. J. E. Hendriks the civil surgeon from Sikhim who had been to Ha with Williamson in 1934, and the Maharaja of Sikhim.

Gould was more than ever impressed by the King who seemed to have 'the gift, as had his father, of picking out good men and sticking to them and their families . . . He treats them in a manner which gives them confidence and inspires loyalty . . . He talks freely with men and women of every class . . . ' The King also had the gift of a light touch and on the last night gave a solo at a sing song.

Reporting on this meeting Gould wrote that the Bhutanese army was
shaping well. In the previous year or so 115 men had gone to the 7th, 9th
and 10th Gurkhas, of the main batch of whom their Colonel had written
that they were 'without exception the finest party of recruits' that he had
ever seen. A hundred and twenty four Bhutanese subjects of Nepalese
origin had joined Gurkha regiments. In Bhutan itself there was now a
very smart platoon, mostly Gurkha trained, and a reserve of 1,900 rifles.
As well as strengthening his own defences at this critical time the King
had given 60,000 rupees out his own slender resources to the Viceroy's
war fund and 10,000 to the Vicereine's Red Cross appeal.

He had shown his acceptance of British guidance over foreign policy
by his request for confirmation that a Tibetan proposal for a mutual
return of population on either side of the frontier was a matter for the
British to deal with and was ready to accede to any arrangement permitting the bulk of the people in the Dirang and Kalaktang areas to
remain in Bhutan.

On the vexed question of finance Gould repeated that the treaty
subsidy still went to the various interests which it had been necessary to
conciliate in 1865. The liquor shop compensation of 100,000 rupees was
renewable on a five year basis and as there had been delays in payment in
1934 and again in 1939 the King requested that it should be on a more
permanent basis; especially as the faithful compliance by the Bhutanese
government had enabled the governments of Assam and Bengal to
establish effective excise control.

The medical problems had not lessened. Captain Hendriks had
discovered that no less than fifty percent of the eighty attendants brought
by the King to the meeting were suffering from gonorrhoea. He also
noted᾿ a high rate of infant mortality and a heavy incidence of goitre.
After discussions with Hendriks the King decided to introduce mass
treatment of venereal diseases in the area of Bumthang and asked for
British assistance with the provision of drugs. Gould supported this and
wrote that the institution in 1940 of a post of civil surgeon to operate in
Bhutan as well as Sikhim and the regular visitations since then had done
much to arouse medical interest; and that there had been no opposition
from the monks or any other parties.

Education was still very limited. There was the small school centred on
the King's son, Jigme Dorji Wangchuk, and 'Raja' Sonam Topgay Dorji
ran his own in Kalimpong and Ha. Very few Bhutanese had been outside
the country to study, apart from Dorji himself in Simla, his sister at a
convent in Kalimpong, his wife at Darjeeling and his son, Jigme Dorji at
the Indian Civil Service training school in Dehra Dun. Gould wrote:
'There seems a good prospect for education in Bhutan but it is likely to
be gradual'. The following year, when the King was awarded the K.C.S.I.,
Sonam Topgay Dorji's services were recognised by the award of C.I.E.

Roads were still poor although the route from Ha to Bumthang was being improved and a mule road from central Bhutan to Buxa Duar was under consideration. The King requested the services of the excellent Indian executive engineer in Sikhim to give some assistance towards re-aligning certain roads.

In the same year 1943, Gould went to Paro with Lady Linlithgow, the Vicereine, together with her daughter-in-law, Lady Hopetoun, Mrs. Joy Wilson, Prince Thondup of Sikhim and Lt.Colonel E. Elliot I.M.S. Gould ended his last report on Bhutan with a plea for restitution of territory and recommended that the Government of India should accede to the King's request for use 'by lease or otherwise' of the Dewangiri area which had been taken by the British in 1865 on military grounds that no longer existed. Dewangiri could then be connected by road with Bumthang and Tashigang. This would bring Bhutan into closer contact with Assam and 'promote medical, educational, agricultural and sylvicultural progress'. He pointed out in justification that whereas the annexation of the duars could have led to 'deep and permanent resentment' the King and his subjects bore no will will towards Britain, rather the reverse. This only received a dusty answer from the External Affairs Department in Delhi who reminded Gould (inconceivably, nearly ninety years and two world wars after the event) that Dewangiri had been kept for reasons of prestige as two British guns had been lost there in the war of 1865 whose last action had been fought there. He was also reminded that when the present King's father had made the same request in 1922 it had been opposed by the government of Assam on the grounds that in an area where prestige counted for so much such an action could be misconstrued. Even though on this occasion Gould had suggested a possible exchange of land with Assam the Government of India saw no reason to reverse the earlier decision.

The war in Europe ended in May 1945 and the Japanese war in August of that year when a change of government in Britain prompted the acceleration of the movement towards Indian independence that had begun in the early years of the century and had only been shelved during the period when India had been threatened by invasion and Britain by defeat. India was in a state of political turmoil which had inevitable repercussions in Bhutan. In 1946 therefore the King asked to have a meeting with the British cabinet delegation then visiting India; but was told that they could not spare the time. However, later that year, two officers of the External Affairs Department in Delhi saw delegations from Bhutan and Sikhim who were obviously very anxious about their future. They were told to anticipate that 'they would have to deal with reasonable people' but in order to help the Government of India in its future relationships, the Political Officer, A. J. Hopkinson, was asked to produce a memorandum on 'particular facts that cause not only Bhutan but Sikhim also to be rather special cases, on geographical, historical, cultural and ethnologial grounds amongst others'. He saw 'Raja' Sonam Topgay Dorji and his son Jigme Dorji who agreed to prepare a paper for the 'interim' Government of India and asked him 'a good many searching questions regarding the consequences for Bhutan under international law, of the transfer of power'. Hopkinson told them that international law was not a codified and universally recognised body and would hardly be applicable to such a special relationship. He felt sure that the new Government of India would probably succeed to the rights and obligations of H.M.G *vis à vis* Bhutan.

Although proved groundless in the end, Bhutanese fears were fully just-ified for had Bhutan been fully accepted as just another Princely state – and the constant reference to the King as 'Maharaja' and to Sonam Topgay Dorji as 'Raja' showed that the British were, to say the least, still ambivalent in their attitude – it would have been swallowed up into the new republic sooner or later. Indeed Sikhim's fears were later to prove fully justified.

In his paper Hopkinson wrote that he had received intelligence reports that the Tibetan trade agency in Kalimpong had written to the Tibetan government advising them to claim suzerainty over Sikhim and Bhutan. There was also some reference to Bhutanese wishes to 'remain' in the Commonwealth even if India left and there was official discussion and a flurry of minuting on the feasibility of the British continuing to pay subsidies; and reference to possible analogies with South Africa where the British High Commmissioner remained responsible for certain trust territories. However it all came to nought, on the whole fortunately for Bhutan, whose favourable treatment by India has at least ensured a steady rate of development.

Hopkinson was the last in the long line of British Political Officers to visit Bhutan, going there with Lt.Colonel L. K. Ledger I.M.S., together with their wives in 1947, just before Indian independence to present the King with the insignia of the K.C.S.I. Like all his twentieth century predecessors, he had become a firm supporter of the Bhutanese and wrote that India needed a friendly and contented Bhutan within the Indian rather than the Chinese orbit. 'Bhutan is now friendly and anxious for continued friendship but negligence or contempt would soon drive it – and much else besides – into the open arms of China or bring in a foreign power, perhaps Russia, to India's doors.' He was afraid that if Indian statesmen were too preoccupied with internal affairs after independence they might not 'sufficiently realise these things, with resultant harm to India's future'. For that reason he suggested that Britain should continue to pay the subsidies for the time being. This recommendation was not accepted.

He need not have worried. In September 1946 a good will message had been received in Bhutan from Pandit Nehru, prime minister of the interim government. On 15th August 1947 India became independent and in 1949 a new treaty was negotiated by which India agreed to be bound by all previous obligations but to surrender any 'colonial rights'; and although Bhutan agreed to be guided in her external relations, the title of 'Druk Gyalpo' or King was emphasised in the treaty. The subsidies were raised to 500,000 rupees and 32 square miles of the Dewangiri region were finally returned to Bhutan.

In 1971, the year before his death, in a speech to the National Assembly, King Jigme Dorji Wangchuk who had succeeded to the throne in 1952, referring to the British connection, said: 'Had they given the assistance that we asked for, Bhutan might have progressed far more than we have progressed today . . . I am prepared to recount how hard we tried for British aid and how reluctant they were to grant that aid . . ' As the King's reign only began after India Independence he was presumably referring to what he knew of events in his father's time.

White would have been the first to agree with him, certainly for the years up to the outbreak of the First World War. Despite the clause in the treaty of Punakha barring Britain from interfering in Bhutan's internal affairs and the fine division between uncommitted aid and interference, there was much that could have been done on the lines so often discussed between White and Ugyen Wangchuk.

By 1918, after the war, things were very different. Britain had lost most of her foreign assets to pay for her fight for survival between 1914 and 1919 in addition to millions of her best men. Before the war she was a great imperial power and still one of the two or three wealthiest, but the post-war years were lean times. Abroad, the spirit of nationalism was on the march and at home labour and coalition governments were uninterested in distant countries. In the twenties Britain was torn by industrial unrest, including the general strike of 1926, and in the thirties subdued by the creeping paralysis of unemployment. In India, and even more in less favoured colonial territories, officials tried to cope on shoestring budgets before the renewed threat of war with the increasingly militant German and Italian dictatorships, the enforced ending of disarmament policies and concentration on arms expenditure. By 1940, less than a year after the start of a six year war, Britain stood alone and virtually destitute. Two years later British India was threatened with the victorious Japanese armies at her borders and in 1944 by their invasion of Assam. All the while the movement for Indian independence grew more clamorous, impatient of the British policy of postponing until the war had been won, completion of the steady move towards dominion status that had begun in 1919.

Understandably enough, there had been neither time nor money to spend on foreign aid between 1913 and 1947. I should also be remembered that the concept of aid, given by one sovereign power to another, or from multi-lateral bodies, was largely a post-second world war phenomenon, associated with the rapid process of decolonisation.

Nevertheless the fact remains that Britain had been asked for aid prior to Indian independence and had not responded, or only grudgingly and in short measure, whereas the Government of India has given massive assistance almost from the earliest days of the republic. Of course, just as all human motivation is mixed, so is the rationale for aid. This is not to gainsay, in some cases, a genuine philanthropic element, but at the same time, as in this instance, there was just as large an element of enlightened self-interest. Bhutan had been of some importance strategically to British India because of the alleged Russian march southwards; but although Independent India feels she has nothing to fear from that quarter, her relations with China, now firmly established in Tibet, have been such as to make Bhutan of vital strategic importance for her defence. This, for a time, affected her attitudes towards Bhutan's internal affairs and the role of other aid agencies. The price of aid therefore has been a greater Indian involvement in internal affairs than the British considered desirable, to some extent inevitable given the size of the Indian contribution and consequent large staff at the Residency, where there was a permanent Resident who wielded great influence. In recent years, since the return of senior Bhutanese from overseas training and taking over control of ministries, the departure of Indian advisers and the transformation of the Residency into an Embassy, this has become much less. Bhutan has benefited immensely from the relationship. India has provided much of the skilled as well as the unskilled labour for engineering, agricultural, irrigation and electricity projects; most of the teachers, many of the doctors as well as economists and specialist advisers of all sorts. Inevitably, as in all relationships when the chrysallis is out-grown, there can be tensions; but the Bhutanese people are far from insensible of the material gains the association has brought.

By comparison the British association seems at first sight to have brought little, if any, benefit to Bhutan; and in material terms this, at least until the last decade, is not far from the truth. There have, however, been less tangible benefits, which are not inconsiderable. Bhutan's greatest asset today is the strength of the monarchy, its competence and the loyalty it commands. This might not have been so had Ugyen Wangchuk and Claude White not formed such a close personal relationship. The King could carry out internal reforms and fend off Tibetan and Chinese threats of interference, secure in the knowledge that Britain was firmly behind him.

At a different level, not only were his eyes opened to the possibilities available to a reforming ruler in the fields of education, medicine and public works, by his British sponsored tours of India, but so were those of his wealthier subjects of whom a steady trickle began to visit India from the beginning of the 20th century. They saw an ordered and comparatively sophisticated society and were prepared to accept adaptations relevant to Bhutan. Their children and later their grandchildren were exposed to a British system of education in north India where the emphasis was no longer on the rote learning to which they were accustomed; and they acquired some proficiency with the language that was to unlock the door to the wider world as the essential tool for development and communication. It is therefore particularly appropriate that most of British aid nowadays should be in this important field.

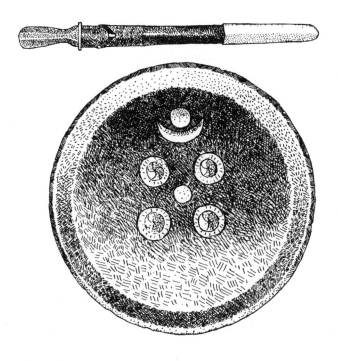

EPILOGUE

1947 to the Present

After Indian independence and the new treaty the way was open for a slow but steady increase in the pace of development. In 1950 new primary schools were built in the ten main towns and Indian teachers were recruited in annually increasing numbers. This laid the foundations for an educated class without which all other plans would be hampered. At the same time there were improvements in health care and in public works.

In 1952 the King died after twenty six years of successful rule during which he had consolidated the great work of his father. He was succeeded by his son, Jigme Dorji Wangchuk, who visited India the following year, where he was welcomed by Prime Minister Nehru. This was a period of acute tension in the whole Himalayan region, following the Chinese invasion of Eastern Tibet toward the end of 1950. Nehru had stated that his government could not permit the Himalyan barrier to be penetrated and had asserted that India could not permit upheavals in Nepal. The Bhutanese, who shared his fears, realised that this applied to them also. This was therefore a ·particularly opportune meeting for the two Heads of State.

A year later began the first of a series of constitutional developments towards consultative government when the Tshogdu, the National Assembly, was established. Although increasingly consultative the Tshogdu was still not a legislative body. At that time, however, this suited Bhutanese requirements better than the form of government demanded by the small Congress party mainly composed of recent Nepali immigrants. Its activities, especially those based on Indian soil, were not encouraged by the Government of India and it never acquired much credibility, even amongst most of the Nepali Bhutanese, who were granted proportionate representation in the Tshogdu. A decade after the Tshogdu's establishment the King set up a Council of Ministers to assist him, so that a form of constitutional government now began to operate. In 1968 he himself initiated changes whereby the King's approval was no longer required for legislation. He also proposed that all officers of the government, including even himself, would resign if subject to a motion of no confidence. This was rather too radical for the members to accept and only a modified version of this law was passed. Even this was rescinded in 1973, reputedly also at the Tshogdu's initiative.

After a temporary period of stability following the Indo-Chinese treaty of 1954, a revolt against the Chinese in Eastern Tibet set off political shock waves across the Himalayan states. In 1958, when the rebels established themselves not far north of the Bhutanese border, Nehru visited Bhutan, proposing Indian economic aid and the building of a road from India to central and western Bhutan, with strategic as well as economic advantages, and advocated the ending of Bhutan's policy of isolationism. This was finally ended when the nation-wide Tibetan rebellion was followed by border clashes between India and China, Chinese incursions into Bhutan in 1960 and the apparent resurgence of Chinese claims to suzerainty. From this time onwards there was increasing alignment with India, starting with the training of the Royal Bhutanese Army by the Indian Army whose training team has retained a permanent presence.

Between 1961 and 1966 the first of three 'five year plans' was initiated. A pact was made with India to harness the Wangchu river at Chukha for hydro-electric power and Indian aid was forthcoming for many other aspects of development. However, not all Bhutanese approved of the pace of change, for when on the 5th April 1964 Jigme Dorji was assassinated, many people thought it was because of opposition to him as the Indianised representative of a new type of society. He had not been vested with such high dignity as his father and grandfather although referred to as Lonchen (Prime Minister) and had never received the orange scarf given to his family predecessors. However, his job as Agent had been greatly increased when Bhutan prepared for entry onto the world stage by joining the Colombo Plan nations. Under his father, foreign affairs, which were within the Agent's sphere of responsibility, had been of comparatively minor importance as they were guided by the Imperial government of India, as indeed they were under the republic of India although they had now assumed much greater importance. Jigme found himself in increased contact with senior Indian ministers and officials, and regarded as virtual foreign minister of Bhutan. According to Nari Rustomji (then on secondment as Adviser to the King) in his book, *Bhutan, The Dragon Kingdom in Crisis*, this role was probably resented.

In 1971 a great turning point was reached when Bhutan joined the United Nations. This was probably the greatest achievement of the King in his nineteen year reign which came to an end the following year when his seventeen year old son Jigme Singye Wangchuk, the fourth hereditary monarch, succeeded. Development now became more rapid as the third five year plan began to take effect. In addition to continued aid from India, particularly with the Chukha hydro-electric project and the building of cement plants, there was now a United Nations Development Programme and a UNDP Resident Representative and staff were appointed to supervise U.N. projects. There were also the beginnings of bilateral aid from a few countries of whom the Swiss were the forerunners. These also included Australia and Britain.

After their departure in 1947 the British had had little further contact with Bhutan for some years. In the sixties three or four teachers were engaged privately to educate the royal family and selected children; but few officials from the British High Commission in Delhi visited the country until the young King's coronation in 1972. There was some preliminary contact with the Ministry of Overseas Development (later renamed the Overseas Development Administration) in London; and a visit by an administrative officer, following a Bhutanese sponsored mission of three British headmasters who reported on the needs of the education system, preceded the appointment of the first aid-funded British headmaster to a Bhutanese secondary school in 1974. The following year a three man official mission (referred to in the preface page (viii) visited Bhutan to discuss, at Bhutanese request, an extension of aid to education. Their proposals, welcomed by their hosts, for two more headmasters and teachers of English and Science, as well as training for educators in Britain were, with the exception of the latter, largely aborted for reasons beyond their control or those of the Bhutanese hosts. However, by the early eighties when India's internal and external difficulties appeared to have lessened and her anxieties about allowing intrusive foreigners into sensitive border areas had, to some extent, been allayed, when a number of senior Bhutanese educators had returned from training in Britain and when the U.N. and other bilateral aid presences had been strengthened, another British official visit (also mentioned in the preface, page (viii) was more successful and a variant on the original project was agreed. At the same time the Bhutanese government welcomed the proposed appointment of young British and Irish volunteer teachers sent by Voluntary Services–Overseas (VSO) to help in the expanding education system; together with United Nations Volunteers (U.N.V.) from many countries.

The British Political Officers of the first half of the twentieth century whose enthusiasm for Bhutan became so suspect to their superiors were replaced by aid officials who were no less impressed by the attributes of the Bhutanese and the beauties of their country and were no less vigorous in their recommendations. Best of all, the administrators and soldiers have been replaced by young teachers who are the first to admit that they have as much or more to gain from contact with this fabled land and its charming people as they have to impart.

CHAPTER NOTES

Further details of all publications and records mentioned below, including full India Office Library references, can be found in the Bibliography.

Introduction
My own personal experience and knowledge of the country were augmented by two UNESCO publications, Y. Imaeda (1984) and G. L. Harris (1973), as well as by the Royal Government of Bhutan handbook (1979). Dr Michael Aris's definitive work (1980) is the main scholarly source of information on the earlier period of Bhutan's history.

Chapter One
For primary source material the Fort William–India House Correspondence, Vols. VI and VII, Advices from Bengal concerning Military Operations against the Bhutanese, Correspondence between the Governor-General and the Deb Raja, and S. C. Grier (1905) were all useful, but my main source for the latter part of the chapter was George Bogle's own report as recounted in Clements R. Markham (1879).

For the Indian background I relied to some extent on my own fairly long experience of India and knowledge of Indian history, but for much factual detail I am indebted to one of my former Cambridge supervisors, the late Dr P. G. Spear, whose *History of India* (1961), although now superseded by later works written by Indian scholars, was very useful for the limited purposes required here. For particular aspects of the text I used Peter Auber (1837), M. E. M. Jones (1918), and G. R. Glieg (1841).

For Bhutan, the following books were used to a limited extent throughout the first six chapters: S. Gupta (1974), Nagendra Singh (1978), Arabinda Deb (1976), Manorama Kohli (1982); and for the first three chapters only, A. C. Bannerjee (1946).

Chapter Two
In addition to the Hastings material already mentioned and the Fort William–India House Correspondence, Vol. VII, Samuel Turner's own published account (1800) and Samuel Davis's diary as edited by Michael Aris (1982) were main primary sources.

Chapter Three
The main source of information was Kishen Kant Bose's report of 1815 as reproduced in *Political Missions to Bhutan* (1865). The Fort William–India House Correspondence was also used.

Chapter Four
Most of the information in this chapter came from Pemberton's *Report* (1839) and Griffith's *Journal* in *Political Missions to Bhutan*. Secret Letters from Bengal 1839–40 provided some useful background material.

Chapter Five
Political and Secret Home Correspondence 1841 and 1842, Secret Letters from Bengal, Political Department Collection 1862, *Papers relating to Bhutan*, No. 47, 1865, and *Further Papers*, No. 13, 1866, were all used. However, the main sources for the progress of the Eden Mission were Eden's *Report* in *Political Missions to Bhutan*, 1865, with appendixes by Godwin Austen and Lance.

Chapter Six

The most interesting accounts of the war were in the unpublished private papers of Capt. (later Col.) A. H. Lewes and the private diary of Maj. (later Maj.-Gen. Sir Charles) Gough, V.C. Surgeon Rennie (1866) is useful although he did not actually reach Bhutan until the campaign was over, unlike Maj. (later Gen. Sir Colin) MacGregor whose report (1866) and autobiography (1888) were also of some use, as was Lt.-Col. J. M. Adye's account as edited by Col. R. Biddulph (1895).

For the political background and for the period before and after the war, Despatches to India 1858-72, Letters to India 1861-66 and 1866-74, *Further Papers* (1866) and Letters from India 1885 were referred to.

The main secondary sources included the Intelligence Branch Report of 1907 and J. Grant (1897). Regimental histories including those by G. Pigot (1946) and E. D. Roberts (1925) yielded disappointingly little. More useful were various issues of the *Illustrated London News* and *Spectator* during the period 1864-5, as listed in the bibliography.

Chapter Seven

Letters from India 1885 and 1904, and the Political and Secret Subjects 1902-11 files were referred to, but the main sources of information were provided by John Claude White's writings, in particular his book of 1909 in which he describes his various missions, and to a lesser extent his article of 1910. Almost more interesting is an unpublished report of Capt. W. L. Campbell on the 1906-7 mission. For the Younghusband Expedition Peter Fleming's study (1961) was most useful.

Chapter Eight

A hitherto unquarried mine of information, and the main source for this chapter, was provided by the reports of Political Officers, most of whom visited Bhutan from their base in Sikhim, and almost all of whom wrote annual reports, which are included in Political Collections — Bhutan 1906-1947. F. M. Bailey's article of 1934 augments his reports. A most useful secondary source was Charles Allen and Shirada Dwivedi's enjoyable book (1984), as was Harold F. Fletcher's study (1975) of the botanical explorations of Frank Ludlow and George Sherriff.

Epilogue

Nagendra Singh's useful book (1978) and to a lesser extent Bikrama Jit Hasrat (1980) provided factual information and for the rest I used my own memory and experiences, albeit constrained by the dictates of the Official Secrets Act. Nari Rustomji's two books (1971 and 1978) provided an interesting personal background to Indo-Bhutanese relations and post-independence developments, as did Leo Rose (1977).

BIBLIOGRAPHY

This has been compiled from a number of sources, among which the most useful was Julie Marshall's exhaustive bibliography *Britain and Tibet 1765-1947; The Background to the India-China Border Dispute*, La Trobe University Library, Publication No. 10, Bundoora, 1977, which was given to me by Dr Michael Aris of Wolfson College, Oxford, and to which readers are referred for additional material. An extensive bibliography loaned to me in Thimphu by Mr Yoshiro Imaeda, Adviser to the National Library of Bhutan, proved invaluable, as was my major resource area, the India Office Library,

London. For sources on the Anglo-Bhutanese war the National Army Museum library proved very useful. Titles of books and periodicals are listed alphabetically by author or editor when known, and records are listed in chronological order.

PRIMARY SOURCES

1. *Records* (India Office Library references) and *Parliamentary Papers.*

Fort William–India House Correspondence: Vol. VI (1772), Vol. VII (1773-6), Vol. X (1786-8), Vol. XVII (1792-5).

Advices from Bengal concerning Military Operations against the Bhutanese 1773: H/Misc/108 & 115.

Correspondence between the Governor-General and the Deb Raja 1814: H/Misc/548

Secret Letters from Bengal 1839-40: L/P&S/5/9; L/P&S/5/64.

Political and Secret Home Correspondence 1841: L/P&S/3/9.

Political and Secret Home Correspondence 1842: L/P&S/3/12.

Political Department Collection 1862: L/P&S/6/52.

Papers relating to Bootan, House of Commons Reports and Papers, 47, London, 1865, and *Further Papers relating to Bootan*, House of Commons Reports and Papers, 13 (in continuation of the above), London, 1866.

Despatches to India 1858-72: L/P&S/6/11.

Letters to India 1861-6: L/P&S/6/12.

Letters to India 1866-74: L/P&S/6/13.

Letters from India 1885: L/P&S/7/44.

Letters from India 1904: L/P&S/7/168.

Political and Secret Subjects 1902-11: L/P&S/10/221.

Political and Secret Subjects 1912-30: L/P&S/11.

Political Collections, Bhutan 1906-47: L/P&S/12/2222-8.

2. *Memoirs and Reports.*

Adye, J. M., *Recollections of a Military Life*, London, 1895.

Aris, Michael (ed.), *Views of Medieval Bhutan: The Diary and Drawings of Samuel Davis, 1783*, London & Washington, 1982.

Anon., *The Truth about Bhutan by one who knows it*, Calcutta, 1866. Reprinted in *Political Missions to Bhutan*, Delhi, 1972.

Bogle, George, see Markham, Clements R.

Bose, Kishen Kant, see *Political Missions to Bhutan*.

Campbell, Capt. W. L., unpublished report of 1907 Mission (copy obtained from Mrs Caroline Tsering in Thimphu).

Davis, Samuel, see Aris, Michael.

Eden, Ashley, see *Political Missions to Bhutan*.

Easton, John, *An Unfrequented Highway*, London, 1928.

Godwin Austen, Capt. H. H., 'Survey Report' and 'Notes on the Government, Religion, &c. &c. of the Booteahs', June 1864, in *Papers relating to Bootan*, 1865, pp. 244-60.

Gough, Maj. C. R., Private diary, National Army Museum.

Griffith, William, *Journals of Travels in Assam, Burma, Bootan, Afghanistan and the neighbouring countries*, Calcutta, 1847.

————, see *Political Missions to Bhutan*.

Hyslop, Capt. Harold, *Extracts from my diary, while accompanying the British Mission to Bhutan 1907-08*, privately printed, n.d.

Intelligence Branch G.H.Q., *Frontier and Overseas Expeditions from India*, Delhi, 1907.

Lance, Capt. W. H. J., 'Report on Bhutan, from a military point of view', 1st June 1864, in *Parliamentary Papers relating to Bhutan*, 1865, pp. 233–41.

Lewes, Capt. A. H., Private papers, National Army Museum.

Markham, Clements R. (ed.), *Narratives of the Missions of George Bogle to Tibet and the journey of Thomas Manning to Lhasa*, London, 1879. Reprinted New Delhi, 1971.

MacGregor, C. M., *A Military Report of the Country of Bhutan: containing all the information of military importance which has been collected up to the present day (12th July 1866)*, Calcutta, 1866.

———, *The life and opinions of Major-General Sir Charles Metcalfe MacGregor*, Edinburgh, 1888.

Morris, C. J., 'A Journey in Bhutan', *Geographical Journal* LXXXVI, Part 3, pp. 201–97.

Pemberton, Capt. R. Boileau, *Report on Bhutan*, Calcutta, 1839. Reprinted New Delhi, 1976.

———, see *Political Missions to Bhutan*.

Political Missions to Bootan, comprising the reports of the Hon'ble Ashley Eden, 1864; Capt. R. R. Pemberton, 1837, 1838, with Dr. W. Griffith's journal [1837–8]; and the account of Baboo Kishen Kant Bose [1815], Calcutta, 1865. Reprinted New Delhi, 1972.

Rennie, S. D. F., *Bhotan and the Story of the Dooar War*, London, 1866. Reprinted New Delhi, 1970.

Ronaldshay, L. J. L. D. [Earl of, later 2nd Marquess Zetland], *Lands of the Thunderbolt: Sikkim, Chumbi and Bhutan*, London, 1923. Reprinted New Delhi, 1977.

Rustomji, Nari, *Enchanted Frontiers — Sikkim, Bhutan and India's North-eastern Borderlands*, Bombay, 1971.

———, *Bhutan: The Dragon Kingdom in Crisis*, Delhi, 1978.

Turner, Capt. Samuel, *An Account of a Mission to the Court of the Teshoo Lama; Containing a Narrative of a Journey through Bootan and Part of Tibet*, London, 1800, 2nd edn. 1806. Reprinted New Delhi, 1977.

White, J. Claude, *Sikkim and Bhutan; Twenty-One Years on the North-East Frontier*, London, 1909. Reprinted New Delhi, 1979.

———, 'Journeys in Bhutan', *Geographical Journal* XXXV (1910).

———, 'Castles in the Air; experiences and journeys in unknown Bhutan', *National Geographical Magazine* 25 (1914).

Younghusband, Sir Francis, *India and Tibet*, London, 1910.

SELECT SECONDARY SOURCES

Aitchison, C. U. (comp.), *A collection of treaties, engagements, and sanads relating to India and neighbouring countries*, Vol. II, 4th edn., Calcutta, 1909.

Allan, V., 'A Journey to Lhasa in 1811', *History Today* 12 (1962), pp. 188–96.

Allen, Charles and Dwivedi, Shirada, *Lives of the Indian Princes*, London, 1984.

Adye, J. M., 'The Umbeyla Campaign 1863 and the Bhutan Expedition 1865-6', ed. H. Biddulph, *Journal of the Society for Army Historical Research* 19 (1940), pp. 34–47.

Aris, M. V., *Bhutan: The Early History of a Himalayan Kingdom*, Warminster, 1979.

———, *A Preliminary Survey of the Photographic Records of Bhutan 1864-1949 preserved in the United Kingdom*, manuscript, 1985.

Auber, Peter, *The Rise and Progress of British Power in India*, Vol. I, London, 1837.

Bailey, F. M., 'Travels in Bhutan', *Journal of the Royal Central Asian Society* 17 (1930), pp. 206–20.

———, 'Through Bhutan and Southern Tibet', *Geographical Journal* LXIV (1934).

Bannerjee, A. C., *The Eastern Frontier of British India 1724-1826*, Calcutta, 1946.

Das, Nirmala, *The Dragon Country: The General History of Bhutan*, New Delhi, 1974.

Deb, Arabinda, *Bhutan and India: a Study of Frontier Political Relations 1772-1865*, Calcutta, 1976.

Fleming, Peter, *Bayonets to Lhasa*, London, 1961.

Fletcher, Harold F., *A Quest of Flowers; The Botanical Explorations of Frank Ludlow and George Sherriff*, Edinburgh, 1975.

Glieg, G. R., *Memoirs of the Life of Warren Hastings*, London, 1841.

Grant, J., *British Battles on Land and Sea*, Vol. 3, London, 1897.

Grier, S. C. (ed.), *The Letters of Warren Hastings to his Wife*, London, 1905.

Gupta, S., *British Relations with Bhutan*, Jaipur, 1974.

Hailes, W. L., *War Service of the 9th Jat Regiment*, Aldershot, 1938.

Harris, G. L., *Area Handbook for Bhutan, Sikhim, Nepal*, Washington, 1973.

Hasrat, Bikrama Jit, *The History of Bhutan*, Education Department, Thimphu, 1980.

Illustrated London News. No. 46, 1865: 28 Jan., 29 Apr., 6 May, 24 June. No. 47, 1865: 30 Sept.

Imaeda, Yoshiro and Pommaret-Imaeda, Françoise, *Bhutan; A Kingdom of the Eastern Himalayas*, photographs by Guy van Strydonck, London, 1984.

Imaeda, Yoshiro, *Bhutan*, Bulletin of the Asian Cultural Centre for UNESCO, Summer/Autumn 1985, No. 35, 3.

Jones, M. E. M., *Warren Hastings in Bengal*, Oxford, 1918.

Keay, John, *When Men and Mountains Meet: The Explorers of the Western Himalayas 1820-1875*, London, 1977.

Kohli, Manorama, *India and Bhutan: a Study in Interrelations 1772-1910*, New Delhi, 1982.

Longford, Elizabeth, *A Viceroy's India: Leaves from Lord Curzon's Notebook*, London, 1984.

Mehra, G. N., *Bhutan: Land of the Peaceful Dragon*, New Delhi, 1974.

Olschak, Blanche C., *Bhutan: Land of Hidden Treasures*, London, 1971.

——, *Ancient Bhutan: A Study of Early Buddhism in the Himalayas*, Zurich, 1979.

Pigot, G., *History of the 1st Battalion 14th Punjab Regiment, Sherdil-Ki-Paltan (late XIX Punjabis)*, New Delhi, 1946.

Singh, Nagendra, *Bhutan*, New Delhi, 1978.

The Spectator. No. 37, 1864: nos. 86, 92, 100-1, 123, 124, 136, 149, 158, 186-7, 205, 369, 449, 461, 483, 507, 514, 555, 575, 892, 916, 994, 996-8, 1123, 1127, 1368, 1487-8, 1499, 1506, 1534, 1818. No. 38, 1865: 350-1.

Rahul, Ram, *Modern Bhutan*, London, 1976.

Rose, Leo, *The Politics of Bhutan*, London, 1977.

Royal Government of Bhutan (Dago Tshering ed.), *Bhutan — Himalayan Kingdom*, Thimphu, 1979.

Poynder, F. S., *The 9th Gurkha Rifles 1817-1936*, London, 1937.

Roberts, E. D., *Historical Records of the 5th Bn. 7th Rajput Regiment (late XI Rajputs)*, Allahabad, 1925.

Spear, P., *History of India*, London, 1961.

White, John Claude, 'Sir Francis Younghusband', *Geographical Journal* LI (1918), pp. 497-8.

INDEX